COACHES

The Best NHL Coaching Legends
from Lester Patrick to Pat Burns

ABOUT THE AUTHOR

Stan Fischler is regarded as the dean of North American hockey writers. The prize-winning author has written more than 60 books on hockey. One of them, *The Hockey Encyclopedia,* which was co-authored with his wife, Shirley, is regarded as the bible of the sport. Fischler also writes a weekly column, *Inside Sports,* which has been carried for the past 20 years by the Toronto Star Syndicate. Among other publications which have carried his byline are *The New York Times, Sports Illustrated, Newsweek* and *The Village Voice.*

The versatile Fischler is also a prominent hockey broadcaster, having done analysis for 20 years. Stan has taught journalism at Columbia University, Fordham University, and Queens College.

A native of Brooklyn, Fischler lives in Manhattan with his wife and two children.

COACHES

The Best NHL Coaching Legends from Lester Patrick to Pat Burns

STAN FISCHLER

W

Warwick Publishing Inc.
Toronto   Los Angeles

ISBN 1-895629-41-1

Published by Warwick Publishing Inc.
24 Mercer Street, Toronto, Ontario M5V 1H3

Distributed in the United States by:
Firefly Books Ltd.
250 Sparks Ave,
Willowdale, Ontario
M2H 2S4

Cover design: Dave Hader/Studio Conceptions
Text design: Jacqueline Lealess
Editorial services provided by Word Guild, Toronto

Canadian Copyright © by Stan Fischler
Published in Canada by:
McGraw-Hill Ryerson Limited
300 Water Street
Whitby, Ontario
L1N 9B6

Printed and bound in Canada by Metropole Litho Inc.

Contents

Part One: *THE INCIDENTS*

1. THE NIGHT THE SILVER FOX PLAYED GOAL : Lester Patrick 2
2. A CASE OF ORGANIZED CONFUSION: Emile Francis 6
3. THE FAT GOALIE AND THE LOUD COACH: Phil Watson 9
4. THE CURSE OF PETE MULDOON 14
5. THE PLOYS AND PRANKS OF RUDY PILOUS 18

Part Two: *THE CHARACTERS*

6. THE ZANIEST - Eddie Shore's Springfield 24
7. THE BEST COACH OF ALL TIME - Toe Blake 34
8. THE WINNINGEST COACH - Scotty Bowman 40
9. THE YOUNGEST COACH - Kevin Constantine 50
10. THE HAPPIEST COACH - Terry Crisp 61
11. THE TOUGHEST COACH - Pat Burns 73
12. THE LOSINGEST COACH - Rick Bowness 85
13. FROM PRESIDENT TO COACH - Pat Quinn 91
14. THE KILLER COACH - Brian Kilrea 96
15. THE HIDDEN GENIUS - Ted Sator 105
16. THE SUTTER - Darryl Sutter 118
17. THE GOALIE COACH - Jacques Caron 127
18. THE OUTRAGEOUS COACH - Don Cherry 138
19. COACH GRAVEL-VOICE - Tom McVie 145

Part Three: *A TALE OF THREE COACHES*

Introduction 155
20. ARBOUR'S LAST HURRAH - Al Arbour 158
21. THE MAGNIFICENCE OF LEMAIRE - Jacques Lemaire 171
22. DOUBLE-CROSS OR DOUBLE-CROSSED? - Mike Keenan 196

Part Four: *CHICAGO STADIUM*

23. The Coaches' Asylum 210

ACKNOWLEDGEMENTS

The way to put together a comprehensive work on coaches is not unlike the manner in which a Mike Keenan or a Jacques Lemaire handles his bench. Several "players" had to be coordinated into the primary winning thrust. These included researchers, transcribers and, of course, reporters.

These players were integral in the attack, so to speak, and merit recognition.

Thus, we are very grateful for the contributions of Dave Levy, Dave Kolb, Susanna Mandel-Mantello, Ira Gitler, Rick Middleton, Alan Goldfarb, Tom Losier, Jim Ramsey and Rick Sorci.

Part One:

THE INCIDENTS

1

THE NIGHT THE SILVER FOX PLAYED GOAL

Maybe, they felt, if he stops a few in practice,
the old boy will think he can stop a few
in the game.

Lester Patrick was one of the most distinguished defensemen ever to grace a professional rink before he retired to become manager of the New York Rangers in 1926. Tall, with white combed-back hair, Patrick was behind the Rangers bench when the Blueshirts went up against the Montreal Maroons in the 1928 Stanley Cup finals.

This was only the second full season of NHL hockey for the New Yorkers, and to reach the Cup finals was a remarkable accomplishment. Nobody really expected the Rangers to go all the way and when they lost the first game to the Maroons, 2-0, very few eyebrows were raised.

The second game of the series at Montreal's Forum was a tight defensive battle that featured the superb goaltending of Lorne Chabot in the Rangers nets. A tall French-Canadian, Chabot girded himself at the cage as Nels Stewart of the Maroons bore down on him in the second period.

Stewart, who was to the hockey of the 1920s what Wayne Gretzky and Mario Lemieux are to the game in the '90s, boomed a shot that took off with surprising velocity. Chabot seemed temporarily mummified by the blast as it sailed straight at his head. Before he could duck, the six-ounce hunk of vulcanized rubber crunched into his head just above the left eye.

Chabot fell backward to the ice and crumpled up into a ball, bleeding profusely. It was obvious at a glance that he would be unable to complete the game. A stretcher was dispatched to the ice and the unconscious Chabot was carried out of the rink and sent to Royal Victoria Hospital.

Still very much in the hockey game, the Rangers' problem now was to find a goaltender. But where?

Lester Patrick dashed around the rink to the Maroons dressing room and conferred with their coach, Eddie Gerard. Patrick had an idea. "I'd like permission to use Alex Connell of the Ottawa Senators," said Patrick. "He's in the rink and I'm sure he'd play for us."

By contemporary standards "borrowing" a goaltender is a primitive practice, but in hockey's early years it was a customary procedure, if the opposing team agreed to it. In fact, Patrick himself, when he was running the Victoria team, had allowed the Toronto St. Pats to use the very same Eddie Gerard in a playoff series against Victoria. So there was precedent for Gerard to approve Lester's request.

Eddie mulled over the bid for about ten seconds and unequivocally replied, "Hell, no. You can't use Connell!"

Stunned and furious, Patrick stormed out of the room and headed straight for the Ranger players who were huddled in their own quarters. "We don't have a goalie," said Lester, "and Gerard won't let us use Connell. Frankly, gentlemen, I don't know what we're going to do."

The late James Burchard, who covered hockey for the old *New York World-Telegram*, was there at the time. A rollicking sort who thought nothing of swimming across the Hudson River on a dare, Burchard fancied it a stroke of genius when he suggested that Lester don the pads himself. "G'wan, Lester," urged the big, gravel-throated Burchard, "show 'em what you're made of."

Nobody took Burchard's latest brainstorm very seriously. After all, Patrick was 45 years old and had never been a goaltender by profession. But he suddenly startled the onlookers. "Okay," he muttered, "I'm going to do it."

While some of the Rangers attempted to persuade him that he had no business making a comeback — in goal, no less! — Lester diligently strapped on Chabot's bloodstained pads.

"Okay, gang, let's go," he shouted as he headed for the ramp leading to the ice. A chorus of oohs and ahhs came from the grandstand as Patrick made his way to the net for the traditional practice shots. Realizing the hopelessness of the situation, the Rangers attempted to bolster Lester's hopes as well as their own by pumping some mild shots at his pads. Maybe, they felt, if he stops a few in practice, the old boy will think he can stop a few in the game.

The referee signaled the resumption of the game and Patrick rapped his pads in the symbolic goaltending gesture of readiness. Finally the puck was dropped and the Rangers pounced on it. They scarcely let the Maroons touch the disk, and when the Montrealers did manage to get off a shot at Patrick, old Lester turned it away.

Somehow Patrick blanked the Maroons in the second period, and when the the teams trooped into the dressing room for the ten-minute break, the score was still tied, 0-0. All of a sudden the Patrick ploy no longer seemed like a joke. His decision to play goal was a catalyst for the Rangers and they returned to the third period more determined than ever.

Within 50 seconds Bill Cook had barreled through the Maroons defense and lifted the puck past goalie Clint Benedict. But the Montrealers weren't about to give up easily. They counterattacked more fiercely than ever, yet the old Silver Fox stood his ground, groaning with every kick-save that strained his aging physique. At last, with only five minutes and 40 seconds remaining, Lester cracked. Nels Stewart skirted the Ranger defense, feinted once, and then skimmed the puck past Patrick, making the score 1-1.

Lester held fast after that as the clock ticked its way to the conclusion of regulation time. Then it was sudden-death overtime — the first goal would win. The Maroons were counting on the ancient Lester to fold in the stretch. After all, there was just so much a senior citizen could take.

But somehow Patrick managed to foil the Maroons in the early minutes of overtime, and soon the momentum — as so often happens in the kaleidoscopic game of hockey — tilted in the Rangers' favor. Frank Boucher, their creative center, captured the puck and made his way up the ice. He zigzagged past a Maroons defenseman and swerved toward the goal. Benedict crouched in the Montreal goal as Boucher cruised in. The shot was hard and low and the puck flew past the Maroons netminder. The Rangers had won, 2-1, and Lester Patrick was the triumphant goalie.

To a man, the Rangers clambered over the boards and surrounded Patrick. He was hoisted to their shoulder and carried off the ice in victory. One of the broadest grins of all was worn by Jim Burchard, who patted Lester on the back. Years later, he composed a poem to him:

'Twas in spring of twenty-eight
A golden Ranger past,

That Lester got a summons
To guard the Blueshirt cage.
Chabot had stopped a fast one,
A bad break for our lads,
The Cup at stake — and no one
To don the Ranger pads.
"We're cooked," lamented Patrick,
"This crisis I had feared."
He leaned upon his newest crutch
And wept inside his beard.

Then suddenly he came to life
No longer halt or lame.
"Give me the pads," he bellowed,
"I used to play the game."
Then how the Rangers shouted.
How Patrick was acclaimed.
Maroons stood sneering, gloating,
They should have been ashamed.

The final score was two to one.
Old Lester met the test.
The Rangers finally won the Cup,
But Les has since confessed.
"I just spoke up to cheer the boys,
"I must have been delirious.
"But now, in reminiscence,
"I'm glad they took me serious."

James Burchard
November, 1947

2

A CASE OF
ORGANIZED
CONFUSION

A total of ten Rangers scaled the tall glass barrier,
but they were too late to prevent damage to their boss.
Francis was cut over the left eye and left cheekbone,
requiring stitches.

Arthur Reichert, a short, wiry man, crouched forward as the Detroit Red Wings headed toward the New York Rangers zone. It was just past the nine-minute mark in the third period on Sunday night, November, 21, 1965, and the Rangers were leading 2-1 at Madison Square Garden. Reichert, who had been a goal judge for more than 20 years, was at his usual position — just behind the Plexiglas barrier at the west end of the arena, directly facing the goal cage.

At the same time Emile "The Cat" Francis, the equally small general manager of the Rangers, was sitting in his seat somewhere in the side of the arena urging his defensemen to thwart the enemy attack.

Parker McDonald of the Red Wings carried the puck over the center red line with Norm Ullman, his center, speeding along at his side. The two Detroiters burst through the New York defense with Ullman now in control of the puck.

As the Wings milled about in front of the goal, Floyd Smith of Detroit added another poke. The Ranger netminder, Ed Giacomin, thrust out his gloved hand and nabbed the puck. A split second later Reichert pushed his right thumb against the button and the red light illuminated above the Plexiglas, signaling a Red Wing goal.

The moment Francis saw the red light he leaped out of his seat,

6

dashed along the aisle, and then rushed down to the goal judge's area. By that time five Rangers were milling around on the ice directly in front of Reichert, protesting that the puck had never gone in. Francis bulled his way past the spectators surrounding Reichert. "I was watching that play clearly," Francis shouted, "and that puck never crossed the red line."

Reichert, who also happened to be an accomplished tennis player and a certified public accountant, stared Francis in the eye and replied, "I've got two witnesses here to prove I'm right."

"I don't give a damn about any witnesses," screamed Francis. "You're the guy that makes the decision and you just made another rotten one."

Suddenly a burly spectator who was sitting near Reichert yelled at the Ranger manager, "Bug off, Francis, that puck was in."

Francis turned to the fan, whereupon another spectator joined the anti-Francis brigade. "One of them," the 140-pound Francis later remembered, "weighed at least 250 pounds."

A flurry of punches spread among the gaggle of fans who surrounded Francis. "Someone, I don't know who, threw the first punch," said Francis, "and things just went from there."

Three spectators jumped him and the four men rolled in the aisle directly in front of the protective glass barrier. One fan ripped Francis' jacket off his back while the second crawled on top of the Rangers boss, tossing lefts and rights.

Vic Hadfield, the big, blond Ranger left wing, was looking directly at Francis as the manager went under. Hadfield dropped his gloves and stick, dug his fingers into the small opening between the glass panes and lifted his skate blades onto the wooden boards. Straining, he pulled himself over the top of the barrier and fell on top of a spectator's seat on the other side. After recovering his balance, Hadfield leaped on the fans who had smothered Francis. "I saw one guy had Francis by the throat," said Hadfield.

One of the spectators pulled away from Francis and fled down the aisle. Meanwhile, Hadfield was followed over the Plexiglas barrier by Arnie Brown, Mike McMahon, Reg Fleming and Earl Ingarfield of the Rangers. "By this time," said Francis, "the players were all around me. They caught up with the first fan and they bagged the second."

A total of ten Rangers scaled the tall glass barrier, but they were too late to prevent damage to their boss. Francis was cut over the left eye and left cheekbone, requiring stitches.

Reichert had sidestepped the brawling by moving to an adjacent aisle while the fuss brewed. Garden police moved in to restore order and nobody, neither Francis nor any of the fans, pressed charges. "I don't want to press charges," said Francis. "I just want that goal back."

The Rangers did manage to score another goal, but Detroit tied the game less than two minutes from the finish and the contest ended in a 3-3 tie, which just served to intensify the bitterness already surrounding the tumultuous scene. Francis and Rangers president William Jennings stormed into the press room and blasted Reichert.

"I had a perfect view of the shot and puck did not get past Giacomin," Francis insisted. "The light didn't go on immediately, and no one seemed to know who had scored — if you could call it a score. Why, none of the Red Wings even lifted their sticks to signal a goal."

Livid over the fact that referee Art Skov had upheld Reichert's decision, Jennings went a step further and said he would attempt to ban the goal judge from handling Ranger games. "I'm backing up Francis completely," said Jennings. "I am not speaking in haste when I say that Reichert is no longer welcome in Madison Square Garden and there are ways of keeping him out. There are just too many antediluvian minor officials in this league and the Rangers have to do something about it."

Jennings, a National Hockey League governor and one of the most important men in the big-league hierarchy, made his most forceful statement after the game. "The goal judges are employed by the league," Jennings went on, "but he [Reichert] won't get into this building again. Clarence Campbell, the league president, will have to come down from Montreal to get him in."

Needless to say, Ranger goalie Ed Giacomin supported his employer. And naturally Detroit Red Wing coach Sid Abel claimed the puck had gone in. "Certainly," said Abel. "The red light was on, wasn't it?"

"Reichert could have gotten 18 witnesses by going over to the Red Wings bench," said Francis.

A few days later, tempers had cooled. NHL president Clarence Campbell supported Reichert and insisted that he would continue judging at Garden games. Overruled by Campbell, Jennings had no choice but to permit Reichert in the building. Francis also complied, and soon all that was remembered was the sight of ten Rangers scaling the glass barrier.

"It was," concluded Francis in a capsule summation of the scene, "a case of organized confusion."

3

Phil Watson

THE FAT GOALIE AND THE LOUD COACH

"It's not true that Watson and I disliked
each other," Gump explained.
"Hated would be a better word."

If ever there was a Mutt and Jeff or Laurel and Hardy combination in the National Hockey League it was found on the New York Rangers (originally on the farm team, the New York Rovers) in the characters Lorne "Gump" Worsley and coach Phillipe Henri "Fiery Phil" Watson.

Gump was a short, crew-cut goalie out of Montreal who was brash at his most conservative moments. Watson was a short-tempered, extremely emotional and hockey-wise coach who had been a superb center on the Rangers 1940 Stanley Cup championship club. The pair — who together were almost as combustible as gasoline and a lit match — first met when Watson was coaching the Rovers and Worsley was a a 20-year-old, fresh out of Junior hockey, trying to make the grade with the New York minor league club.

Worsley made it fast! He had been with the Rovers only a couple of weeks when he was temporarily promoted to the New Haven Ramblers of the American League for two games. The Ramblers regular goalie, Emile "The Cat" Francis, had been sidelined with a shoulder separation and Worsley was his replacement. Gump beat Buffalo, 3-2, and Springfield, 3-2. "I returned to New York," Worsley recalled, "feeling pretty chipper. The Eastern League seemed like small potatoes after that experience."

The moment Worsley returned to Broadway, Watson picked up on his cockiness and was determined to reduce his ego to what Phil regarded as the proper size. "Worsley," he snapped at their first encounter, "you think you're hot stuff now. Well, YOU STINK!"

Worsley was young enough — and tough-minded enough — to absorb the needles, but the incendiary quality of the relationship was there from the start. "Watson," Worsley explained, "was an egomaniac. When we won he took all the credit. When we lost it was our fault."

It was difficult for Watson to barb Worsley too often because Gump was the best young goalie in the league. He posted a 2.83 goals against average and led the Eastern League in shutouts with seven. "Watson was still calling us lousy players when we went into the playoffs."

The Rovers soon defeated Atlantic City in the finals and then played Spokane for the United States Senior Amateur Championship. "You guys better win," Watson warned the Rovers before the series started, "or I'm going to send you home in a bus."

The Rovers lost but they returned by train. "Watson," laughed Worsley, "was overruled by the front office."

Watson and Worsley eventually parted — temporarily — when Gump was promoted through the Rangers system; first St. Paul, then Saskatoon and Vancouver before returning to the Big Apple. Watson was also moving up, and in 1955-56 they met again. Worsley was the Rangers varsity goaltender and Watson was the coach.

And they still didn't like each other.

"Watson," wrote Worsley in his autobiography, *They Call Me Gump,* "stuck his nose into everything. He always wanted to know what we were up to — even when the team was home. He would call our homes at night, sometimes even late at night, wake up the kids and get the wife screaming too. You expect bed checks on the road, but not at home. It was ridiculous."

The relationship between Worsley and Watson was analogous to the one endured by Reggie Jackson and Billy Martin of baseball's New York Yankees. "It's not true that Watson and I disliked each other," Gump explained. "Hated would be a better word. During my second season with him, he really bled me. The bastard made me so mad I was ready to choke him."

As Gump had learned from his Rover days, a win would put Watson in the limelight, and a loss would put Gump on the spot. Once, Worsley gave up three goals to a relatively low-scoring Chicago forward named Hector Lalande. Even worse, Lalande's club came from behind a 3-5 deficit to gain a 6-6 tie in the third period. After the game, Watson went bananas. "When a dopey Frenchman like Lalande scores three goals in one game, how good can the goalie be?" Watson realized that picking on Worsley had a built-in boomerang. Much as he may have loathed his netminder, Phil knew that the fans and New York hockey writers loved him. "Every time I hop on Worsley people accuse me of picking on him," Watson charged. "But the same guys who pat him on the back after a game are the guys who are buying him a beer. YOU CAN'T PLAY GOAL WITH A BEER-BARREL BELLY."

When that remark was relayed to the ever-so-slightly corpulent goaltender, Gump was insulted. "Beer Belly!" he snapped. "I don't drink beer. YOU TELL WATSON THAT I ONLY DRINK V.O."

The Watson-Worsley dialogue took on Alphonse-Gaston proportions. First the newspapermen would tell Worsley what Watson had said about him; then they would dash back to Watson and relate Worsley's remarks. And so it went on into the night. On this occasion, Worsley conceded that he played a "lousy" game. This concession was worth relaying to Watson who barked "Hell, I've seen games when he's been lousier than that."

With pads flying in their wake, the reporters sped back to Gump and relayed Watson's latest epigram. To that, Worsley delivered the perfect (for the situation) squelch: "Tell Watson he is full of crap!"

Through it all, however, Gump and Phil managed to talk to each other even without the benefit of intermediary newsmen. One of their most memorable confrontations involved a challenge leveled by the loud coach to his fat goalie. The two were sitting in a tavern when Watson dared Worsley to drink him under the table. "We matched slug for slug," wrote Worsley in *They Call Me Gump*, "while a lot of the players watched. And who wound up under the table when it was over? Not Lorne John Worsley."

As coach, Watson theoretically held the upper hand over Gump. But Worsley usually came out on top because he had 17 other teammates on his side. One of the most clever was Parker MacDonald, a workmanlike forward who was an accomplished mimic, a talent that was unknown to Watson. The coach was easy prey for Parker since Watson had a penchant for delivering pep talks at the drop of a puck.

Worsley recounted the scenario: "Watson would stand in the middle of the dressing room, shouting and waving his hands. Every time he turned his back on MacDonald, Parker would go into his act — imitating all of Phil's gestures. I used to sit across the room from Parker and would bury my face in a towel to keep from laughing.

"Watson would see this and say 'What the hell's wrong with you, fat man?' To that I would answer 'Nothing, Phil. I just felt a sneeze coming on.' Then Watson would spin around quickly to find Parker looking very serious. But the moment Phil turned his back, Parker would start moving his lips again and waving his hands like Phil."

Likewise, Watson was never able to nab Worsley during any of Phil's numerous crackdowns on post-game drinking in the vicinity of Madison Square Garden. Even after practices, Worsley defied the explosive coach. Once, Worsley went so far as to suggest to a friend that they drink at The 322 Club, directly across the street from the Garden. "We can't go in there," Worsley's friend protested, "Watson is sure to spot us."

"Don't worry about that," Gump replied, "Phil's so dumb he'll never think to look in there."

As usual, Gump was right, but Phil did fool his goalie at least once. It happened at training camp for the 1958-59 season. At the very first meeting Watson stood before the players and announced: "Every position on this club, bar one, is wide open, and I kid you not. Nobody's job is safe except Worsley's. He's my goalie."

Worsley was stunned to the very core. It marked the first time Watson had ever give him a vote of confidence. "I sat there," said Gump, "in a trance. He shocked the hell out of me."

Watson, as they say, was dumb like a fox. He later reported his speech to reporters and chuckled at the thought of it. "You should have seen the little son of a bitch's face. His chin nearly hit the floor but I wasn't fooling. Until Gump goofs off, and maybe he won't, he's my man."

The honeymoon lasted about a week or until the first serious practice. "Then," Gump remembered, "he was back giving me the same old guff."

But Worsley was privileged at least one more time during the fast-waning Watson regime. Late in the season the Rangers were blown out by the Canadiens on Gardens ice. Montreal won, 5-1, and Watson followed his club into the dressing room whereupon he delivered an unprecedented order: "NOBODY TAKE OFF YOUR UNIFORM. WE'RE GOING BACK ON THAT ICE AND DO A LITTLE SKATING. WORSLEY, YOU DIDN'T PLAY THAT BAD. YOU CAN GET DRESSED AND GO HOME."

Worsley escaped before Watson changed his mind. Instead of going home. Gump climbed to a high seat, out of the coach's view, and watched Watson put the already tired players through an hour's stiff skating drill. "It was a terrible punishment," said Worsley, "especially after such a tough game. No coach had ever done such a thing before, and I don't think it's been done since."

The Watson-Worsley feud percolated into the 1959-60 season. Once Worsley asserted, "Phil, I was here when you came and I'll be here when you're gone."

The coach's stand-by was "Watson goes on forever."

But by mid-November 1959, the Rangers were going nowhere and Watson, hospitalized with a bleeding ulcer, was replaced by Alfie Pike. "I outlasted him by only a week," said Worsley. "The new coach, Alfie Pike, shipped me to Springfield and brought in Marcel Paille to play goal."

The paths of Watson and Worsley crossed briefly when Phil took a job coaching the Bruins, but that was Watson's last NHL position. Worsley remained a Ranger until June 1963 when he was traded to Montreal and starred for the Canadiens, and finally the Minnesota North Stars. Watson's last coaching fling was in the World Hockey Association with Philadelphia and Vancouver.

Years later, Worsley was scouting for the North Stars and wound up in Vancouver, when he bumped into none other than Watson himself.

"He told me," Worsley recalled, "'Gump you're still fat.' But I weighed 183 pounds, just what I weighed when I was playing!"

4

THE CURSE OF PETE MULDOON

As Muldoon was walking out of McLaughlin's office, he wheeled and looked his opponent in the eye. "I'm not through with you. I'll hoodoo you. This club will never finish in first place."

At times it is difficult, when dealing with hockey legends, to separate fact from fiction. It is a fact that in Chicago for many years, hockey fans believed that their Blackhawks were victims of "The Curse of Pete Muldoon." But the curse itself could very well be fiction. In any event, the Muldoon saga began when the Blackhawks were born.

Chicago's application to join the NHL was accepted in 1926, the same season the New York Rangers and Detroit Cougars (later to be known as the Red Wings) entered the league. The Blackhawk entry came by way of the Pacific Northwest.

Multi-millionaire Major Fredric McLaughlin of Chicago purchased a minor league team known as the Portland Rosebuds.

Even his most generous followers felt that the major was a man given to grave eccentricities. The purchase of the Rosebuds was considered one of his lesser aberrations. Hockey was not regarded with enormous affection in the Chicago of the mid-1920s, and there was considerable speculation that the major had been taken for a financial ride. But the Blackhawks' performance in their rookie season indicated that the major wasn't so foolish after all.

Coached by Pete Muldoon, the Hawks finished third in the five-team American Division, ahead of Pittsburgh and Detroit and only four points behind second-place Boston. They had obtained hard-

14

shooting "Babe" Dye from Toronto, and Dye wound up fourth in scoring in the American Division, hard on the heels of league-leading Bill Cook of the Rangers. All in all, it was a more impressive debut then Major McLaughlin's Detroit rivals could boast.

Unfortunately for Coach Muldoon, his first-round opponents in the Stanley Cup playoffs were the Boston Bruins, who had the benefit of two years' big-league play behind them. Even worse, arena-leasing problems made it impossible for the Blackhawks to play their first game in Chicago, so the series opened in Boston, and the Bruins romped to a 6-1 victory. In those days the semi-finals were decided on the basis of total goals scored in two games. To win, the Blackhawks would have to make up the five-goal deficit on unfriendly Boston Garden ice. The challenge was too much for the men of Muldoon. They fought Boston to a 4-4 tie and lost the series, ten goals to five.

Although impartial observers regarded this as a not too disgraceful turn of events for the Blackhawks, the perfectionist Major McLaughlin was not at all pleased. According to legend, as reported by Toronto columnist Jim Coleman, McLaughlin summoned Coach Muldoon to his office and reprimanded him for allowing the Blackhawks to go to the pot. "Why," said the major, "this club was good enough to finish in first place." "You're crazy," the infuriated Muldoon reportedly shot back.

"You're fired!" shouted the offended major.

As Muldoon was walking out of McLaughlin's office, he wheeled and looked his opponent in the eye. "I'm not through with you. I'll hoodoo you. This club will never finish in first place." And so, a hockey fable was born.

Major McLaughlin laughed contemptuously as his former coach stalked out. But as the years passed, the laugh turned to a frown and the Muldoon declaration became known as "the Muldoon jinx." For, try as they might, the Blackhawks could not get past second place.

Apparently the "hoodoo," as Coleman had put it, began taking effect as soon as Muldoon was fired. When the Black Hawks reported for training camp for the 1927-28 season, their hopes for an improved record rested on the heavy shooting of "Babe" Dye, who had scored 25 goals the previous year. "From what I saw of him in Winnipeg," recalled Marvin "Cyclone" Wentworth, a Blackhawk defenseman, "he appeared to be headed for another good winter."

By this time the Chicago players had established a reputation for horsing around, and Dye was no exception. One of his favorite foes was teammate "Cye" Townsend, also a forward. The two would elbow and butt each other on the ice like a pair of friendly goats, and they weren't at all reluctant to throw in an occasional trip or high stick.

One afternoon the Dye-Townsend rivalry escalated to a point where they were fouling each other on almost every rush down the ice. As Wentworth recalled, "It developed into quite a contest."

On one rush late in the workout, Dye collected the puck and began accelerating in the direction of Townsend. For some unaccountable reason, Dye kept his eyes on the puck and overlooked the fact that Townsend had extended his foot as a barrier.

"Dye was caught off guard and off balance," said Wentworth. "Townsend's boot plunked into him just above the ankle, and 'Babe' went down in a heap. He couldn't get up. His leg was broken."

Nobody blamed Townsend. The trip was all part of the horseplay. Nobody really thought that the accident was particularly tragic, either. But as the weeks passed and Dye's condition failed to improve noticeably, it became obvious that the playful trip was ruining Chicago's bid for first place. One could almost hear Pete Muldoon cackling in the distance.

"The accident closed Dye's career," said Wentworth. "He was out of hockey that winter. And though he later attempted two or three comebacks, he couldn't regain his old stride."

Without Dye to bolster their attack, the Hawks finished a dead fifth in the American Division and wound up out of the playoffs.

Year after year, the curse held. In 1926-27, they finished third in the American Division. In subsequent years they finished fifth, fifth, second and second. Then in 1931-32, when they looked like they might be winners, they failed again.

They finished seven points behind the American Division leaders, the Rangers, and were rapidly eliminated by the New Yorkers in the opening playoff round. By this time, Major McLaughlin must have been wishing that Pete Muldoon had never entered his life. However, there was little he could do but continue to experiment with his personnel and hope for the best. In 1934-35, the Hawks looked good enough to break the jinx. But when the 48th and final game of the season was completed the Bruins and Hawks had each won 26 games. And since Boston had lost only 16 games to Chicago's 17, the Bruins finished on top by the margin of one point. Blackhawk goalie Lorne Chabot could not be faulted in the opening playoff round against the Montreal Maroons, for he permitted only one goal in the total-goal, two-game series. Unfortunately for Chabot, his teammates got him none and Chicago was eliminated.

No matter what the Blackhawks did on the ice, they were unable to break the curse through the 1930s, 1940s and 1950s. In fact, it appeared to be holding well into the 1960s.* Despite this fact, nobody believed that 1966-67 would be any different from previous seasons, even though the Hawks had obtained a strong defenseman in Ed Van Impe and had convinced goalie Glenn Hall and center "Red" Hay to give up their retirement plans.

Blackhawk critics took mischievous delight in viewing the traditional early spurt of the Chicago club. They watched with even more glee when the Hawks opened up a big lead into the homestretch, believing that soon the Canadiens would put on the pressure and Coach Billy Reay's troops would fold. But this time Reay was not only getting high scoring from his two all-star forwards, Bobby Hull and Stan Mikita, but his young defensemen, Doug Jarrett and Pat Stapleton, were playing a cool, calculated game. And centers Phil Esposito and Fred Stanfield, with winger Ken Hodge, were giving the team more balance than it had ever boasted before.

This time the Blackhawks refused to fold, and when the 1966-67 curtain dropped they were sitting atop the NHL standings with a 17-point lead over Montreal. For the first time in 40 years, the point championship belonged to the Blackhawks.

Which proved, if nothing else, that for 40 years Pete Muldoon knew whereof he spoke when he uttered those deathless words: "I'll hoodoo you!"

---

* The Blackhawks finished in third place when the won the Cup in the 1960-61 season.

THE PLOYS AND PRANKS OF RUDY PILOUS

"Bobby Hull's uncanny accuracy on the slap shot can probably be attributed, in large measure, to Rudy Pilous' old wooden dummy."

Among post-World War II hockey personalities Rudy Pilous ranks with the most successful — and amusing — to have coached on the Junior and professional level. It was Pilous who coached the last Chicago Blackhawks team to a Stanley Cup (1961) championship and it was the Pilous-managed Winnipeg Jets that won the Avco-World (WHA) Cup in 1976. When he coached the St. Catharines Tee Pees of the Ontario Hockey Association's Junior A division, Pilous led them to the Memorial Cup, emblematic of the Junior championship of Canada. And always, Rudy managed to do it with a smile and a quip. "I wasn't taken as seriously as I should have been," said Pilous. "Why can't a person be funny, be entertaining and still know his job?"

Pilous did basic training for his ultimate jobs as manager and coach back in the 1930s when he was an amateur ace, but Rudy's development in hockey was unusual to say the least. One day late in the summer of 1936 he was perched on a telephone pole working with a crew stringing wire in the remote Slocan Valley of British Columbia. A man from camp headquarters came by with a message. A London (England) promoter had cabled asking if Rudy would consider playing hockey in Great Britain. Pilous called to his partner on the ground, 20 feet below. "Say, Mac, throw me up a quarter."

The other man was perplexed by the unusual request. "You can't buy anything up there," he replied.

"I know," said Pilous, "but I got a hell of a decision to make."

Once he had the coin, Pilous flipped it into the air, saying: "Heads I go to England, tails I stay up on this pole."

The coin turned up heads and a week later Pilous was en route to the British Isles. In time Rudy would return to North America and play for the New York Rangers farm team in the old Eastern League, the New York Rovers, before heading for St. Catharines, Ontario where he launched Junior hockey in 1943. He coached there for three years and then took off for hockey jobs in Houston, San Diego and Louisville before returning to St. Catharines in 1950 to coach and manage the Junior club. Within seven years he had won four OHA championships and one Memorial Cup and played a major role in developing such NHL stars as Bobby Hull, Stan Mikita, Elmer "Moose" Vasko and Pierre Pilote.

It was in St. Catharines that the zany side of Pilous surfaced. One night he executed a daring ploy during a playoff game between the Tee Pees and the Toronto Marlboros. With 28 seconds left on the clock and the club trailing 5-4, Pilous pulled his goalie.

Even worse, the face-off was in the St. Catharines end of the rink.

Onlookers were amazed. No coach within memory had ever made a move like that. "Coach," screamed Tee Pee goalie Marv Edwards after returning to the St. Catharines bench, "are you crazy or something?"

Pilous winked at his goaltender: "Just watch and see what happens."

As soon as the puck was dropped the overanxious members of the Marlboros fought with each other for possession of the puck and a shot at the yawning Tee Pees net. In the process, they flummoxed so badly that, with 12 seconds remaining, Hugh Barlow of St. Catharines grabbed the rubber, sped down the ice and scored the tying goal. Inspired by the move, Pilous' skaters went on to win the Memorial Cup.

According to Canadian author Earl McRae, Pilous' greatest psychological coup also took place while coaching St. Catharines. This time the Tee Pees and Marlboros were tied at three games apiece in a best-of-seven playoff. "The big game was coming up," McRae wrote, "and Pilous' players were going down. They were moody, edgy, complaining to people around town that Pilous was working them too hard, yelling at them, picking on them. Pilous knew there was no way his team could win the all-important game in that frame of mind."

Rudy went to his bag of tricks and came up with a beauty. He invited Jack Gatecliff, sports editor for the *St. Catharines Standard,* to the club's dressing room. "Just knock on the door, Jack," said Pilous, "and walk in and I'll act surprised to see you. Just do it and don't ask any more questions."

Gatecliff complied with his pal's request and walked in on the Tee Pees meeting just as the bored players listened to Pilous' monologue about not working hard enough in practice. "Oh, hi, Jack," said Pilous, wearing a straight face. "Come in, come in, you're just the man I want to see. Fellows, you all know Jack Gatecliff here, the sports editor of the paper? Well, I keep hearing from you guys and people on the street how tough and mean I am to you guys. I keep hearing how tired you all are, how some of you are hurt and shouldn't be playing.

"Dear, dear. Isn't that awful? Well, I have an idea. I want each and every one of you to tell Jack here personally just what it is that's wrong with you, just what it is that's so terrible about me, what I'm doing wrong. I want you to tell him why you don't think we'll win tomorrow night's game. And, Jack, I want you to talk to every one of these guys. And I want to see them in tomorrow's paper. Names and all. All right gentlemen — I now leave you. Jack — they're all yours."

Exit Pilous.

As instructed, Gatecliff talked to each of the Tee Pees and then wrote a major story which ran as the lead the next day in the *Standard*. Curiously, nobody on the Tee Pees beefed in print about Pilous and his policies. "They were all in the best of health," said McRae, "and thought the coach was a most wonderful guy."

The Pilous charges predicted that they would beat the Marlboros — easily. And that is precisely what they did, 5-1, to take the series.

When Rudy wasn't making young hockey players into better young hockey players, he was regaling them with stories of his growth and development as a player and a humorist. Rudy candidly admitted to his skaters that he had been as wild a youngster in his playing days as any of them. Once he told about the night he was engaged in an all-night card game with teammates on the Rovers. The next morning Lester Patrick, general manager of the New York Rangers, who owned the Rovers, entered the dressing room and gave the players a searing critique of their lackluster play.

"I want everyone who stayed up playing cards last night to raise his hand," Patrick ordered.

Pilous responded by raising first his left and then his right hand.

"What are you, a comedian?" demanded Patrick.

"No, Mister Patrick," Pilous replied. "One hand is for my roommate, Walt Cunningham. He was too tired to make the meeting this morning!"

Pilous did so well coaching the St. Catharines Tee Pees that he became the talk of Canada. One of his interesting techniques — although not original — was removing his goalie from his practices and installing a wooden dummy instead. The dummy was so constructed as to allow a few inches of opening at either side and the top. Rudy told his players that he was installing the dummy because the real goalies' hands are very tender early in the season.

"What happened," wrote McRae, "was that hardly any of the players could score on the wooden dummy. Their shots bounced off the wood, making an awful noise. The players fired harder, cursed louder and the noise was terrific. Pilous chuckled to himself. The strategy was working. The loud noise emphasized the lousy accuracy of the shooters, making them more and more frustrated and angry as the practice went on. When Pilous finally did install the real goalies, shooting accuracy was much improved — and then the goalies worked harder to fill the gaps. Bobby Hull's uncanny accuracy on the slap shot can probably be attributed, in large measure, to Rudy Pilous' old wooden dummy."

Rudy's success in St. Catharines inspired the Chicago Blackhawks to hire him as coach in January 1958 after the club had finished last, eight of its ten previous seasons.

Within six seasons the Pilous-piloted Blackhawks had made the playoffs five times, had reached the Stanley Cup finals twice and were coached to its first Stanley Cup in 22 years. "There were people who said I was a better storyteller than a coach," Rudy reflected. "Being funny doesn't mean you aren't smart, but a lot of people have that crazy idea."

Pilous always figured that he was misinterpreted in Chicago, that he was regarded more as a clown than a sage. In his final season of coaching in The Windy City, the Blackhawks were edged out of first place by only one point. In a sense it was a tragi-comedy because Chicago was favored to win it all and then blew the duke right at the wire. Rudy claimed that he was victimized by a cocktail party which he never wanted his players to attend.

"We blew first place," he explained, "because of that party at the Canadian Consulate in Chicago. Tommy Ivan [Chicago's manager at the time] insisted the team, the coach, the management — everybody go to the cocktail party at the consulate. We were in first place then, in the stretch drive, and I said no, I didn't want the players there. Guys get drinking, management gets too chummy with the players, people say things they shouldn't say, arguments start and the first thing you know you got dissension on the team. But Ivan made us go. And exactly just what I said happened. The bad feelings hung on and affected our play. I knew it. So a few players put the rap on me and, bang, I'm fired!"

And the Blackhawks have never won a Stanley Cup since.

Part Two:

THE CHARACTERS

6

THE ZANIEST — EDDIE SHORE'S SPRINGFIELD

"I'll never forget how Eddie hated to see his goalkeepers fall to the ice. If he got a player and that poor sap fell down to block a shot — like Nipper O'Hearn or Johnny Henderson used to — Shore'd get a piece of twine and tie the goalie's arm to the crossbar of the net. Then he'd dare him to fall."

No sports franchise, be it in baseball, football, basketball, or hockey, so epitomizes what we have come to understand as "minor league" than the Springfield (Massachusetts) Indians of the American Hockey League, circa 1947-1967.

Only one factor was necessary to set Springfield apart from the others, but that factor was crucial because it involved the most amazing — and easily the most bizarre — personality ever to run a professional athletic team.

His name is Eddie Shore.

Shore was born on a farm in Fort Qu'Appelle-Cupar, Saskatchewan, and he toughened himself early in life, hauling the harvested grain to town and riding wild horses. In time he was to become one of the most accomplished and feared defensemen ever to skate in the National Hockey League.

Shore arrived in the big time in 1926 and singlehandedly built the Boston Bruins into an NHL power. His end-to-end puck-carrying rushes soon became legendary, matched in excitement only by his crunching bodychecks and his ability to sustain great pain.

While earning a place on the All-Star team eight times and being named the NHL's most valuable player four times, Shore accumulated more than 900 stitches in his body, not to mention fractures of his back, hip and collarbone. His nose was broken 14 times and his jaw smashed five times.

Shore retired from full-time play in 1940 and invested his savings in the acquisition of the Springfield hockey club. His investment was a major one and, no doubt, helped to shape Shore's budgetary philosophy which, according to some observers, was somewhat to the right of frugality.

"When he first got the franchise," said Jack Riley, former president of the American League, "he used to park cars outside the arena until about ten minutes before game time. Then Eddie would go in, suit up, and play defense for his team.

"His players would take inner tubes from their automobile tires, cut them up into rubber bands and put them around hockey stockings to save the cost of tape. During the ice show at the arena, Eddie operated one of the spotlights himself to save expenses. But you can't knock him. Not when he invested all his hockey money right back where it came from."

Shore paid $42,000 for the Indians — $16,000 in cash and the rest on a note — and he was determined to build Springfield into one of the best hockey cities on the continent. In a sense, he succeeded. Attendance at home games reached a profitable level in time, and Shore developed an excellent hockey program for the young people in the city.

But Eddie was never content to limit himself to the front office part of the business. Over the years he had developed innumerable theories about the way hockey should be played, and he was determined to pass these ideas along to his players. More than anything it was Shore the theoretician, the coach and the manager that marked him as the only one of his kind in the world. His actions also explain why many skaters considered Springfield the Siberia of minor league hockey.

How can anyone believe a man would open a training camp by ordering two dozen rugged hockey players to tap dance in the hotel lobby or to execute delicate ballet steps on ice? Would an ordinary coach tape a player's hands to his stick? Or work out day after day with his players despite four near-fatal heart attacks? Is it conceivable that a club owner would instruct players' wives to diminish sexual relations with their husbands in the interests of a winning team? Is it imaginable, either, that a man would actually lock a referee out of his dressing room as punishment for "poor" officiating? Or order his players to make popcorn, blow up balloons and sell programs when they're not in the game?

"You better believe it happened with Shore," said Don Johns, an alumnus of Shore's Indians. "Once Eddie told me he knew why I wasn't a better hockey player. I'm always willing to learn. So I said, 'Okay, Ed, what's wrong with me?' Know what he says? 'You're not combing your hair right.' He told me to part it on the other side. That way it would help me 'cause I'd have something to think about."

Johns was struck dumb at the opening of training camp. Several players were churning up and down the ice taking shots on goal when a whistle pierced the air. Shore beckoned to a rookie, and the other players stopped to see what Eddie was up to this time. "He wanted the boy to skate with his legs closer," said Johns, "so he pulled out a piece of cord and tied the kid's legs together and told him to skate. Did you ever try to skate with your legs tied?"

Another time, Johns was immobilized on a hospital bed after suffering a 40-stitch cut in his leg. The phone rang. It was Shore. "'Mis-ter Johns,' he said, 'you ought to be ready to play soon.'"

"'But, Eddie,' I told him, 'I can't even turn my leg.' I was babying myself. So I called the doc and told him to look at the leg. He did, and he told me I'd be crazy if I got outta bed in the next couple of days."

By the end of the week, Johns was released from the hospital, and he reported to Shore, who occupied a modest office in the Eastern States Coliseum, the rink he leased in West Springfield, Massachusetts.

"Mis-ter Johns," Shore ordered, "you're playing tonight."

"He played me for three minutes," said Johns, "and then suspended me for a week.

"'When I played hockey,' Shore told me, 'I once had a hundred stitches in my leg, and I was out only three — no, two and a half — days.'"

After a few weeks, Johns had become numbed by Shore's criticism. Johns' feet were wrong, Shore said. He wasn't shooting correctly or bending properly, and so on, ad nauseam.

One day, when Johns was about to quit, Shore pointed at him. "Mis-ter Johns," he said, "what did you do wrong this time?"

Exasperated, Johns said, "I guess I wasn't skating right. Or my hands were too close on the stick..."

"Bul-loney," Shore said. "You're doing nothing wrong."

Johns considered himself rather fortunate that he was sent to Baltimore after only a year in Springfield. Others, such as Billy McCreary, formerly of the St. Louis Blues, who played four years for Shore, cursed the day they were told to report. Up to his ears in Shore-isms, McCreary once threatened to quit hockey rather than to sign another Springfield contract. Eddie finally traded him to Hull-Ottawa.

McCreary said Shore was so cheap he made Jack Benny seem like the last of the great spenders. "We were on strict budgets with him," said McCreary. "He allowed us to tip taxi drivers 15 cents. After a while, we got so known around the league, none of the cabbies wanted to pick us up.

"That was bad enough. But some guys had a bonus clause in their contracts. If they got, say, 30 goals, they'd get more money. So a guy would be comin' close to 30 near the end of the season. Does he make it? Hell, Shore would sit him out of the last five games so he couldn't score any more. And if you think I'm joking, just ask any player who skated for Shore."

Still, when polling members of the Shore Alumni Association, a fellow can find as many admirers of the "Old Man" as critics. Everybody agreed, though, that Shore is the wildest, most learned hockey man in the world.

One graduate of Shoresville, Don Simmons, former goaltender of the Stanley Cup champion Toronto Maple Leafs, said Shore's techniques left him limp from shock. "I'll never forget how Eddie hated to see his goalkeepers fall to the ice. If he got a player and that poor sap fell down to block a shot — like Nipper O'Hearn or Johnny Henderson used to — Shore'd get a piece of twine and tie the goalie's arm to the crossbar of the net. Then he'd dare him to fall."

Shore once ordered Simmons into his office. Don had been in a slump and, naturally, feared the worst. But Eddie was convinced Simmons had developed a mental block against goaltending. He suggested that the kid return to his home in Port Colborne, Ontario, for a rest. "He told me to go home to my mother. 'Help her around the house,' he said. 'Wash the dishes and do other chores for her. That'll take your mind off hockey. While you're at it, find a studio and take some dancing lessons.'"

Simmons nearly suffered a nervous breakdown soon after he returned. In a tense game between Cleveland and Springfield, referee Frank Udvari called a penalty against the Indians that so enraged Shore he ordered his entire team off the ice with the exception of Simmons. Udvari pulled out his watch. "You got ten seconds to ice a team," the referee said, "or I drop the puck." Shore ignored the threat.

Udvari dropped the puck, and five Cleveland players charged at Simmons. So amazed were the attackers at this unheard-of scoring opportunity, they fought among themselves over who would take the shot. Finally Bo Elik of Cleveland shot and missed. Three succeeding shots went wild, and Simmons fell on the puck, stopping play. Finally, Shore sent his team back on the ice.

The players' wives became involved in the bizarre world of Eddie Shore one day in the 1950s during a losing streak. A notice was posted on the team bulletin board: "Players and Wives Report to Dressing Room at 3 P.M."

"We thought it would be a party," said Simmons, "because the Old Man threw a party once in a while. We told our wives to get dressed up real fine. When we got to the dressing room the girls expected to see decorations. Instead, the room was filled with dirty uniforms and stunk of liniment. That shook them up a bit, but nothing like what was to come.

"After we all sat down, the Old Man looked at our wives and said the team wasn't doing as well as it should. He told the girls he wanted them to pay less attention to their husbands so we could play better hockey for the rest of the season. Then he sent us home. That was the end of the party."

Although Shore had four heart attacks, he would throw himself into furies, even fighting opposite players. Such combat was relatively simple for Eddie since the Coliseum's penalty box was directly across the aisle from the Springfield bench. All Shore had to do was leave his seat behind the bench and walk a few feet to the penalty box.

On one such walk, Shore nearly gave his doctor a heart attack. Aldo Guidolin, the tough former Cleveland defenseman, was penalized after manhandling several Springfield players. As Guidolin stepped into the penalty box, Shore charged him. "He told me," said Guidolin, "if he was 20 years younger, he'd kick the crap outta me. That didn't satisfy him 'cause we beat 'em in overtime. So, after the game, he ran down to the announcer's box, turned on the loudspeaker, and called the referee every name in the book. You could hear it all over the rink."

Another alumnus of Shore Academy, class of 1959, Guidolin shudders when he recalls the hours of grim instruction with Eddie. "He harped on three points," said Guidolin. "He wants the hands two feet apart on the stick, the feet 11 inches apart on the ice, and he wants you to skate in a sort of sitting position. You better do it exactly right, or you're in big trouble."

Guidolin discovered this one morning during a practice. He had just completed what he considered a perfect pass that resulted in a goal. What's more, he had skated at top speed while doing it. Then he heard the whistle and saw Shore motion to him. "Mis-ter Guidolin," he said, "do you know what you did wrong?"

"The pass was perfect," said Guidolin. "I was in the sitting position. My two hands were on the stick. What more do you want?"

"Mis-ter Guidolin," Shore said, "your legs were two inches too far apart."

As outlandish as Shore's ideas may appear, they were well grounded in physiological theory developed and harbored in his encyclopedic mind. "Studying under Shore is like getting your doctorate in hockey science," said Kent Douglas, once Toronto's star defenseman. "The Old

Man taught me things about the game nobody else ever mentioned. He showed me you don't have to hit a man real hard — just get a piece of him. He showed me how you maneuver a man till he's off balance. Then you take the puck away from him."

When Douglas complained about being overweight, Shore stayed up nights analyzing the problem. Finally, he had the solution. "You're drinking too much water," Eddie said. Douglas eliminated excess water form his diet, lost weight, gained speed and stamina, and won the American League's outstanding defenseman's trophy.

Shore startled Guidolin and a dozen other players when he ordered them to try several dance routines. But Eddie could see nothing to be surprised about. Not when his lesson made all the sense in the world.

"Tap dancing," Shore explained, "improves balance, and balance is the foundation of an athlete's ability. From balance he obtains power and maneuverability. I want a player to move forward, backward, to one side or the other without actually taking a step, just by shifting his balance. Add those up each time he has to make a move during a game, and he's saving himself a tremendous amount of energy."

Another Shore theory was that players should skate from an almost sitting position. "You fellows were in the Boy Scouts," he'd say. "Remember when you were on a hike in the woods and had to move your bowels? You'd have to bend your knees and squat. Well, that's the way I want you to skate."

Eddie felt that the hockey stick is as delicate a tool as a gyroscope. He urged his players to use nothing but a six-to-eight-lie (the angle between the blade and the shaft) stick. This often disturbed players who had been used to four-or nine-lie sticks. Springfield's former star scorer, Bill Sweeney, always preferred a four-lie, but rather than quarrel with Shore, he told him that he would use six-lie sticks.

"Sweeney fooled the Old Man," said Guidolin. "He had his four-lie stick stamped six, and Shore never knew the difference."

Eddie's severest critics were members of the "Black Aces"— Indians who were out of the lineup as a result of injury, illness, or Shore's desire to bench them. However, they often were compelled to work considerably harder than regular members of the team. "Shore used to tell the Black Aces he's paying like any other job where you put in an eight-hour day," said Hershey defenseman Larry Zeidel. "So he'd have 'em at the rink all day and told 'em to bring a lunch bucket."

The Black Aces said they were forced to do such odd jobs as paint arena seats, sell programs, make popcorn and blow up hundreds of balloons before ice shows. Once, when some Aces were particularly angry, they gave Shore a special lesson in balance. It happened when

Eddie was changing a light bulb in the Coliseum's high ceiling — he never required anyone to perform a job he wouldn't do. To do this, he had to climb a platform which the players on ice pushed from bulb to bulb. At one point Shore was hanging onto an overhead cable with one hand, screwing in a bulb with another, when someone "accidentally" pushed the tower from under him. "He was just hanging there from the cables like a trapeze artist," said a former Ace. "The fellas finally got around to pushing the platform back so he could get down."

According to several men, Shore treated his coaches the same way he treated his Black Aces. Pat Egan, the erstwhile Springfield coach, reportedly painted the arena seats, scraped the ice and repaired Shore's house.

Opposing coaches suffered, too, when they were in Springfield. When King Clancy was coaching Cincinnati, Shore said he'd allow Clancy use of the Coliseum ice for morning practice. The Coliseum was a barnlike structure with a seating capacity of 5,600 and rows of windows near the ceiling on either side of the ice. Late in the morning, the sun beamed through the windows, giving the rink its only natural light and warmth. But this, of course, was contingent on the sun coming out.

"We got on the ice at nine in the morning," said New York Rangers manager Emile Francis, then playing for Cincinnati. "The place was dark as the Dickens, so I asked Clancy to get the lights put on. Just then, Shore came by.

"'Hey Eddie,' Clancy yells, 'how about giving us some light for the practice?'"

"Ya know what Shore tells him? He said, 'Wait a half hour till the sun rises and comes through the windows, then you'll have plenty of light.'"

At the game the next night, Clancy climbed over the boards, marched solemnly across the ice, and presented Shore with a lantern.

Shore managed to antagonize almost every coach in the league, but none more than Jackie Gordon. In a February, 1960, game with Cleveland, Shore suffered a fit of pique when referee Lou Farelli disallowed a Springfield goal even though goal judge Bill Tebone had flashed the red light signifying the score.

Gordon, then the Cleveland coach, couldn't believe it when Eddie reacted by removing Tebone from his post behind the net. Shore said that if the referee could overrule the goal judge, there was no point having one. Gordon insisted the least Shore could do was appoint a new judge. Farelli ordered Shore to comply, but Eddie wouldn't hear of it. The referee resumed the game — minus one very important official.

"I did not pull out the goal judge," Shore said. "He saw the puck go in and put the light on. The referee would not take his decision. So the judge said: 'I seen the puck go in. I'm not a liar. If I am, I don't want the job.' So he walked away.

"The referee asked me to put in another judge. I said, 'This man is honest. If I put in another man it would be saying the first man is a liar and a cheat.' I told the referee: 'Either he goes back in there or else you don't have a goal judge.'"

Ultimately, the then-league President Richard Canning fined Shore $2,000 for the stunt. Eddie suffered a heart attack thereafter. "When he had the attack," said the late Jim Ellery, secretary-treasurer of the American League, "we decided not to press him for the money. And never did."

Fining without collecting was a formula followed by Shore himself. This was the other side of Shore, the side as hidden from the public as the far side of the moon. He was steel on the outside but soft as cotton candy underneath. But he never talked about it. You have to talk to Shore's friends to learn that Shore covered the expenses when forward Doug McMurdy's son was seriously injured. Eddie would not tell you that he gave Bill Sweeney $1,000 to pull him out of a financial jam or that he performed countless other acts of benevolence.

One night Shore caught a couple of players drinking after hours and fined each $200. At the end of the season each received a $200 bonus. Another time, Eddie criticized Ken Schinkel for a mistake during a workout. Normally mild-mannered, Schinkel was upset because his wife had just lost a baby. "Eddie," Schinkel shouted, "you can go to hell."

"That'll cost you $100," snapped Shore.

After the playoffs, Schinkel dropped into the hockey office to say goodbye to his boss. "Wait a minute," said Shore, reaching into his pocket and pulling out $100. "I don't know why I'm so good to you."

"Funny thing about him," said Schinkel. "He fined me every year I was there, but every year he gave me the money back. One thing you gotta say for Eddie — he stuck up for his players all the way."

Eddie's bizarre behavior reached in many directions, including the world of medicine. He always fancied himself an amateur doctor, trainer and psychologist, and he insisted he cured himself twice of cancer, once of the bowels and once of the liver. "He went on a special starvation diet," said Larry Zeidel, "and he says he eventually passed it out of his system."

Eddie himself didn't care to discuss the bouts with cancer. "All I can say," he said, "is three specialists gave me only six months to live in 1940."

Shore passed his medical advice to his players. One afternoon he noticed Schinkel sniffling. Ken had a cold and, having tried the usual remedies without success, was simply waiting out the ailment. Shore had other ideas. "You know what he prescribed?" said Schinkel. "Twelve drops of iodine. And you know what? It worked!"

Sometimes the Shore cure — or diagnosis — disagreed with the patient. Eddie once told Schinkel he was suffering from jaundice. "The Old Man gave me his special 'Market Treatment,'" said Schinkel. "It was a laxative made up of oils. I was scared of it, so I only took half of what I was supposed to. I lost 12 pounds in no time, so I cut it out. I think if I'd taken the whole business it would have been suicide."

The surest form of suicide in Springfield was a full-scale attempt to buck Shore's will. Occasionally, he'd put up with a player who disputed him if he believed the player had a point. But it wasn't any healthier to quarrel with Eddie off ice than it was on.

Former Springfield broadcaster Bob Jones once accused Shore of having him fined for discussing player gripes on the radio. "When I took up the cudgel and aired some of the grievances of my friends on the team I was removed from the air," said Jones. "I thought Shore's penchant for having players sweep the ice, pick up debris and sell score cards was anything but funny.

"What has made the whole era of Shore-dominated sport so mystifying to the average Springfield fan was this: they didn't know anything about it. The two local papers never printed a derogatory word about him. The miserable morale of the Springfield club, which led to a succession of losing seasons, was glossed over or completely ignored."

Perhaps it was, but in the 1966-67 season the Springfield hockey players rose in revolt against their master, in what developed into one of the ice game's rare full-scale mutinies. The players laid it on the line with Shore — either he shaped up, or they would ship out. This was not the first time that Shore had been challenged, but it was one of the rare times when he was defeated.

The pivotal factor was timing. It had become the age of revolt throughout the world, and NHL players had turned to Toronto attorney R. Alan Eagleson for help in organizing a Players' Association. When the Springfield players heard about Eagleson, they contacted him, and he immediately became the general of their uprising.

"I got tired of Shore talking to me like an animal," said Roger Cote, a defenseman who had challenged Shore's practices. "I haven't been paid for weeks. But Mr. Eagleson says not to worry."

The players remained firm in their stand, and public opinion in the hockey world soon turned against Shore. He eventually yielded to the pressure. Shore turned the team over to his son, Eddie, Jr., and eventually delivered control of it to the Los Angeles Kings when Los Angeles joined the NHL in the first major expansion.

Shore himself always believed he was doing the right thing — for hockey, for his players and for himself. In an interview during his heyday as owner of the Indians, he discussed his image and his impact with the authors.

"To me," Shore said, "the $64 question isn't whether you can hand it out but whether you can take it."

Asked about his image and its not-so-positive side, he said: "I'll tell you what's the matter. Shore has always been in the wrong. He doesn't mean to be, but he gets in people's bad graces. He's been outspoken even if it hurts. But his shoulders are fairly broad. I see no point in bragging. I've always felt the truth will out."

Each year the NHL presents the Lester Patrick Trophy. It is given to the man who has done outstanding work for hockey in the United States. Gordie Howe has won it. Bobby Hull has won it.

In March 1970, the winner was Eddie Shore.

"Most of us are a little crazy in some form or other," Shore once said. "Some of us admit it. As for me, I'm not sorry about anything I've ever done in life. As long as I can be close to hockey, I'm happy to be alive!"

7

Toe Blake

THE BEST COACH OF ALL TIME

"I could see immediately," said Blake, "that we would have good harmony in the club. The boys were greatly disappointed with the way they'd finished the last two years. One year a bad goal beat them, the next year a bad fuss. They were determined they were not going to let anything beat them this time, least of all themselves."

Hector "Toe" Blake is rated the best coach of all time for a very simple reason: he accomplished more in fewer years than any other coach in big-league hockey.

Starting with the 1955-56 season and concluding with the 1959-60 campaign, Blake won five consecutive Stanley Cups.

Nobody had been able to do it before, nobody has done it since and, certainly, nobody will ever do it again. Period.

Blake was the perfect coach. He had been an expert player, earned great respect as a performer, played on weak teams and Stanley Cup-winners and experienced everything there was to feel as a performer.

When his time came to move behind the bench — first in the minors with Valleyfield and Houston — he knew everything there was to know about how players feel and how they play the game.

Since Toe never had been a perfectly natural athlete, he took nothing for granted, and since he was an extremely dedicated performer, he understood the value of a strong work ethic.

Blake's entrée to the NHL came about because of dissension in the Canadiens ranks. Although Montreal had a winning club under veteran coach Dick Irvin, they failed — in the eyes of managing director Frank Selke, Sr. — because Irvin allowed his emotions to interfere with his directing of the hockey club.

34

Specifically, Irvin mishandled the tempestuous Maurice "Rocket" Richard, who was allowed to explode with the coach's encouragement. As a result, the Rocket was constantly in hot water. Prior to the 1954-55 playoffs, Richard accosted linesman Cliff Thompson during a melée at Boston Garden and was suspended for the remainder of the season *and* the entire playoffs.

Selke was shaken not only by the suspension but by the unprecedented riot which shook Montreal after the suspension was announced (and which forced the forfeiture of the Canadiens-Red Wings game on March 17, 1955 at The Forum). Fortunately for all parties, Irvin was offered the Chicago Blackhawks coaching job for 1955-56 and was quickly granted his release by Selke who now sought a replacement.

Surely, there was an abundance of qualified coaches to choose from, but the task of controlling Les Canadiens was something special. No team in the NHL had the distillation of French- and English-Canadians that the Montreal team possessed. Selke would have to find a man who, like Irvin, would be able to maintain harmony in the club. On top of that, he required a personality who could command the respect of aces such as Richard, Beliveau and Geoffrion, and who could follow in Irvin's difficult footsteps as a winner. A big winner.

One rumor had it that Selke would be obliged to select a French Canadian. One suggestion was Butch Bouchard; another was Roger Leger, both former players and both well respected in the French-speaking community. Others speculated that Billy Reay, though not a French Canadian, would wind up with the job. Several of the Forum directors were partial to Reay and he was the only choice seriously in the running for the job along with the favorite, Hector "Toe" Blake.

"The Old Lamplighter" had studied coaching well in the Quebec Senior League. He was partially French Canadian and he was admired by all the players, particularly Richard. Kenny Reardon, who had moved up to a key front-office position with the Canadiens, was a strong advocate of Blake, and ultimately the opinions of Selke and Reardon prevailed. On June 8, the signing of Blake was officially announced before a standing-room crowd at the Forum, and Les Canadiens were ready to become the greatest team in hockey history.

Toe Blake wielded a dictator's baton over Les Canadiens, but at first he ruled them like a benevolent despot. This was easy at first because the players, to a man, respected Blake, and vice versa. The pivotal personality on the team was Rocket. He went out of his way to assure the Canadiens hierarchy that he backed Blake to the hilt, and he meant every word of it.

Now it was up to the Old Lamplighter to produce. All the ingredients were there: a young competent goaltender, a strong, intelligent defense, and the most explosive collection of scorers in history. It was simply a matter of stirring them to the proper boiling point without creating the fire hazard of previous years. Richard riots were to be avoided at all costs.

"Blake and Selke were trying to give the Rocket all they had by way of a tranquilizing program," said author Josh Greenfeld. "They started giving him de-pep talks long before the season began. They pointed out to him that he was 35 years old, that he did not have to carry the emotional burden of victory alone, that he still would be treated with sufficient respect by the other players around the league even if he went a little easier on the roughhouse, and that the important thing was not one game, not one fight, but to lead the team to a Stanley Cup victory."

The Canadiens organization, not to mention the city of Montreal, was still smarting from the black eye it had received from the St. Patrick's Day disaster. A unique community spirit seemed to engulf the team right from the start of training camp in nearby Verdun, Quebec. "I could see immediately," said Blake, "that we would have good harmony in the club. The boys were greatly disappointed with the way they'd finished the last two years. One year a bad goal beat them, the next year a bad fuss. They were determined they were not going to let anything beat them this time, least of all themselves."

Blake directed the Canadiens to a Stanley Cup in his rookie season, but it was no fluke. A year later the Habs won the championship again and Blake's blend of toughness and savvy won all the players to his side, but especially Richard.

The Rocket enjoyed playing for Blake more than for any other leader and the results were evident on the ice. The Maurice Richard-Henri-Richard-Dickie-Moore line was one of the NHL's best, partially because of the Rocket's élan.

Under Blake, the Habs won an unprecedented five straight Stanley Cups but when Maurice Richard retired in 1960, Blake was unable to replace the special energy the Rocket brought to the team. In the 1961 playoffs, the Habs were eliminated by Chicago, thus ending their remarkable reign.

Blake never was able to regain his dominance of the Richard Era but his Canadiens remained competitive and won their next Cup in 1965.

Inevitably, Blake clashed with some of his stars, most notably goalie Jacques Plante, with whom he had feuded since the late 1950s. Plante was finally traded to the Rangers in 1963 as defenseman Doug Harvey was two years earlier.

Blake remained coach after Sam Pollock replaced Selke as managing director in 1964, although some thought he might leave.

Blake's decision to continue was a wise one for both himself and the hockey club, even though Les Canadiens finished second to a surprisingly strong Detroit sextet in March, 1965. This placed Montreal against Toronto in the first round of the playoffs and they disposed of the Leafs in six games with Claude Provost and young Bobby Rousseau leading the attack. They had even less trouble with Chicago in the final, winning the Cup in five games. A new award, the Conn Smythe Trophy for the most valuable player in the playoffs, was won by captain Jean Beliveau.

The success formula devised by Blake was interpreted in various ways by different analysts of the game. One theory had it that Toe was the ultimate tyrant who frightened his players by slamming doors, shouting at them on the bench, and doing sardonic dances in the dressing room. Selke, who was admittedly closer to Irvin than Blake, insisted that Toe was not a martinet. He contended that Blake empathized with his skaters more than most coaches and was a master psychologist. This was an amiable chap who could go along with a jape.

Once, after Montreal had won the league championship, the players were celebrating at a banquet in downtown Montreal. When they reached the banquet hall, somebody remarked, "This is room six. Does that mean number six [Ralph Backstrom] is paying the bill?"

Backstrom laughed. "It means the guy who wore it before me [Floyd Curry] can take care of it. But he's not here, so it's the guy who had it before Curry and that's the coach."

Blake was standing there at the time. "Not me," he shot back with a leer. "Who wore number six before me?"

"Before you," chided Backstrom, "they used Roman numerals."
Blake was less amiable during a losing streak but, then again, so was Irvin and so many of the other excellent NHL coaches.

"The Canadiens consistently deliver a greater percentage of their capabilities than any other team in hockey because of their respect for Blake," said Jim Proudfoot, *Toronto Daily Star* columnist. "Blake is the best coach in the National Hockey League."

Goalie Gump Worsley, who was playing the best goal of his life for Les Canadiens, put it another way: "There isn't a man on this club so important that the coach won't bench him if he doesn't move his butt. We all know that. Toe doesn't humiliate you or mouth off to the press. A guy just finds himself sitting the next one out and he sees some kid skating like the wind in his spot."

This was not a unanimous opinion. One who later rose to stardom under a different coaching technique was Gordon "Red" Berenson, whom the Canadiens signed after he had completed his studies at the University of Michigan. Berenson, a tall, rangy center, would have been a superb replacement for Beliveau had Blake managed to nurse him along properly, but the two never quite got along.

"I was a different kind of player compared to the ones Blake was accustomed to," Berenson once said. "He knew I was a college man and I don't think he believed I could make it. When your coach is thinking that way, your chances are not too good."

Berenson's problem, aside from his college diploma, was that he shied away from heavy physical combat. By contrast, little Henri Richard seemed to enjoy mixing it with the muscle-men and endeared himself to Blake right from the start. The coach liked to kid about the Pocket Rocket's diffidence. One day a magazine writer approached Blake and asked the coach whether young Richard spoke English. "The guy's so quiet," Blake replied, "I don't even know if he talks French."

Blake's humor became less apparent with each year, and as he grew older, he seemed to enjoy coaching less than he had during the halcyon years of the five-Cup dynasty.

"Toe was no longer a happy man," said forward John Ferguson. "He would have frequent and persistent headaches, and he didn't sleep well. Besides that, he had become a loner, was angry at some who had been his good friends, and appeared to be within himself all the time. On the road he would shake his depression by walking the streets, but usually he was found in his hotel suite late at night, alone and moving from the bed to the chair and back to the bed again. Once in a while he would turn on the late show and just when it was catching his attention, he would start thinking of Big Jean, the Rocket, goaltending problems and why he wasn't getting even more out of the team — even though nobody could possibly have done better.

"Having to cut players who had been loyal to him but were over the hill was difficult and it hurt Toe. 'It's a very difficult thing to do,' he once said. He also was aware of the deep scar coaching had left. 'Once I was a very happy man,' he had said to me a couple of years ago. 'I am a bitter man now, a very bitter man.' Then, we'd go on a winning tear and he'd cheer up again."

But there was no cheering Blake during the 1967 Cup final against Toronto. Of the stars of the Montreal team that had won the Stanley Cup in 1960, only Henri Richard and Beliveau remained. The total power of the fifties' dynasty was missing, and the goaltending of Worsley and Vachon could not match the perfection of vintage Jacques Plante. As a result, Toronto bumped Montreal out of the finals in six games.

In a sense the defeat marked the end of an era for Montreal as it did for the other five NHL clubs. Expansion had finally come to hockey, and in June 1967, representatives from Pittsburgh, Los Angeles, Oakland-San

Francisco, Minneapolis-St. Paul, Philadelphia, and St. Louis participated in the draft to stock the six new teams of the Western Division. The Canadiens were on the spot because they owned the most abundant stockpile of young talent in the NHL and figured to be riddled by the hungry new clubs. But that was where the genius of Sam Pollock intervened to protect the glittering herd. Wheeling and dealing with expansion teams, Pollock peddled off enough fringe talent to enable Les Canadiens to retain the nucleus of a future winner and they entered the 1967-1968 season as strong as possible under the circumstances.

This time it required more than the usual time for Les Canadiens to get going. They were in last place in December 1967, but soon began a relentless climb to the top that placed them first in the newly created Eastern Division of the NHL. They then wiped out the Bruins and Black Hawks in short order and proceeded to the East-West final against the St. Louis Blues for the Stanley Cup.

The expansion sextet extended Montreal in each of the four games, but Les Canadiens gave the impression of a German shepherd toying with a kitten. At any time, the Montrealers suggested they could have devoured the Blues whole. It was merely a question of how much energy they wanted to generate.

The four-straight sweep was Blake's last hurrah. Toe finally gave in to his better judgment and his nerves and retired after the 1968 championship. In his 13 years as coach, Blake had finished first nine times and won eight Stanley Cups. Few would argue that he was the finest all-round coach the NHL has known.

"Under Toe's stabling influence," said Jim Proudfoot, "the Rocket earned the stature he surely would have missed otherwise. This might have been Blake's finest achievement as a coach. Another would be the rehabilitation of the Montreal club after it came apart in 1961 and 1962. In two years, the Canadiens were back in first place and, a year after that, they won the Stanley Cup again."

Blake was one of a kind. There were good ones to follow, especially Scotty Bowman who won four straight Cups from 1976 through 1979, but nobody ever had five in a row like Toe. That's why he's the best — ever!

8

THE WINNINGEST COACH

*"There's nothing like a home-ice Cup victory,
especially when it's the fourth consecutive Cup."*

*Scott Bowman is both the most appreciated and misunderstood man in
major league hockey. He also is the winningest coach in NHL history.*

*Bowman is complicated yet simple; warm but distant; introverted, yet
effusive. It all depends on the time of day and season of the year.*

*The Great Expansion of 1967-68, when the league ballooned from six to
twelve teams, spawned Bowman's career. St. Louis Blues general manager
Lynn Patrick signed Bowman , and he has been winning ever since.*

*But during stints in St. Louis, Montreal, Buffalo, Pittsburgh and, most
recently, Detroit, he has perplexed both friend and foe alike. But there's no
disputing his intensity. Bowman is what the trade calls "a hockey man's
hockey man." He has been steeped in the game dating back to his Montreal
youth and was a gifted Junior level player until a serious head injury ended
his career.*

*Without missing a beat, he moved into amateur hockey as a coach, then
scouted for the Montreal Canadiens and, finally, the big break, being named
first-year coach of the expansion St. Louis Blues in 1967.*

*"At first the Blues weren't a factor in the race," recalled Larry Zeidel, a
defenseman with the rival Philadelphia Flyers at the time, "but later in the
season Scotty took over as head coach and St. Louis was primed by playoff
time."*

*In fact, the Blues upset Philadelphia in the playoffs and went all the
way to the Stanley Cup finals before losing to the Canadiens in four*

straight. Bowman directed them to the finals again in 1969 (vs. Montreal) and 1970 (vs. Boston), and although St. Louis didn't win a game, Bowman was highly praised for his efficiency.

Following a dispute with Blues ownership in 1971, Bowman became the Canadiens head coach for the 1971-72 season and thereby launched one of the most impressive runs behind the bench the NHL has known. He won the Stanley Cup in his second year piloting the Habs and, starting in 1975-76, ran off four consecutive champion-ships, culminating with a Cup win in 1979.

At the time it was freely predicted that Bowman would ascend to the general managership in Montreal, succeeding Sam Pollock, but when it became apparent that Scott would be aced out of the job, he left the Habs to both manage and coach the Buffalo Sabres.

Although the Sabres finished first in 1979-80, Bowman could not win a Cup during his Buffalo stint which became less successful than anticipated. He left the Sabres in 1987 to become a television analyst and, for all intents and purposes, his coaching career had come to a dead halt.

To everyone's surprise, the Pittsburgh Penguins hired Bowman in June 1990 to become director of player development and recruitment. But when Penguins coach Bob Johnson became ill shortly before the 1991-92 season, Bowman moved behind the bench once more and directed Pittsburgh to its second straight Stanley Cup.

The Penguins were favored to make it three straight in 1993 but were upset by Al Arbour's New York Islanders in a seven-game Patrick Division final series. Bowman was criticized for being too aloof and hands-offish in his orchestration of the champions.

Whatever the case, Scott moved on to Detroit where he signed a lucrative contract with the Red Wings. Owner Mike Ilitch made it abundantly clear that he expected Bowman to do what he had done six times before: produce a Stanley Cup-winner.

Bowman responded by first leading the Red Wings to a respectable (46-30-8) finish in the regular 1993-94 race. After a shaky start, Detroit moved into a contending position and emerged as one of the NHL's élite teams. Nevertheless, Bowman was unhappy with Tim Cheveldae's goaltending and finally prevailed upon GM Bryan Murray to obtain Bob Essensa from Winnipeg. Essensa was less than superb upon his settling in Detroit, but Bowman nevertheless brought his club to the playoffs.

In the playoffs, Bowman failed where he was expected to succeed. The Red Wings opened against the little-respected San Jose Sharks and suddenly found themselves behind the eight-ball.

What was expected to be a breeze turned into a death struggle. Armed with such stars as Sergei Fedorov, Steve Yzerman and Paul Coffey,

Bowman nevertheless could not firmly establish Detroit superiority. Ultimately, he gambled on rookie Chris Osgood in goal over Bob Essensa and Osgood blew the deciding game.

Bowman and his favored Red Wings were humiliated by the first-round elimination which eventually resulted in the firing of Bryan Murray. As expected, Bowman accepted the defeat with equanimity. He has endured many years and lost a few before this one. Besides, hockey isn't everything to this complex character.

Away from the rink, Bowman is a homebody who loves to tinker with model electric trains, eat lobster and read books like The Rise and Fall of the Third Reich, *see films like* Rain Man *and never tires of visiting Montreal which, as he puts it, "is my home town." He is an insatiable teacher, always willing to impart hockey knowledge to younger coaches.*

"Scotty made me what I am today," said St. Louis Blues coach Mike Keenan. "He got me started in the coaching business." Ditto for Pierre Maguire, who made his head coaching debut with the Hartford Whalers in 1993-94. Bowman discovered him at St. Lawrence University.

"If it weren't for Scotty taking a chance on a 28-year-old kid, I wouldn't be where I am right now," said Maguire. "I'm eternally grateful to him. Scotty doesn't talk about himself much. That's why I love to brag about him. I want people to know that as much of a champion he is as a coach, he's more of a champion as a father and a husband."

Like so many others who have worked with Bowman, Maguire was amazed at Scotty's mental acuity when they were colleagues in Pittsburgh. Pierre spent two years with the Penguins as an assistant coach and now owns a pair of Stanley Cup rings for his efforts, although Pierre fully credits Scott for the jewelry.

"I've seen Bowman out-coach people, just eat them up," said Maguire. "They knew what he was going to do and still were defenseless. He knows how to get the star players on the ice at the right time, especially on the road and in the playoffs."

That's why Ilitch imported Bowman from Pittsburgh. But nobody is infallible and, after all these years in the NHL, Bowman might just be a bit passé for the hockey player of the 1990s.

In an effort to glean what's behind Bowman, Stan Fischler huddled with Scott, an old friend, during one of his frequent visits to New York. Their conversation follows.

SF: What surprised you most about the Detroit situation?

SB: Hockey interest in Detroit. I didn't realize how intense it was. There are four major league teams and, frankly, I don't know exactly where we stand on the list but I know we're not number four.

SF: Explain the difference in coaching the Red Wings as opposed to the Penguins.

SB: When I took over in Pittsburgh, the Penguins already had been a winner under Bob Johnson. They had won the Stanley Cup and were a very confident group. When a club takes a championship, it means a lot of groundwork already has been done, so what I had to do in Pittsburgh was win again. With Detroit it's a lot different, starting with the age of the players. Dino Ciccarelli was the oldest at 33, then there was Steve Yzerman who's 28. Then we go down to Ray Sheppard and Shawn Burr at 27. Then it drops right off. We had about nine players under 24. That's a big difference compared with Pittsburgh.

SF: How have you changed your coaching style from 1968 to today?

SB: I've had to adapt to the new style of play which is certainly more offensive-minded. Players are more individual nowadays. It's much more difficult to think as a a team now. But the values haven't changed. You still need good self-discipline. You still need players to come to the rink and play, and come to the rink and practice.

SF: What has been the most dramatic change in hockey that you've seen since you came into the NHL as a coach?

SB: Certainly the goaltenders' equipment has changed an awful lot. We have cages and all kinds of headgear. Equipment becomes a part of a goalie's play now right up to them using the masks to stop shots. We didn't have that before. Also, the advent of the offensive defenseman is a change; the one who can pressure-forecheck. When I first started, if you couldn't go in and really forecheck you stayed back.

SF: From a coaching viewpoint, which was your most satisfying Stanley Cup win?

SB: The first one is always the most cherished. Whether you're a player or a coach, you want to win at least one Stanley Cup. In another way the fourth Cup [in a row] we won in 1979 was very important to me. That was the season when we went to the finals against the Rangers after they had upset the Islanders in the previous round. There was a tremendous amount of hype involved in our series with New York because we were gunning for a fourth straight Cup and Freddie Shero had the Rangers sky-high. The first game was at the Forum and they beat us. Game Two was also in Montreal and New York took a two-goal lead before we came back and won the game. The other thing that made it so special was that this was the only Stanley Cup of the five that the Canadiens had won for me that was won at the Forum. My family was able to enjoy it more and they were all a little bit older. There's nothing like a home-ice Cup victory, especially when it's the fourth consecutive Cup.

SF: Even though you won it four games to one, it was not an easy series for you because some weird things happened.

SB: One of the strangest things was the goal that was "stolen" from us in the second game at Madison Square Garden [fourth game of the series]. This was in overtime when Larry Robinson took a shot that beat John Davidson in the Rangers goal, but the light didn't go on and play didn't stop. That goal should've ended the game and I had a hard time restraining my players and keeping them going, which was important because the Rangers had a counterattack going and moved into our end. We were fortunate to stop them, and then within a minute or two after we had scored the goal that was never counted, Serge Savard beat Davidson and this time the goal counted. But we had good fortune behind us in that series.

SF: What do you mean specifically by "good fortune"?

SB: The Rangers had us reeling after Game One. We were concerned because Fred Shero had brought this team from really nowhere and he had them believing they could win. They had a strong goaltender in John Davidson who was at the top of his game. I had planned to make a goalie change for Game Two. I've always gone on the assumption that when things aren't going well you have to try something. So, I decided to remove Ken Dryden and insert Bunny Larocque, who was our second goalie. Talk about good fortune! In the pre-game workout, Bunny got hit by a shot and had to leave the ice. He was injured enough so I had to start Dryden after all. Ken went back in and shut the door on the Rangers. In the end I was fortunate that I didn't have to experiment with Larocque because we went with Kenny all the way to the Cup.

SF: You've pulled yourself out of other desperate situations as a coach, haven't you?

SB: A lot of people remember the Bruins series when we were down by a goal in Game Seven against Don Cherry's club and Guy Lafleur saved us after they got penalized for too-many-men-on-the-ice. It was quite a game. We had previously fought back to tie the game and then Boston went ahead again with a goal from behind the net. That's when I was experiencing that special coach's feeling that I could have stayed there all night and we weren't going to win the game. But they got called for the extra man and Guy did his thing. It was odd because we were going on to the power play and we weren't doing well with the power play up to that point. And even then, Lafleur's shot wasn't a result of setting up well. What happened was that Guy came down the right side and took a routine shot from just over the blue line — and scored!

SF: Jacques Lemaire had a lot of trouble coaching Lafleur. How difficult was he for you?

SB: I had no problem with Lafleur. At the beginning it was a bit of a challenge to make him realize how good he could be. We had been upset that fellows like Marcel Dionne and Richard Martin, who had been drafted after Guy, were putting up big numbers on the board while Guy wasn't, at first. Then, Guy finally realized he could be the best player and from that point on it wasn't really difficult. He was a very coachable player because he enjoyed coming to the rink. He enjoyed playing and he enjoyed practicing as well.

SF: The first Cup win of the string — in 1976 — must have been especially satisfying since your Canadiens stopped the two-year Cup streak of the Philadelphia Flyers. It was your Good Guys against the Broad Street Bullies.

SB: That was a series we won in four straight and yet, strangely enough, it was a close series. Actually, it easily could have gone seven games. We won the first two games in Montreal by a goal but we still were concerned because they were a strong home-ice team. That's when Dryden shut the door on them for the most part and we got key goals from our top players. But that was some challenge for us because Bobby Clarke was the premier centerman in the league and it took Jacques Lemaire's ability to play two-way hockey against him for us to win. Plus two other centermen came through for us: Doug Risebrough and his feistiness and Doug Jarvis' defensive ability. I wound up throwing three different players at Clarke because I remembered how we couldn't shut him down the other way during the regular season.

SF: What sort of emotion do you experience these days? People who watch you get the impression that you're emotionless.

SB: I try to control my emotion more than I try to let it out. I can be emotional at times, but what I try to do is structure it so that the team itself feels that the coach at least is in control. The Red Wings were not as emotional a team as they should have been. That's one of the points we discussed; the fact that we had to get more emotion into our game. It's hard to give it every night, but they have to do it.

SF: How close are you with fellow long-time coach like Al Arbour who retired after the 1993-94 season?

SB: We talked a lot but more about things that were not involved in hockey. I thought nothing of picking up the phone and asking Al about a certain player. When I was coaching Pittsburgh, it was a little strained because then we were in the same division. But when I moved to another conference, we talked more. You see, our families grew up together in St. Louis when he played defense for me on the Blues. My wife, Suella, is very close to Al's wife Claire. We share a lot of the same interests. Al is a good friend to have outside of hockey, but when I was involved in the games themselves I didn't consider him as a friend because in hockey you have no friends (*laughs*).

SF: You went up against Al in the 1993 playoffs and he beat you. What went wrong?

SB: What happened was that Mario Lemieux's problem of not playing in two or three of the games. That, plus the Islanders goaltending of Glenn Healy. Everybody dumped on our goaltender, Tom Barrasso, but the difficulty was that we ran into a hot goalie.

It's been proven over and over again that a hot goalie in the playoffs can win a series. We couldn't put the puck in the net and, ironically, it was the seventh game when we felt we really got our offense going. But the Islanders got the goaltending you need to win. Also, it didn't help that Kevin Stevens got hurt early in Game Seven. It had been said that Kevin needs Mario, but Stevens is also the one player who has been able to play constantly in the past few seasons without Mario. Remember, Mario was back in that game feeling pretty good so that when we lost Stevens we really never replaced him in that game. If you examine Mario's games in the playoffs, you'll see that this wasn't one of his vintage games.

SF: It's often said that the regular season is a war of attrition. How do you view an 84-game schedule?

SB: I look at it in segments often and by quarters. We had a poor first quarter in 1993-94, and I determined that we couldn't have another poor quarter or we'd be in jeopardy. The one thing I don't like about the present set-up is that the conference we're in has tougher points to get for all of the teams. What I care about is the playoffs; I don't really care about being the overall winner although I'd like it. The thing is we were in a division without an expansion team and more established clubs are not easy to beat up on. The facts are that in 1992-93 Detroit had nine games with Tampa and I think they won eight of them. In 1993-94 we played them maybe two, maybe three times. Our division points became much tougher in one year.

SF: Who is the favorite player of all who you've coached?

SB: I'll go back to my first coaching years when I was with St. Louis, but I won't limit myself to just one or two players. Red Berenson, who came into his own when he joined the us in St. Louis, is one and Glenn Hall, who played goal for me with the Blues, is another. In Montreal I enjoyed Bob Gainey, Guy Lafleur and Ken Dryden. Lafleur was the best offensive player in the league and Gainey was the best defensive forward. We also had Larry Robinson, Serge Savard and Guy Lapointe. I have a hard time distinguishing which of those three I enjoyed the most. Then, in Pittsburgh, I had Tom Barrasso, Mario Lemieux, Ron Francis, Joey Mullen and Kevin Stevens. I can't pick one player from among them.

SF: Pick one.

SB: The one player who contributed for me for a longer period of time than the others was Guy Lafleur.

SF: You've been a general manager and a coach. Which is more fun?

SB: Coaching. It's the job where when the season is over, you can totally focus on something else. Which is good. So, I had two or three months in there. If I'm manager, there's always something to do; signing or negotiating of some kind. And you're at the mercy of both players and coaches.

SF: What aspect of coaching gives you the most satisfaction?

SB: The game gives me a sense of accomplishment. But there are many factors in coaching; obviously the practice and the preparation — not only game preparation but the game itself. When the game is on and you're coaching, you're doing things, putting certain players together, experimenting.

SF: Name the player you coached against who you would have wanted on your club.

SB: I would have to say Bobby Clarke. He was a special type of player for the Flyers. Looking further back than that, I'd pick Gordie Howe.

SF: Name the player who played for you who succeeded more on drive and motivation than he did on ability.

SB: Al Arbour, because he had to work for every inch of the ice. He played in an era when you had to do all of the little things right. It took total concentration for him to really be an effective defenseman. When I was in St. Louis, Al was at the end of his career but he was still the glue for our team. Another player like that, who I had in Montreal, was Doug Risebrough. Also Yvon Lambert. They were very underrated players who would come to the rink every day and put their work shoes on. When I was in Buffalo, Craig Ramsey was like that — a special player. When those guys were on the ice, you had the feeling that they were doing more for the team than people realized. Terry Crisp. Looking back, it's not hard to imagine why people like Arbour, Gainey and Crisp became coaches in the NHL.

SF: You got Mike Keenan his coaching break; how close are you with him now?

SB: Mike and I have been pretty good friends from the time he came to Rochester in the American League. When he started as head coach in Philadelphia, we talked and we've stayed close. When I made the decision to leave Pittsburgh for Detroit, I talked to Mike quite a bit. He talked to me as well about his plans.

SF: Do you remember giving Keenan his first coaching opportunity?

SB: Actually, Mike would have been my choice to coach in Buffalo after he had been in Rochester. What happened was that Red Berenson had joined us the year before and Red and Mike became very good friends. Mike respected the fact that Red might come back. In late August of that year, Red changed his mind, which was a bit of a tragedy because we were scrambling and we never really replaced him. If we had known that June that Red was not coming back, Keenan would have been the coach.

SF: How intense was it to coach against Keenan in the 1992 Stanley Cup finals?

SB: It was not insane like some people might have thought. A coach doesn't get on his uniform against the other coach. At least I don't feel that I do. When we played against Chicago, both teams were on a roll. There was a fine line and the line was so fine that it set the stage for the rest of the series.

SF: Why did you leave Pittsburgh?

SB: In Pittsburgh I was sort of an interim coach and I didn't think I was going to be compensated for the experience that I had put into the game. Obviously, I had wanted to keep coaching, but the contract that I had signed the year before with the Penguins was not the type of deal that I wanted to end my career with, and then came the chance to go to Detroit. I knew that the Red Wings had a young team and they were one of the teams in that conference that had had a good season the year before. Besides, Detroit was the same distance from my home as Pittsburgh. It was also a good move for me because one of my children was trying to get into the University of Michigan and my son was probably going to go to the University of Dayton, the same school that Al Arbour's daughter went to.

SF: Your salary in Detroit was considered astronomical by previous coaching standards. You're getting more than some managers are making.

SB: Times have changed. Salaries have gone up and all you have to do is look at what has happened with players. Then, you have to remember that the coaching business is very volatile. And in the end, you have to average it out just like they do on the stock market. They look at a stock and average what it has done for three, four, five years.

9

THE YOUNGEST COACH

"The way I looked at it, everything depended on how we judged ourselves. If I believed we wouldn't do well, then we wouldn't do well. We had to raise our expectations, set out from the beginning to win the Stanley Cup. We had to believe that something good would happen, or it never would. We had to set our expectations as high as possible because life is self-fulfilling."

In a 1993-94 season filled with unusual happenings, there were no stranger hockey events than those which unfolded in California's Bay Area. The previously hapless San Jose Sharks impressed absolutely no one when they hired totally unknown Kevin Constantine as head coach.

Addressing 800 downtown San Jose businessmen, the crewcut redhead unabashedly said, "I encourage you to simplistically and mindlessly enjoy the game. That way you won't second-guess me."

But the second-guessing began within a week of the season opener. In no time at all, the Sharks fell to the bottom of the National Hockey League and actually staggered through nine games (0-8-1) without even winning a single contest. It was freely predicted that Constantine would be gone by Christmas — if not Thanksgiving — and the brand-new San Jose Arena would be less than half-filled of its splendid 17,190 seats.

Then, something happened; nobody is quite sure what it was but it was SOMETHING! Under the severely intense gaze of 35-year-old Constantine, the Sharks began to win and win and win. By mid-season, they had not only become a respectable hockey club, but actually developed designs on a playoff berth.

Still, it wasn't until March that experts began taking Constantine's Sharks seriously. In the absence of a superstar, San Jose challenged the Los Angeles Kings for the final playoff berth in the NHL's West Conference. It *seemed preposterous. This was the very same Kings club that reached the 1993 Stanley Cup finals with Wayne Gretzky leading the way, battling the no-names from San Jose.*

Yet, somehow, Constantine guided his patchwork quilt of a team into the playoffs while the ritzy, glitzy Kings finished out of the running.

How did the miracle of San Jose occur? Considerable credit belongs to Constantine, one of the unlikeliest leaders to ever pilot a big-league hockey club.

His saga began in International Falls, Minnesota where he was on skates just about the time he learned to walk. "I think," Kevin recalled, "that I was was skating as soon as I could breathe."

Constantine wanted to be a goaltender and, as a youth, idolized Pete Wasalavich, varsity netminder for International Falls High School. Kevin aspired to follow Wasalavich's skate steps and eventually reached the varsity as team captain. Already his leadership qualities had become apparent.

"There was no question that he'd be captain even though he was our goalie," said coach Larry Ross. "Kevin was highly respected by everyone."

So respected, in fact, that he received a full scholarship offer from the prestigious Rensselaer Polytechnic Institute in Troy, New York. But the RPI experience was a disaster and Kevin was out of there faster than you can say Constantine. He had a tryout with the Montreal Canadiens that was less than a hit and decided that he had had it with hockey.

"I tried to find the furthest spot away from hockey," he said. Constantine moved to California where he alternately built houses (with his brother, a carpenter), sold cars and tended bar.

Never in his wildest dreams did he expect to become a professional hockey coach. He subsequently had jobs as a ski lift operator and raft-renter on the Truckee River. The turning point occurred during a visit to Squaw Valley, site of the 1980 U.S. Olympic gold medal triumph.

"I stood along the boards and watched about ten kids learning how to skate," Constantine told Ann Killion of the San Jose Mercury News. *"Some parents and I started talking. After I said that I'd played hockey, they asked me if I'd come out and help their Learn-to-Skate program every Wednesday night. That was how it all started. I spent 40 hours a week on the coaching side without getting paid, but I was really enjoying it."*

Serious about coaching now, Constantine went to the University of Nevada-Reno, obtained a bachelor's degree in business administration and then began seriously climbing the ladder. He coached a junior team in Mason City, Iowa, then was an assistant at Northwood Prep in Lake Placid, took another Junior job in Rochester, Minnesota and directed the team to the national championship.

While at Rochester, he was introduced to Peggy Kos who happened to be dating two players on Kevin's Rochester team. He traded both of them and began dating Peggy himself, and two years later they were married. "She would say about me that I have an enormous sense of humor," said Constantine, "but it comes out in a dry and sarcastic side." Meanwhile, he continued his hockey progression until in 1991-92 he was named head coach of the Kansas City Blades in the International Hockey League.

"The NHL never was my primary goal," Kevin insisted, "but as I got closer and closer and made it to The I, I said to myself, 'One more move and Holy Cow, I might be in the NHL.'"

Kansas City was the Sharks' premier farm team which meant that Constantine was closely watched by the San Jose high command. After he led them to a league championship, they couldn't help but be impressed. "He doesn't like losing," said forward Ray Whitney who played for him in both Kansas City and San Jose, "and he's not crazy about ties."

Constantine didn't enjoy the first weeks of his rookie NHL season. He lost game after game and he seethed. He was a marked contrast to the Sharks previous coach, George Kingston, and the players knew it immediately.

"Under Kingston, after a loss, we knew nothing was going to happen, bad or good," said goalie Arturs Irbe. "The coach [Kingston] wasn't going to say anything. George was not tough enough. But Kevin pushes us very hard."

Constantine: "If you ask my players what I'm like, they'd say, 'pretty serious, intense.' Coaching forces that personality on you."

Away from the rink, he can be a laugh riot. Like just before Christmas 1993, he promised his wife a new table for the holiday — except that he bought the table and immediately had it delivered to his neighbor's house. On Kevin's instruction, the neighbor dressed up the table as if it was his own and then invited Mr. and Mrs. Constantine to visit.

"This is the kind of table I wanted," said Peggy Constantine. "Maybe we should take it home," snapped Kevin. And they did!

His Sharks also took home more wins than anyone in the NHL imagined would happen in 1993-94 and Constantine eventually got mention as an Adams Trophy (Coach of the Year) candidate. All the while, he kept a healthy distance from his troops.

"I'd love to be one of the guys," he told Oakland Tribune *columnist Dave Newhouse. "When I played hockey, I was one of the guys — to a fault. If there was a party, I'd be there. As for having a few beers with the guys, and telling old stories, I'd like that but my assignment is direction, organization, to lay out the dream. I don't know where this is going. No one does. But there's a common mission, and to have that, there has to be a hard-core feeling."*

In time, that common mission helped push the Sharks right past Wayne Gretzky's Kings and right into the playoffs where they upset the Red Wings and took Toronto to seven games before losing. One would have been hard-pressed to have found a happier coach in the NHL.

"I'm one of only 26 coaches in the big league," Constantine concluded. "I'm the only one born in America and I'm coaching in a place where the sun shines. You can't beat that!"

During a respite in his schedule, Constantine chatted with Oakland reporter Alan Goldfarb about his hockey life.

Hockey has been my life almost from the second I put on my first pair of skates at our home in International Falls. Not that there weren't other thoughts on my mind. I played the piano and people still say that I write well, but I was purely attached to hockey. I even skipped my sister's wedding to play a high school hockey game.

My day went something like this: up for breakfast; then to school; then it was right to the rink over the yard. The rink was fifty feet away. I'd be there for all kinds of games and practices and my father would even bring me a meal every night so that, after I ate, I could referee and supervise public skating. I'd go home at 10 p.m. Without knowing it, my parents turned me into a pure hockey person.

You see, I came from a strict Baptist family that didn't believe in movies or dances or those things and they certainly didn't believe in me spending a lot of time out at night. I had to be home or, if not, then playing hockey. So, hockey became my substitute for a social life which was why it was so tough for me when I was away from the game later on — after I left RPI and came out to see my brother in California.

I was no different from any other American — just wandering around, wondering where my niche would be. One thing I did learn was how much I missed hockey. They say you never really know how much you really love something until it's taken away from you. In that sense, I learned that lesson and now I consider myself one of the luckiest people on Earth; doing something I truly enjoy. I mean, how many people can work 16 hours a day and want to get up and do it again every day? I love people and I love coaching.

There are two distinct personalities that exist within a coach and within most good players. The game itself requires a demeanor that's borderline pathological. Maybe anti-social would be a better description. Or sociopath. Hockey is a tough game that borders on warlike. It's a battle. There's a direct parallel to war and you certainly need that kind of mentality to be successful.

The ultimate player is the one who can switch to that personality once he starts preparing for the game and can build that to its maximum until the game is over. That same, ultimate, player away from the ice would be one of the easiest-going, nicest people, with a sense of humor, a family man, loving and caring.

As a coach, I try to surround myself with players like that. I hope that my personality doesn't vary too much from the players. I try to get myself worked up for the game so that I'm peaking mentally, I'm focused and I can make sharp decisions.

Teams take on the personalities of their coaches. When I'm not very "up" on the bench, then, most of the time the team is not "up." When I'm really intense, the team takes on that same personality. That's why I feel an obligation in each game to be as excited about it as I would want my players to be excited about it. After the game, it's back to life, laughs and giggles.

Of course, sometimes it's hard to leave a game. I often carry the game to sleep all night long and it bugs me the next day. Like most coaches, I have a routine on the day of our games. I try to go home in the afternoon to take a nap for a couple of hours.

Most people are at their freshest when they get up in the morning and that's when they peak mentally. As the day drags on, people fatigue a little. I nap in the afternoon so that when I awaken, I'm mentally fresh. Then, I go to the rink and go through a series of goal-setting methods. I try to pick out four or five things the team needs to work on that night and try to do the same thing for the units playing. I set individual goals for each of the players playing. Most of the time each of the players choose those goals themselves; two or three things they feel are real important. By the time I walk myself through that process I've convinced myself of the things we need to get done for that night and try to present those things to the team. Then, I have a mood check on myself.

I ask myself if I'm emotionally ready. I don't want to be too high emotionally because then I can make frazzled decisions. But I don't want to be down, so I find the mood that fits me best to be at my coaching best. Then, I have to get antsy by walking around or jumping down the hall; just getting the mood right. If I feel I'm getting myself too much into it, I have to back myself up a bit.

It's the same with good athletes. They find that perfect balance. Which explains why there are so many routines with players, so many superstitions. The hockey player tries to get into that same frame of mind to maximize his game.

As for my coaching, I've tried to learn something from every kind of coach — baseball, football, basketball and hockey. From them I've been able to find my own way of coaching, although defining it isn't easy. It's like asking Wayne Gretzky to explain what he does and, for years, he probably didn't even know. He just went and did it.

I demand a lot from players and at the same time I have to learn to relate to them and appreciate what they're going through. In that sense it's a tough-love approach. I'm always thinking about what they're thinking and, at the same time, I have to be the guy who pushes them really hard and get them dedicated and disciplined and a little defense-oriented while taking advantage of their various skills.

I've always had teams that won because of good defense and not necessarily because of a great offense. Being an ex-goaltender, I believe in building from your goaltender. Because I've had great goaltenders, it's worked out all right.

There's a common thread with teams I've coached. They've been defense-oriented and they had a common goal; a dream of chasing down the best there was. Right now I'm determined to win the Stanley Cup. There's no satisfaction being in the NHL for just being here although it's unbelievably satisfying. But that's not my only reason; I want to win it all down the road.

To get there, I believe there's a certain best way to do things and I try to push in that direction. On the way, I hope that my passion for the game and for people is evident when I'm doing that. It's not like I'm simply a taskmaster or I'm Mister Drill Sergeant. I always hope that the players recognize that I have their best interests at heart.

If I'm maximizing their abilities for the best interests of the team, only good could come out of that for the individual players. The frustration of the job along the way is that sometimes you have to push so hard to get the results that everyone commonly shares that it may give the appearance that it's all work and no fun. The truth is, there's nothing more I like than to laugh. That's one of the reasons why I like coaching; the players are characters and they keep doing things just strangely enough to keep things exciting. I don't mind guys who are a little wild or guys who make me laugh or guys who talk a lot. At the same time my ultimate obligation is to make sure everybody is doing as good a job as he can, so if that means I have to be hard-nosed, then that's my job. As they say, life's a stage and we're the actors.

You have to go through the bad to experience the good. In my last year in the International League, I experienced that when we went through an eight-game losing streak. The first thing I would ask the players to do after a loss was to look in the mirror first and find out if they were at fault before starting to pin blame on other players.

The first person I had to scrutinize during that losing streak was myself. It made me question everything about myself; whether I was good at this or whether it was the players or luck or if the system was correct. Ultimately, the lesson learned was that we really didn't change our principles at all. We didn't change the way we did things. We didn't change what we believed in; we just went even harder at what we had done in the past and the situation righted itself. We went on to have the best record in the league during the last 52 games of the season. That created strength in me. Things went wrong, but it created strength in me and it taught me, even after I got to the NHL, to have strength in my convictions. It's not necessary to do a 360-degree turn when the chips are down.

When I took over the Sharks in September 1993, there were lots of comparisons between myself and my predecessor, George Kingston. The media was always into that but I said then that I wouldn't compare the two of us because there was no value in doing that. The only reason I ever look back is that there may be a lesson to be learned in terms of going forward but never to look back. I organized my training camp with no thought to the way it had been done before. I was going to do it my way whether the previous Sharks had been highly successful or not successful.

But since the Sharks had not been successful in the previous two years, there was an open door for me to come in and build a foundation. That foundation is a high degree of organization and a certain way of doing things. In the process, we were forming an identity. Once we had the identity, we built on that. But that's the way I've always done things.

When we launched camp in the fall of 1993 I had everything organized. Positionally, on the ice, I had everything covered. It provided a structure and once everybody had an assignment, they became dependent on each other to fulfill obligations. If they didn't, everything would break down. That interdependence produces a power that grows and it's far greater than having five people independently trying to figure out what's going on on a need-to-react basis. The game changes quickly and there are situations where a player must react constantly to go from offense to defense to offense a number of times in a shift. Once the players learn to trust each other, a real power grows from that.

When we started the 1993-94 season, we were not a very mature team. We were still a two-year-old team in a 77-year-old league. We didn't know how to deal with success. Then, good things began to happen. By the middle of January we were still in the middle of the playoff race, which fooled a lot of people. But I could see the pieces of the puzzle starting to come together. We just had to find the rest of the pieces.

I kept looking for junctures that would show that we were better than we were before; markers along the way that help us pursue the real goal of being as good as we can be. One of them was our goaltending. Arturs Irbe improved significantly and that gave us a big boost.

As we won, we gained confidence but, at the same time, I had to guard against that winning creating complacency. Fortunately, we pretty much stayed on keel and kept in the playoff race and that enabled me to focus on the broader goal of being a championship team.

The way I looked at it, everything depended on how we judged ourselves. If I believed we wouldn't do well, then we wouldn't do well. We had to raise our expectations, set out from the beginning to win the Stanley Cup. We had to believe that something good would happen, or it never would. We had to set our expectations as high as possible because life is self-fulfilling.

If you tell yourself you won't be good for five years, you won't be good for five years. If you tell yourself you're pursuing the Stanley Cup, you might surprise yourself. Whenever you've shown people what you can do, you become obligated to keep doing that.

I have been described in some places as a "workaholic" and my wife would agree to that description. My answer to that is this: isn't everybody in life a "holic" of some sort? We're all into something. Some people are couch potatoes; their holicism is nothing; they're into doing nothing. I'm 35 years old and I've been into some things that were good for me and some that weren't so good for me. Hopefully, the only difference between me now and the past is that age has provided, if any, a small degree of wisdom.

Why shouldn't I addict myself to something that will provide good for myself and other people? In that sense, coaching provides me with a way to have a life that is fulfilling and, at the same time, positively affect the people around me. I get up, I work and I go to bed. In the meantime, I have to eat so I stop for a second and do that. The only time I try to walk away is when I think putting in too many hours is making me less productive. I need to walk away long enough to refuel.

Over the course of time I find myself saying I have to back off a second here or there because I'm not thinking sharp. I'm spending 16 hours getting eight hours of work done. If I back off and work 12 hours, I'll get 12 hours of work done.

The first year I worked in Kansas City, I went at it a little too hard. I was trying to maximize what I could get out of myself. I hope I get my players to want to do that. But if I'm going too hard and it slows me down, then I have to back off.

I remember the year we won the Turner Cup (IHL) championship, I would stay in the office until 11 at night. If there were two hours in the day left, I wanted to make sure I was using them well. In the end, it became counterproductive. The year after that, I went home at 9 p.m., turned on the TV and watched a sitcom and had a few laughs. To me there's nothing better to do than laugh. When I did that, I found that I slept better at night and was more refreshed when I woke up the next day.

You learn all the time. When I was in high school, I was an all-American teen, same in college. I didn't go to some classes; I had a few beers; got terrible grades. Would I do it differently now if I had a chance to do it over again? Yeah, I would. But if I had done things differently then, I wouldn't be where I am now, and I don't want to be anywhere else.

It wasn't as if I planned to make it all the way to the NHL. When I played the game, I never thought about coaching. Period. As a goalie, I was one of the lonely guys down there, just stopping pucks. Coaches don't focus on goalies and, if the truth be known, I had no interest in coaching until I began doing it as a volunteer. But, in retrospect, the elements were in place, just waiting for the opportunity. I really like young people and I like working with them, so the seeds were just waiting to be planted. Of course, once I got started, I never thought of going to the bigs until I was named head coach at Kansas City. When that happened, I then said to myself, "Hey, I'm one step away from the NHL." The thought finally occurred to me that I could go right to the top some time in the future.

When I took over the Sharks, one of the first things I came to realize was that some of the players were my age. In camp we had Igor Larionov and Sergei Makarov, two of the best world-class players of all time. I said to myself, "Who the hell am I to tell them how to play the game?" They probably knew more than I'll ever know about playing, but that didn't relieve me from my obligation as a coach to tell them how I wanted it done. I had to tell them because that's my job. But once in a while, I'd think about it and slap myself and say, "Yeah, right, you are gonna tell Makarov and Larionov how to play the game of hockey."

Every player is motivated by different things, but there are certain fundamental things that hold true with every player and as a coach I have to hold every player to those fundamentals. Past relationships can't dictate my current decision-making and I have to guard against that. The hardest day in coaching is the day you cut the players. If you don't care about that day, then you're just a callous person. I don't know of any person who can do that without anxiety.

Take training camp, 1993, Mike Kravets. Cutting him was not easy but the consolation was that the cut was not terminal. He could be brought back up at any time. But at the time of the cut, I didn't have to watch him anymore because I knew exactly what he would do because I watched him every time he stepped on the ice. I've never seen a player differ. If you judged guys and gave them a ranking from one to ten in every game, his ranking would never change. If we feel we need his ingredients some time down the line, we'll bring him back.

He was the last one we told we'd cut and we saved him purposely for last because we were just a little chicken to do it at first. But we wanted to let that meeting go as long as it needed and not pressure to get him to the next one because that's the kind of respect we had for the guy. But in those emotional moments, you never know whether a player really understands. Still, you have to say it anyhow.

In my job, respect is of the utmost importance. But I can't go out and just demand their respect; I have to earn it. I know that if they don't respect me, they won't follow through with the same conviction. If they don't perform with conviction, then they're not as good as they could be. So it's my job to show that I care more about them and their careers and, hopefully, I can gain their respect through that.

Take the case of Igor Larionov. When he came to the club, I knew that he was an intelligent human being who prided himself on that. He had seen a lot and been through the Soviet way of doing things. I knew it would be fun to see how he trusted me because I doubted that he trusted his coaches through his whole life.

In the end, if I've had any success, it's that I base my decisions on common sense. Tradition says that the game of hockey belongs to North Americans in the NHL. Common sense says that the game belongs to people who are the best players. That's why it was intelligent of the Sharks to pursue the best players and why we've drafted more Europeans than average. A common-sense decision was made.

Another example: tradition said that players came to camp out of shape and used training camp to get in shape. Common sense says that if you lose 71 games, let's figure out a way to get ahead of the competition and come to camp in shape.

On the other hand, tradition says it's a tough, rough game and they need to play that way. Common sense agrees with it. In that sense, the two things coincide. But my philosophy is that if I find that traditionally things are done one way but common sense is staring me in the face saying, "Do it a new way," then I'm going to try the new way. For one season, at least, it's worked in the NHL.

After a while, our success caused a ripple among the media. The Sharks got noticed; I got noticed. There would be hockey stories and offbeat stories. One fellow, Mark Purdy, sports editor of the *San Jose Mercury*, even did a column on the gum I chew behind the bench. I told him, honestly, that when I broke in as an amateur coach I was a sunflower seed guy. But that doesn't work so well when you're walking behind the bench and spitting out seeds with the players in front of you.

Now I chew two pieces of Bazooka bubble gum in the first period and, depending on how the game goes, two more pieces in the second and, maybe, two more in the third. Purdy figured that I had a 5.2-Bazooka per-game average.

I figured out that there's a small amount of logic to chewing the gum. People who are really into something tend to be physically demonstrative in some way while they are into it, either walking back and forth or chewing gum or whatever.

Anyway, I had plenty of reason to chew. We stayed in the hunt right down to the home stretch and, in the end, we set a club record winning streak and outplayed some elite teams and won respectability when the Sharks made the playoffs for the first time in the franchise's history. All things considered, it was one of the biggest turnarounds ever in the NHL.

As I told Mark Purdy, unless you're dreaming about something, you don't have anything to shoot for. I've never been around a professional athlete who doesn't have a goal of some sort. My goal is the Stanley Cup!

10

THE HAPPIEST COACH

*"My most important influence was Shero.
I watched him operate through two Cup wins and
learned a lot. He once told me to take the letters
P and R with me wherever I go. P is for Patience
and R is for Reputation."*

Only twelve individuals have had the distinction of having won a Stanley Cup as both a player and a coach. Terry Crisp is one of those select few, skating for the championship Philadelphia Flyers in 1974 and 1975 and directing the Flames bench in 1989 when the first Cup was delivered to Calgary.

A native of Parry Sound, Ontario—also home to Hall of Famer Bobby Orr—Crisp was one of the most respected foot-soldiers in the National Hockey League in a career that spanned eleven seasons, beginning in 1965. Terry played for Boston, St. Louis, Philadelphia and the New York Islanders before retiring in 1977.

Over a 536-game career as a two-way center, Crisp scored 67 goals and 201 points. He appeared in 110 Stanley Cup playoff games, tallying 15 goals and 28 assists.

"Terry was an asset to every club he ever played for throughout his career," says Al Arbour, for whom Crisp played on Long Island. "One word describes him—dependable."

Following his playing career, Crisp did his basic training as a coach for six years in Sault Ste. Marie with the Ontario Hockey League's Greyhounds after which he did a two-year American Hockey League stint as head coach of the Moncton, New Brunswick Golden Flames. In two seasons, Crisp led the Flames to a combined 77-65-18 record and was instrumental in the development of several players that he later coached in Calgary.

Terry's big-league break arrived in 1987-88 with the Flames. A year later he steered his club to a 54-17-9 record before they went 16-6 en route to the Stanley Cup.

Part of the reason for the triumph belonged to the coach who always was studying the game. It is not unusual for Crisp to scribble lineups on napkins, envelopes or post-it notes. "My wife says that I even make them out on the cuffs of my shirts," chuckled Terry. "The cleaners know my lineup for the first six weeks of the season."

A victim of front office foibles, Crisp was immediately placed in the hot seat the following season when his Flames failed to respond as vigorously as they had a year earlier. Asked in 1988-89 about his coaching philosophy, Crisp shot back, "To win and save my job." He explained that if an NHL coach did not accomplish the first, the second is impossible.

Crisp did win (42 games) but not enough to suit management. After a disappointing playoff, he was released as head coach but remained in hockey doing an assortment of jobs. In 1992 he served as assistant coach for Team Canada during the World Championships and was assistant coach for the 1992 Canadian Olympic Team which won the silver medal in Albertville, France.

He executed his NHL comeback in the summer of 1992, being named head coach of the new Tampa Bay Lightning. Although the expansion club failed to make the playoffs, they surprised many critics with their competitive effort. A similar scenario was followed in the 1993-94 season, when once again the Lightning failed to reach the playoffs but nonetheless displayed a respectable brand of hockey.

During the period from his big-league coaching debut in 1987 and today, Crisp has undergone a significant personality metamorphosis behind the bench. Where once he was a virtually uncontrollable firebrand, he now is more conservative and controlled.

Terry explains that he has learned to hold his tongue, and points out that today's coaches are expected to count communication skills as a strength more than ever before. "When there was a six-team league and you asked a player to go through the wall for you, he'd do it, no questions asked," Crisp recalled. "Now if you ask a player to go through the wall, he'll do it, too. But first he'll ask why, how big a hole and what direction to go."

One of hockey's most charismatic characters, Crisp discussed his attitudes toward coaching over lunch on Long Island, New York, with Stan Fischler and with Tampa Bay reporter Tom Losier.

The general public thinks everything is just beautiful after you win a Stanley Cup and it is—for a while. The biggest thing is that you don't get a chance to really enjoy the first Cup until you're completely out of the game.

Freddie Shero told us after we won our first Cup in Philadelphia in 1974, "You guys won't appreciate what you've done—or truly enjoy it until ten years down the road." And he was right. I remember when we won the Cup in Calgary; a week later I was down in the Co-Op, shopping at our grocery store. Everyone was congratulating me on a job well done and telling me I was going to win it again in 1990. I had exactly one week to enjoy that 1989 win. That's all they would allow me; one week to enjoy the Stanley Cup!

It wasn't easy for me in Calgary. I led the Flames to a .700-plus winning percentage during three regular seasons but there still was criticism. They said that [his predecessor] Badger Bob Johnson did a tremendous job and Crisp inherited it. They said [General Manager] Cliff Fletcher gave Crisp a lot of talent and he won. It was all true and it was all right. The only satisfaction I had was that I could walk home and sit down with my coffee and say to my wife, "Hon, I did a pretty good job."

I wasn't going to win no other way. I was not trying to convince the media that Terry Crisp was the coach who won it, because I wasn't. I just considered myself a big part of it, the same as Tim Hunter, Doug Gilmour and any of them. We were part of the puzzle. Sometimes they say that only a coach can screw this up. Well, maybe we're not smart enough to screw it up. At least we're smart enough not to screw it up.

Naturally, there are going to be problems with players from time to time. After we won the Cup, there were rumors about Gary Suter wanting to be traded, but Suter was like everybody else — he wanted to play. We were going through a rough period at that time and the players who weren't playing much weren't happy because they all felt that they should play. It's inevitable; when a coach takes ice time away, for whatever reason, the dissatisfied minority are the vocal ones.

Gary Suter was a helluva hockey player. Offensively, he was one of the best in the league. He had proven over the years that he was one of the best and a key on our power play. I had nothing against him and he was one of the mainstays of our defense corps. After a while he wasn't getting the ice time he felt he wanted, and it was blown into a great dissension story. I called Suter and I told him, "If you've got something to say, let's discuss it." He said, "No, I told 'em I wanted to play more." Gary Suter was like all my other players. They're not happy when they don't play. Where a player's ice time is limited, you never hear a player blame himself.

A year after we won the Cup was when the first major influx of Russian players made it to the NHL and we got Sergei Makarov. To say that it was difficult to integrate him into the lineup would be accurate, but I wasn't taken by surprise. That year we were on a pre-season tour of the Soviet Union and I made a point of spending an afternoon with the great Russian coach, Anatoli Tarasov. I went over to his place with my assistant coach Tommy Watt and my other assistant, Doug Risebrough.

We got as much as we could out of Tarasov. At one point, I asked, "Mister Tarasov, who are the best players you have ever had in Russia?" He picked Vladimir Krutov and Makarov even over Vladislav Tretiak, the great Soviet goaltender. So, I asked, "How do you coach them?" He said, "They play, they play. You let them play."

Well, it was easy enough for him to say, "Let them play," but I had nineteen other guys who I had to keep happy, too. I had a decision to make about Makarov and what I did was consult with my other coaches and we decided that we were getting a world-class player and it would not be wise to make him something that he doesn't want to be.

We agreed that for the first 40 games we would play the guy come hell or high water. We found a spot for him with Gary Roberts and Joe Nieuwendyk, and we talked a lot with them. What happened was that Makarov had done some things that we weren't happy with and we had done some things that he wasn't happy with. After the 40 games I called him into my office with his interpreter. I said to the interpreter, "I want this verbatim. Word for word what I say, and I want word for word what he says back to me—good, bad, indifferent." It was interesting because he had never had the opportunity to talk to a coach, and in the Soviet Union you didn't talk back.

Well, he got a lot of stuff off his chest and it was neat. Lots of his points were very valid from his point of view. For example, in the Soviet Union he was used to getting so much more ice time than we were giving him. And in Russia they didn't match lines the way we do. We watch Wayne Gretzky, Mario Lemieux and the other great ones. We'll pull a guy off with two minutes to go and put out our best checking line to hold them down. He wasn't used to being pulled off in the last two minutes so I could put out our best checking line.

Marakov got it all off his chest and it was really good. He told me a good story. He said, "You must learn to call 'time-out' at the right time. Then change. Call 'time out.' It's your job." I said, "Okay, that's fine." A week later we were up at Edmonton and winning, 3-2. The clock was counting down and we had about one minute and 20 seconds left. Marakov was on the ice and turned around and said to me, "Time out." I said, "Okay, Sergei, we'll get time out for you. No problem." At that moment, the whistle blew and—what do you know—Edmonton's coach at the time, John Muckler, called a time-out. Sergei looked down at their bench and then looked at me and said, "Smart coach!"

Another interesting player for me to work with at the time was Theo Fleury who was in his second year after we had won the Cup. He had a lot to do with the chemistry of the team and what we were looking for in an agitator. We needed somebody to stir the pot, to get everyone else bubbling. We had the guys who would bubble but no one would light the fire. Besides being very talented, Fleury was a pistol and feared nobody. Nothing. He worked the power play and killed penalties and took a regular shift.

At the same time, there were stories about his teammates being upset with all the opportunities given him. In the world of sports, people say about a kid, "Who is this guy? Where is he from?" And that's a natural reaction from the veterans. It had nothing to do with me; the players work that out between themselves. Only Fleury could handle that. In time he would mature and learn, too.

He came to Calgary to do a job as good as the veterans did. He was doing the same thing they wanted to do. As a coach, I monitored it but I didn't try to guide it. I just made it stay within the confines of the hockey club.

As for myself, my emotions behind the bench were very apparent. I warned my guys that I was loud. I would get into the game. I cheered. The guys told me, "Coach, we don't mind you yelling. We don't mind you being in the game as long as it's possible. If you want to yell, that's fine with us." What they were saying is, "If you're going to get into it, you've got to be a controlled-into-it coach and know what you're doing."

That was good advice and from then on I accentuated the positive. Not one negative word came out of my mouth because my players had been teaching me. That was a far cry from the way I had coached earlier.

When I started out as a coach I'd say, "God what a dumb pass." I'd say it because it was a dumb pass. But the guys didn't want to hear that. I don't know if I wanted them to dislike me. Granted, I may have said a few things to get them riled up, to put a fire under them. If that meant they were mad at me...so be it. I go back to what Fred Shero told me: "If you want to be a good coach, you'd better be a great actor."

That means that I sometimes do things or say things that I don't want to say. But, given time, you say, "Hey, this is needed. Things have been quiet for a week. Nobody had phoned and called me a fink for a week. I'm going to do something because I think it needs to be done." So I do it. I don't want to do it any more than I want to fly to the moon, and I know I'm going to end up on the short end of the stick when some guy says "Screw you!" A lot of times I feel I have to do something I know I'm going to pay a price for, whether it's in the papers, or on TV, or with the players.

Confrontations with players are always interesting. I remember when I was still in Calgary, some reporter asked me how I handled the "aftershock" of a yelling bout with a player. I told him, after I've done it, I'll get the player off ice and explain to him, "Last night I said to you, 'Take the eggs out of your pants. Get in the corners.' I did that for a 30-second jewel. That is my feeling. I'm not going to apologize to you, but we were just hoping we would get you up a little bit for that night." When I feel it's time for the whip, I whip 'em. You just can't be predictable. You can't have it every day where they say, "Here he comes. Here we go again." Sometimes you have to think. Sometimes you have to make them think.

Meetings are always a challenge. I learned from Tommy Watt, who was a schoolteacher, that if I go in the dressing room and do all the talking, I get nothing. It becomes a ho-hum kind of thing. I'll come in and give a statement and ask for an answer, too. You'd be surprised at the amount of time you catch guys saying, "Huh?" As soon as you catch one guy, the rest wonder "Is he gonna get me next?" At least then I know that I have their attention. Long meetings are B.S. The mind will only absorb what the rear end can endure.

Coaching in the NHL always is helped by the fact that you once were a player, as I was. I had very limited talent, I admit, but I also enjoyed the game. I had to work hard for every job I got and I was never certain that I had a job until after training camp. That meant that I had to work hard every training camp for a job. But since I loved playing hockey, it was no problem working hard at it.

I was a foot soldier, and if I had to compare my playing style with someone in the league today, I'd say that I resembled players like Robbie DiMaio, Kevin Dineen and Pat Verbeek. I don't know if I was as skilled as they are, but I like that attitude. They know what they have to do to keep a job. Somebody once compared me to Teeder Kennedy, which was really something because he was a Hall of Famer center who played on several Toronto Maple Leafs Stanley Cup-winners in the late 1940s and in 1951.

Naturally, coaching is a kick but there's nothing like the feeling you get when you're actually playing in the NHL. For me, my number one thrill above all was hearing the final buzzer when we won our first Stanley Cup in Philadelphia in 1974. I knew then that, as a player, I had reached the pinnacle of my chosen career. The picture in my mind of me standing there with my teammates and the coaches in celebration will never be erased from my mind.

I felt then that if I never did it again, at least I was there for once but, sure enough, we won a second Stanley Cup in 1975. And it was just as fulfilling. They're all very, very good, but you can only have a first once: your first steps as a baby, your first stroke as a swimmer. The first one is always IT.

But playing for Fred Shero in Philadelphia was something special. They called us "The Broad Street Bullies" and we loved it. Of course, the press made it what it was and they did our job for us. At that time, the press was the greatest ally we had because they went ahead of the team and softened up our opposition with their stories and their tales.

The media, at that time, was looking for a swashbuckling team to hate and we lived up to the image. But the thing most people fail to realize is that we were a very talented hockey club along with all that tough stuff. You don't win two Stanley Cups if you don't have talent and we had a lot of skill on that team.

Except that when we're discussed today, the thing that's most remembered is that we were the Bullies and we let them fall into that trap. We were disguised as tough but we had a lot of skill, not to mention plenty of camaraderie. The players were close and the families were close.

It's funny how life goes because none of this great NHL stuff would have happened had it not been for a fellow who took an interest in me when I was a teenager. I had been playing Junior B hockey but I had decided that I was going to give it up, go back home, go to school and go on to be a high school teacher. My coach, Stan Miller, drove up to see me in the middle of the night and brought me back to the team. He said, "No, you're going to play hockey. You're not going to stay in this town for the rest of your life." Now if Miller hadn't come and taken me back, my career would have taken a whole different road. He was the one who got me back on track with hockey.

When I was coming up through the ranks, the NHL still was a six-team league and it was mighty tough to crack that nut. I finally made it to the Boston Bruins camp in 1965-66, but it wasn't easy. It was an old-boys club and they could really freeze out a rookie like me. I got to play three games with Boston and went zero, zero, zero in the stats. You could look it up!

Then, in 1967-68, the NHL expanded from six to twelve teams and I was signed by St. Louis. Lynn Patrick started out as our coach and then Scotty Bowman took over. We started off slowly and then began to get stronger. Glenn Hall, who they called Mister Goalie, was in the nets for us and we had Red Berenson at center. He blossomed into the first real superstar of expansion; once he scored six goals in a single game against Philadelphia.

The Flyers finished first among the expansion teams but we knocked them off in the playoffs. Veterans like Doug Harvey, Camille Henry and

Dick Moore played great hockey for us and we went all the way to the finals where we played the Montreal Canadiens. They beat us in four straight but, still, to get that far was really something for a kid like me.

I played in 18 playoff games, got a goal and five assists and was feeling pretty good about myself. I played five years in St. Louis and loved every minute of it. We went to the finals again in 1969, got beaten by Montreal and also in 1970 when the Bruins took us out; both series went four straight as well.

When expansion came again in 1972, I was drafted by the New York Islanders. I stayed on the Island for a season and then was traded to Philly for Jean Potvin and Glen Irwin. After we won the two Cups, I finished my NHL career in 1976-77.

It's pretty obvious that I didn't put a lot of points on the board. I liked Crispy, the player, although I don't know if Terry Crisp the player would have liked Terry Crisp the coach, although I do think I could play for me. After all, I played for Scotty Bowman in St. Louis and some guys hated him, but I enjoyed playing for the man.

Everywhere I went, from St. Louis to Philly, each team was a family. In St. Louis the Salomons—owner Sidney, Jr. and his son, Sid III—ran the team and were very close to the players. On the Island it was Bill Torrey and Al Arbour, and in Philadelphia the Sniders—owner Ed and his son, Jay—we were very much involved.

I'm still in touch with many of them because the hockey circle is funny; once you're in that circle, it's yours for life. Fred Shero said it best right after we won the Cup: "We won today; we reached the top of the mountain and we will walk together forever."

Family is always very important to me whether it be the hockey family or my wife and kids. From the day I got married my wife knew what she was in for when it came to hockey. She knew that once she was connected to professional sports, she had to be a strong lady and she certainly has been that.

In our business there are miserable days and miserable times and it's important to me, the coach, to have a lady who's going to stay with me and tell me if I did it right or wrong out there. We've been married 28 years and she's been right there all along. Any good times we've had, she's certainly earned. I'm a lucky guy with a strong lady.

I've been especially lucky since I've won the Stanley Cup as both a player and a coach, and not many men can make that statement. In a sense I was lucky to get into coaching full-time. Actually, I had my eyes on two possible post-playing careers: coaching and TV work. I knew I wanted to be involved somehow in hockey and I really enjoyed TV analysis, but there's the teacher in me as well. I also leaned toward coaching.

After all the coaching wars I've been through, I can say that I've changed my attitude and I have reflected a lot. I've done a lot of soul-searching and part of that is because Terry Crisp the coach is very intense and wants to win. Sometimes I have to learn to temper my temper and stay very clinical behind the bench—and very objective. If I'm out there tossing in the wind with the rest of them, there's no one there to control the ship. My theory is, be a coach, not a cheerleader or an ex-player.

I still love what I do, especially the everyday interaction with the players and management and coaches and the hanging-out. I enjoy the challenge whether it be during a game or a practice. Right now, there's nothing else I'd rather be doing.

My most important influence was Shero. I watched him operate through two Cup wins and learned a lot. He once told me to take the letters P and R with me wherever I go. P is for Patience and R is for Reputation. Have the patience to repeat it again 1,001 times. He was a mastermind who played the media like a violin, like an orchestra. He pointed out that a coach finds himself in situations for which he has no desire and, in the end, the coach is on stage and had better be a damn good actor. Freddie was a master at it.

In my own evolutionary process, I've gone from fiery to mellow; or, at least, I'm trying. After I got fired in Calgary, I talked to a gentleman named Ron Scott who became the biggest influence on my career. I spent a week with him going through an in-depth computer analysis for management and consulting.

When we were finished, I sat down, read it and realized that what came out was me. It revealed my strengths and what I did wrong, and to this day I hope I'm learning from my assistant coaches, management and players. If I'm not, then I'm fooling myself.

It's quite a difference coaching in the NHL today than it was when I quit playing and started coaching Juniors in Sault Ste. Marie. During the six years I coached Juniors, I was handling kids from sixteen to nineteen years old from the bench.

I got into a mode then where I coached from the bench, not only in practice but during play in a game. It was a habit I had to break — trying to get away from coaching as a player on the ice.

Really, the hardest thing is separating yourself as a player from a coach, and breaking the habit that I had while coaching Juniors of coaching from behind the bench during the game. These NHL guys don't need to be yelled at during the game. They're professionals so now when somebody makes a mistake on a shift and returns to the bench, instead of yelling, I'll quietly say a key word in the player's ear. The one thing I can't lose is my power, as well as my zest and enthusiasm. They'll always be there.

From time to time, there'll be incidents that really test a coach's patience. In my case there was the classic still-discussed goal Calgary scored in the sixth playoff game which was not counted. We knew it was in because we had the video set right behind our bench and I sent a guy to look at the thing. I said, "Make damn sure because we only have half-a-minute here." That referee was floating around out there in the middle of nowhere; I don't know what the hell he was doing.

My guy came back and said, "Coach, it's in. It's definitely in!" I knew I had to do something in a hurry to get my point across and he wouldn't come over. I stood up on the bench and pointed to the camera and screamed at the referee, "CHECK THE CAMERA! CHECK THE CAMERA! IT'S IN THE DAMN NET!!"

I asked my guy if he was sure and he said, yes, he was sure. So, I'm up there screaming and my tie is going and I'm waving to get my point across.

In retrospect, everyone said that Terry Crisp was ranting and raving. It was cold and calculated and done for a purpose. If I had politely said, "Hey, ref, excuse me...," he wouldn't have come over because he was down by the penalty box, listening to no one except his linesmen.

Would I do it over again? I'd do it thirty seconds from now if that was what it would take to win the hockey game. The goal was in; it was legal but it was not counted and we wound up losing the game in overtime. And I lost my job.

As I see it, thirty seconds or a minute of a tirade is worth it to save your job, or the series and maybe win the Stanley Cup. I know in my gut if that goal had counted we would have won the Cup. And I would have felt better for the rest of my life. If I had just stood there with my arms crossed and my mouth shut, that would have meant that I had gone down without a struggle, knowing in my heart and mind that it was a goal. I'm a coach and my job is to get my point across.

Over the years people have asked me whether I thought I was unfairly treated, getting fired by the Flames [Cliff Fletcher] and my answer is no. I was fired because he obviously thought it was better for the club. Cliff Fletcher, who originally hired me in Calgary, was my best friend when I got the job and he was still my best friend. And we are still best friends; not only Cliff and I but our families as well. What happened to me was part of the business. Unfortunately, getting fired is a part of the business that's not nice, but I know as well as anyone else that it happens.

I may not have thought so at the time but I benefited from the experience. I came out of it a much better person and, I hope, a much better coach. The only thing I didn't appreciate was that some members of the press out there [in Calgary] took advantage and took shots at my family. And that had nothing to do with hockey and I still don't think that was right.

Fire me, that's fine; I'm a big boy. As a coach, I know I'm in a fish bowl but what they did to my family wasn't fair to my kids. If that circle comes around, I'll get my turn.

Which is not to say that I don't enjoy the media — I do. The media is a very, very important part of our game and you don't survive without them; right, wrong, or indifferent, we need the press. Sometimes it's going to be good press and sometimes I'm not going to like them, but we need them. You have to have your team in the public eye. I say, just don't print lies; anything else is fair game. It's stupid to try to go head-to-head with them.

As for coaching, styles change from person to person. My own style varies according to the personnel I have. If I've got a bunch of grinders and hitters and pounders, I'm not going to have a run-and-gun game. If you're going to be a run-and-gun coach with that type of team, you'll be off-base.

If you've got a bunch of scooters and goal scorers, and you think you're going to go to war, you're going to bomb also that way. The coach has to figure the style best suited for them. You can't think you're God and create something that's not there.

Coming to Florida was quite an experience to me and, naturally, I had to readjust to coaching a brand-new expansion team. It wasn't surprising that there've been bumps along the way, but I've been proud of the team in Tampa. You won't hear the word "disappointed" in my vocabulary when discussing the guys. When we struggled, it hurt us all, especially when we lost before great crowds at the Thunderdome.

These are proud athletes who are paid good money. It's their job to play hard and play well. I remember one game in 1993-94 when we played a losing game against Buffalo. Well, it wasn't because Lightning players didn't care or weren't giving all they had. I was irate for a while, then I realized their bodies had crashed in near-unison. They were brain-dead. Fuel tanks registering past empty. My guys kept putting the pedal to the metal and there was nothing there.

So what could we, as coaches, do in a situation like that? We could beat them to death in practice. We could say that this guy is horse manure, or that guy is horse manure. We could threaten a few moves, trades and send-downs to the minors. But to me, that 's not the answer. We took it easier in practice, allowing some regenerating of the bodies. As for making moves, it is "fear" when a pro worries about losing his job, being traded or getting demoted.

Like every coach in the business, I occasionally daydream about the

"Perfect Team", or the team I'd coach in my dreams. My lineup would be something like this: My goalie would be Jacques Plante who revolutionized the business in the late 1950s, coming out of the net to trap the puck and who also was the first to regularly wear a mask. I'd have Bobby Orr and Ray Bourque on defense. Up front, Bobby Clarke, one of the grittiest guys to ever play the game, would be one of my centers and, of course, Wayne Gretzky. Also, I'd want a tough scorer like Rick Tocchet and stylist like Jaromir Jagr and a heavy shooter like Bobby Hull. Another goalie I'd love to have would be Battlin' Billy Smith who played on the Islanders' four Stanley Cup-winners. That would be a pretty fair team.

How do you motivate a team? All I can do is put together a scenario where the players might motivate themselves. One of the greatest motivators is fear: fear of losing your job; fear of embarrassment; fear of losing a game; fear of being ridiculed. My philosophy is, whatever you do, do it with class. If I'm to be remembered in this business, the one thing that I'd like people to say about me is that I've been honest. You can't ask for more than that.

11

THE TOUGHEST COACH

"When I got behind the bench I looked up to the Forum ceiling and saw all those banners from Stanley Cup victories, and then I searched the building from end to end with my eyes and knew that I had finally arrived. Wayne Gretzky was right; Pat Burns had made it to the NHL."

His steely eyes, car-bumper moustache and bushy mane set Pat Burns apart from his peers. By a lot.

The 42-year-old Montreal native is the quintessential ice cop, figuratively and literally.

If 20th Century Fox wanted to cast for a 1940s gendarme to work alongside Jimmy Cagney or Edward G. Robinson, Burns would get the role without a second audition.

Yet today, he is a cop only in the figurative NHL sense. Just seven years removed from undercover work for the Gatineau, Quebec police force, Burns now patrols a beat behind the bench. Detective work is long in the past and in recent years Pat has moved with extra-ordinary speed through the coaching ranks, most recently in the bigs.

In 1992-93 he converted a ramshackle Toronto Maple Leafs club into a contender that came within one game of beating the Los Angeles Kings and moving into the Stanley Cup finals. In 1993-94, he guided the Leafs past Detroit and San Jose before bowing to the Vancouver Canucks.

"We were told a lot we didn't have much talent, but the heart was always there," says Burns. "I've never been more proud of a team I've ever coached."

That's saying plenty since Burns, as a rookie NHL mentor, led the Canadiens through the playoffs to a 1989 six-game final series before capitulating to the Calgary Flames.

For a time it appeared that Burns would be a fixture on St. Catherine Street West as long as The Forum was intact. He originally arrived in the

73

Habs dressing room upon the departure of Jean Perron's regime and immediately made sense out of chaos.

"That's one place where my police background comes in because I really don't give a damn," says Burns. "I'm just an ordinary person who has been on the street and worked nine to five. It wouldn't bother me to go back to police work, although I would like to stay in the game."

Chances are, Pat Burns will be around NHL rinks for quite a while. He made his first imprint with Les Canadiens and, since coming to Toronto in 1992, restored pride in the Maple Leafs.

"The big thing we did was getting them to understand their roles," he explains. "Not everyone's a scorer, not everyone's a tough guy, not everyone gets the hits. I defined the roles and tried to get everyone to understand them."

Apparently they have. Which explains why Vancouver Sun *columnist Archie McDonald opines that the "most crucial acquisition" GM Cliff Fletcher ever made for the Maple Leafs was Pat Burns. In an interview with Stan Fischler, Burns gives his views of life and the hockey world.*

SF: Very little is known about your early hockey background. How did you become a player?

PB: I started out as a rink rat in a Montreal neighborhood called Saint Henri. I worshipped the Canadiens and hockey was a religion. When I wasn't in school, I was out playing hockey on a rink just down the street from The Forum. We lived in a French community but I was from an Irish group that included the family of [Penguins coach] Eddie Johnston and [former Canadien] Robin Burns, who is my cousin. We had a whole bunch of Irish people in that area who played hockey and that included my brother. I was a centerman and moved right up through the ranks, but after my dad passed away, we moved to Quebec where I wound up playing at the Midget level. I was a big kid who scrapped a lot and I played in the Central League where Larry Robinson played.

SF: Were you any good?

PB: (*Laughs*). I've often said that I had become a good student of the game because I spent so much time on the bench. Actually, by 1967, when the NHL was about to expand, I got a few inquiries [for pro hockey jobs] but I had already made my decision to go out in the working world. Then, I got some more calls but I had decided no — I was getting out of hockey.

SF: What did you decide to do?

PB: I got into police work with the Gatineau police force and enjoyed it very much, but I also stayed close to the hockey community. I played senior hockey and had a lot of friends who were coaching, so it wasn't as if I was totally removed from the game. But police work was my profession and I stayed at it for sixteen years, retiring as a detective sergeant.

SF: But if you were doing police work full-time, how did you get into coaching?

PB: One of my friends, who was coaching a local team, got sick and needed someone to help so he asked me to come down and run a couple of practices. Up until then, I had never run a practice but I had always paid attention to my coaches when I played, so I had absorbed something before I even took over the team. It didn't take me very long to pick up the rudiments of coaching and when my friend decided to give it up, I took over and found that I really liked being behind the bench.

SF: What level were you on when you started coaching?

PB: It was Bantam and Midget. We did well. I had John Chabot, who later made it to the NHL, on my team and a total of eleven guys from my Midget team were drafted into Juniors. Meantime, I'm still doing police work and soon I was asked to be a scout for the Hull Olympiques Junior team. Pretty soon, I was not only scouting but also helping the club with its practices. Slowly but surely, I became more involved with hockey though I still had my full-time job with the police.

SF: Was there a conflict developing between being a cop and a coach?

PB: As I became closer to the Olympiques, there were more hockey demands made. For instance, the club would have liked me to go on the road with them as assistant coach but I was unable to leave the force to do that. Which meant that I only worked home games and practices. The only time I went on the road was when I had time off from the force. But the real time problem came when they asked me to become head coach, and I accepted.

SF: How could you manage doing both?

PB: It wasn't easy. I was working undercover but then they transferred me to a day job but I had to get a lot of time off. So, all my holidays were taken out. I wound up with day-by-day holidays instead of a two- or three-week period. And I'd skip my lunch hour and work instead so that I could leave early enough for hockey. My first year doing that was very, very tough and by mid-season my eyes were glazed but, somehow, I managed to survive the season.

SF: What made you then choose between police work and coaching?

PB: Wayne Gretzky was the reason. He bought the Hull Olympiques. Of course, when I found out about it, I had no idea I'd still be coaching because I figured that Wayne would bring in his own people. I said to myself, "That's it for me and hockey." But during the summer Wayne phoned and said, "Hey, we want you to continue coaching." That's when I told him about the problem with time, the police and working with the kids. Wayne worked something out with the city and I wound up with a year off to do full-time coaching.

SF: Was it worth it?

PB: We had a good club and actually went all the way to the Memorial Cup finals with Guelph. The last game was tied and went into overtime. Luc Robitaille, one of my best players, missed a breakaway and then Gary Roberts scored for them and that was that. Even though we lost, I must have made an impression because I was invited to coach the Junior Team Canada club. Once again, I was granted a year off but the department by now was getting tired of my sabbaticals and they asked me to make a decision — be a coach or a cop.

SF: How did you decide?

PB: I sat down with Wayne and he assured me that I had a bright future in coaching; he even said I'd make it to the NHL someday. He offered me a three-year deal with a bit more than I was making as a cop. That was good enough for me and I left police work to become a full-time hockey coach. Although I thought he was kidding, he kept telling me that the NHL was in my future and he even agreed that if I should get a pro offer, I'd be free to leave the Olympiques.

SF: Was he true to his word?

PB: Sure enough, I got a call not long afterward from [Canadiens GM] Serge Savard. Turns out that Pierre Creamer had left to move up to the Penguins and Serge wanted me to coach the AHL team in Sherbrooke. I wasn't crazy about leaving Wayne that way, but he insisted that I accept Savard's offer and reiterated that I'd be coaching in the NHL before I knew it. Believe it or not, he was right. Jean Perron left the Canadiens in 1988 and I moved up to Montreal.

SF: By this time you were in a position to compare police work with coaching.

PB: I found there's not much difference between the two. How the detective work helped me with hockey was that when you're a policeman you get to know characters a lot; you have to be into character study all the time and in hockey it's a lot like that. I have 25 different players on my team and 25 different characters. I can usually tell when they're trying to get away with stuff.

SF: What did you immediately like about coaching?

PB: It's going into a job every day and not knowing what's going to happen. I live off of that — going to work and saying, "What's gonna happen today? What kind of game is it gonna be? Are we gonna get blown out or are we going to blow out the opposition?" It could be anything. Of course, it was the same thing on the force; day in and day out, it was never the same.

SF: How would you describe Pat Burns to others?

PB: I'm a very regular person trying to get through life — that's all. I don't bestow any genius on myself and I don't consider myself smarter than the next guy. I'm not like a former player who comes back to the league and is known by everyone else. With me coming into the NHL it was different.

SF: What was it like when you went behind the bench for your first game, coaching at The Forum?

PB: We played an exhibition game in Montreal and I was feeling pretty nervous. When I got behind the bench I looked up to the Forum ceiling and saw all those banners from Stanley Cup victories, and then I searched the building from end to end with my eyes and knew that I had finally arrived. Wayne Gretzky was right; Pat Burns had made it to the NHL.

SF: But being a rookie coach, you surely had problems at the start; especially when the club opened with an under .500 record.

PB: I had to take the bull by the horns. The first time I walked into the dressing room I was coaching guys like Bob Gainey, Larry Robinson, fellas who I had looked up to in the recent past. Meanwhile, these guys, who have won Stanley Cups, are wondering, "Who's this guy? Where is he coming from?" My background didn't mean anything to them, so I knew that I had to build on what I had.

SF: How difficult was it for you at the start with the Canadiens?

PB: I was fortunate to have some good guys on the team; people like Robinson and Bobby Smith were pretty supportive for what I was trying to do. They said, "Hey, we know what you're trying to do and we'll back you up." At the beginning it was rough because we played a dozen games and were three wins under .500 and a lot of people were saying that I'd be gone by Christmas. Fortunately for me, I got backing from Serge and after a long team meeting in Hartford, we beat the Whalers and got on track.

SF: That meeting was led by your captain, Bob Gainey. What happened?

PB: Basically, he told the guys, "This is what we're going to do; the way we're gonna go." I knew I had to live with a certain amount of things because there were problems before I came along. My job was to take care of them. We had an old team going out and another team coming in.

SF: How did that meeting change things?

PB: We went into the game against the Whalers with two straight losses. We beat Hartford and then went on a tear. We finished in second place overall — two below first-place Calgary — and I was named Coach of the Year.

SF: You had several confrontations in that rookie coaching year, with Claude Lemieux, Stephane Richer and John Kordic. Which was the worst?

PB: The one with Kordic. John was a guy with problems that no one really knew about or could put a finger on, but I knew that he was not normal and eventually he and I had a bit of a turning-on in my office. He was trying to get his point across because he had done it before with the coach at Toronto and I confronted him. He was an intimidating guy, but I wasn't intimidated at all.

SF: You did pretty well for a rookie coach.

PB: I had some important help. First of all, I became part of the Canadiens tradition, the mystique, so to speak. Like other clubs, the Canadiens have problems but they don't seem to last long. They find a way out.

And one reason is that they usually have good men running the show. Many was the day when I'd be chatting with Larry Robinson and he'd tell me how things had been run in other years with Scotty Bowman coaching. Bob Gainey was the same way; very reassuring. I respected both of them, Gainey and Robinson, but I got to be more friendly with Larry than with Bob. Bob was more reserved.

SF: You kept your job but others got fired. What are your thoughts about the tenuous job of coaching?

PB: I know people get fired but I don't really worry about it because I know some day it's gonna happen and I'm prepared for it.

SF: When he was coaching in Denver, Don Cherry once grabbed a player, Mike McEwen, around the neck on the bench and practically choked him. Mike Keenan lays hands on players. What do you do when you're really upset with a guy?

PB: I'll just whisper something to the guy and the message will get across without anything physical. I wouldn't lay a hand on a player on the bench but the dressing room is another story. I did it to Mathieu Schneider right in the dressing room when we were in Boston. We'd been through a tough run of injuries and had about six or seven AHL players up with us. I remember saying to myself, "Pat, you'd better be a good coach tonight." We actually won the game and played really well, but later in the game Matty cross-checked a guy from behind — which was completely ridiculous — and took a stupid penalty. What I mean is that he didn't have to do it and we even stressed before the game the need to avoid getting dumb penalties and there Schneider does that, which really upset me. So, after the game, he walked past me in the dressing room and I sort of grabbed him — and two coaches wound up pulling me off Matty.

SF: Don't you like Schneider?

PB: I like Matty. In fact, he'd come up to me every day and talk to me. I was just trying to make him realize at that point in time that, "Hey, you're a young kid in this business and a marquee player. You're gonna have to listen and do things for the team, not for yourself."

SF: What aspect of the game drives a coach like you farthest up the wall?

PB: There's nothing worse than dumb penalties. I do a lot of talking about that. When you take a penalty at the start of the game, you don't say anything. But when you're leading by a goal with five minutes left in the game and a guy takes a penalty, that's frustrating. The questionable ones, I can take; like when one of our guys goes for a hit and maybe gets his elbow up. That's gonna happen, but when a guy trips another guy...

SF: In today's player's market, discipline is not easy. How can you punish them?

PB: With the money they're making these days, fining them is insignificant. The only thing we, as coaches, have as a weapon for discipline is the control of ice time. Players want to play; they don't want to be kept off the ice. So by benching a player, you can often get him to respond to your goals.

SF: Who was your favorite player among those you coached?

PB: Chris Chelios would have to be the guy. He lives the game. He's the kind of guy who'll bring his skates home at night and hope for a game to play. Chris lives off a lot of ice time. You saw in the 1993-94 season. One night he got badly cut and had to be taken to the hospital for stitches. Another player would take the rest of the night off, but not Chris. He hustled back to the rink and was back on the ice for the second period.

SF: Some critics argue that Chelios is dirty. Remember that series with the Flyers when Chris rammed Brian Propp into the boards and a big fuss was made of it?

PB: I thought that it was a clean check. Propp had his head down a bit when he was hit. I mean Chelly is like that; if you have your head down, he'll take advantage of that.

SF: You have another Chelios-type in Doug Gilmour. But he's smaller. You have to worry about wearing him out, don't you?

PB: This season I didn't work him as hard as I did last year because the scenario was different then. In 1992-93 we were fighting for a playoff position. This year we were doing better so Gilmour's ice time was cut down about six to eight minutes a game which, for him, is a lot. In the season I used Doug in fewer situations so that at playoff time, he'd be used more. I liken Gilmour to Chelios in that he loves to play the game, anywhere, anytime.

SF: Who was your biggest headache in Montreal, Claude Lemieux or Stephane Richer?

PB: I had problems with Claude but actually I like him; he's a funny guy and I'd take him on my team again. He's the kind of player who gets people pissed off at him in the dressing room, but that's the way he is. He's always had his problems. But Claude is a challenge. He's the type who puts a challenge in coaching but that makes it tough because you have 26 other guys to worry about. But off the ice he's terrific. Richer was never a problem although there was one game when I didn't dress him because he missed curfew. The thing with Stephane was that in the long run he was better off being out of Montreal. He got to be involved with all the rumors — and I said so at the time — that they were all bullshit. I played ball with Stephane's dad and remember coaching him when he was 15 years old. He had as much baseball talent then as he did hockey talent and he could have done anything with it. But he was a small-town boy who came to the big city and he became a popular guy and had trouble living with that every day. But I'll say this about Steph; he's got talent and he's a game-breaker. But his situation in Montreal became frustrating, for him, the team and for management.

SF: You weren't happy about management trading Chelios for Denis Savard, were you?

PB: That happened after my second year in Montreal. No, I don't think I was betrayed. Denis is a great kid and everything but I remember them doing the trade without me being aware of it. I think it was done above management's head. I think Serge was told, "This trade has got to be made." When I heard about it, I was in shock.

SF: How is hockey different than when you originally got involved with the game?

PB: The kids are coming out younger, bigger, stronger and not necessarily smarter. I'm not saying that they're dumb but they expect things now. In the old days, they had to work; nothing was given to them. Now they come up, "The sweater is yours; the money is yours." That's the big difference. In the previous generation of players, someone like a Bob Gainey had to work in the minors before he made it in the NHL. They knew what the minors were like and they didn't want to go back. Today, the players are partners in business with the owners. When you pay a guy $15 million, it means that this guy has become a partner and it makes things a bit different for the coach.

SF: Another change is in the officiating. Mark Messier says far too many penalties are being called.

PB: He's right. And there are other changes. Now the kids are bigger and stronger. Some of them who come out of Junior hockey are monsters.

And the respect that once was there has left the game. Before helmets, a guy could go into the corner and not worry about getting a stick in the face. I don't know how a player like Craig MacTavish goes out there every season without a helmet. What they're trying to do now is "clean up the game," but I say the game was pretty good before. In the past, if you hit a marquee player, the feeling was, "Hey, you have to answer the bell." That was part of the game.

SF: Speaking of tough hockey, Jeremy Roenick says he'd like to play without a helmet but his coach, Darryl Sutter, won't allow it. What would happen if one of your players said he wanted to play helmetless?

PB: That would be the player's choice but I wouldn't support it. In Chicago's situation, I believe that management said to Darryl, "Hey, what are you, crazy? We're paying this guy all this money and you're gonna let him go out without a helmet?"

SF: While we're on the subject of tough guys, Wendel Clark was absolutely useless as a Leaf until the 1993 playoffs. Then, he got hot. What happened?

PB: He matured. He had been in a situation where he hadn't been part of winning [in Toronto] for a long time. In the Detroit series [1993], he didn't do much. But all of a sudden we turned around and were playing in the second series and we had a crack at it. For the first time in his career, Clarkie was surrounded with guys who wanted to win, and were saying, "Hey, this is fun." I know for a fact that Wendel was having fun. After the St. Louis series, he told me, "Christ, I've never played this late in the season in my life. This is fun!" It was amazing to hear him talk.

SF: It was pretty evident that Clark presented a coaching challenge to you.

PB: Wendel is different. Throughout his career he never was really told a lot of things. He was never advised, "Well, you can't do this and you can do that. And if you do that, you might have to sit on the bench." When I've sat him down, I've sat him down for days. Now he's taken more control and responsibility. When he was a Junior and thereafter, he was sent out to win the game, score the goals and beat people up. That's what he had to do and that's why he was hurt a lot. He felt he had to run somebody to the boards, win the game and beat up the best player on the other side. Which is a lot to ask a guy. My perspective with him is different. I tell Wendel you fight if you have to fight. I don't want him running around from one board to the other, just running people and getting hurt.

SF: What did you do about it, one-on-one with Clark?

PB: I took him aside and said that there was a way of playing that he had to respect. "If there's a hit to be made, you're going to do it. And if there's not a hit, you're not going to do it." He understood.

SF: How do you handle losing? Are you a brooder?

PB: A loss the night before stings until the next morning when I jump on the ice. I'm not a very funny person after a loss so the best thing to do is just leave me alone. I've changed. In my first year in the NHL, I would take a lot of the blame and put a lot of the onus on myself. But with more experience, I learned to say, "Hey, wait a minute. There are a lot of other things that you have to look at here." I've learned to break things down.

SF: What was it like in Montreal?

PB: There's a lot of pressure because everybody always expects so much all the time. The players don't get accused because they are the friends [of the media]. You rarely hear someone yell something at a player. But they'd say, "Hey, Burns, do something!"

SF: What's the Burns method for handling referees, especially when the calls are going against you?

PB: There's one thing a coach has to do; let his players know that he supports their point [against the referee]. If I don't support their point, the players will take it on themselves to do something. I always tell the referee, when there's a situation where I'm on his case, "Would you rather have all 20 players yell at you, or just me? If you don't want to hear them, then you have to listen to me." Which is why I tell my players, "I'll handle the referees, you worry about the game." A lot of the referees are smart enough to see what I'm doing; that it's tougher on a ref if 20 guys are yelling at him than just one.

SF: Don't you find the NHL "gag rule," forbidding criticism of referees, a bit unfair?

PB: Sometimes there are things I'd like to say but I can't because of the league rules. I think the league misunderstands that rule because we have to go to the press after a game and explain why such-and-such a thing happened but the referees don't.

SF: How different is the media in Montreal as opposed to Toronto?

PB: First of all, let me say that the media created a lot of misconceptions about my leaving Montreal. And I told one guy [from the Montreal media], "Don't you ever give yourself credit for getting me to leave Montreal. Don't ever do that." The Montreal media is a little more vicious because hockey is the only thing in Montreal. Baseball is secondary, football is nonexistent and politics is very important. People read about hockey every day and they look for something explosive; something that's going to make headlines. It took me a while to figure it out. I told them [the media], "The most important thing is the 20 guys sitting in the dressing room — before you guys. In Toronto, the language thing is not a problem. When I was with the Canadiens, I was dealing with two languages. I had to be very careful what I said in English and what I said in French. In other words, it wouldn't be good for me to say something in English and not say the same in French, or vice versa. Quebecers are always protecting their French-Canadian players. It's part of their heritage and there's nothing wrong with that. They protect their own.

SF: Mike Keenan says he never reads the papers. How about you?

PB: Oh, not really. I'll just look at the standings and that stuff.

SF: What was the real reason why you left Montreal?

PB: It was time. I told Serge [Savard] about my feelings. Serge told me, "I don't want you to go. I want you to stay with the Canadiens. We're gonna make some moves, some trades. We're going to have a good team. You've done a lot to build us up, so stick around." I said, "Serge, it might be easier for you than it would be for me." I felt that I could help another club and my agent, Don Meehan, got permission from Serge to talk to Cliff Fletcher. As a result I wound up being one of only two coaches — Dick Irvin being the other — who had the good fortune to coach each of the two great Canadian franchises, Montreal and Toronto. I left and, to be honest, I think you're going to see more and more of that. I don't think you're gonna see coaches hanging around too long in one place anymore.

SF: Then, how do you account for Al Arbour being on Long Island for so long?

PB: He's amazing. He's my hero. He keeps coming back and he still gains that respect.

SF: Which NHL coach do you feel closest to in terms of off-ice relationship?

PB: Mike Keenan. People don't know Mike. I know him personally and we talk a lot during the season, call each other up. He's an amazing man.

SF: By contrast, you had a feud going with [Kings coach] Barry Melrose during the 1993 playoffs. What was that all about?

PB: What was behind the feud was this: there's one thing I don't respect from a [opposition] coach and that's when he yells at one of my players who's on the ice. There's nothing we're in a position to do about it and that's what happened with me and Melrose. He was yelling at Doug Gilmour and after the situation, he said, "You're gonna get more of this." With that, I felt, "Hey, you're not playing the game; you're in no position to say anything about my best player." He had no business to say he was going to do this or that when he can't do anything. I don't get into yelling matches with players on the ice and I don't think other coaches should. That's what upset me about that incident.

SF: It's interesting — and ironic — that Wayne Gretzky, who got you started in coaching, torpedoed you in 1993 and your ex-team, the Canadiens, won the Stanley Cup.

PB: When Montreal won the Cup last year, I felt that I actually had a lot to do with it because I was the one who brought up those kids. I started with them, worked with them and made those kids into better players.

SF: What kind of satisfaction do you get from your profession?

PB: Something different happens every day. You have new ideas, new things happening every day. Coaching is not a dog-day affair where you come in to the office and say, "Oh, no, not this again!" I don't punch a nine-to-five time clock or flip through papers answering the phone. I come to the rink, have fun with the guys — sometimes get mad at them — praise them, kick them in the butt. If you asked me to pick two words that say what I like most about my work, I'd say, "It's refreshing!"

12

THE LOSINGEST COACH

"This business is very consuming. Some guys talk about 'leaving the game at the rink,' but that doesn't happen with me. The game stays with Rick Bowness 24 hours a day."

Like many coaches who made it to the National Hockey League, Rick Bowness had an undistinguished career as a top professional. He played the NHL yo-yo, moving from team to team over a period of seven seasons.

The Bowness dossier lists the Atlanta Flames, Detroit Red Wings, St. Louis Blues and Winnipeg Jets among his employers. It was in Winnipeg, during the 1980-81 season, that Rick endured the brand of adversity which would prime him for his excrutiating years coaching the hapless Ottawa Senators.

During his stint with the Jets, Bowness and colleagues suffered through 30 consecutive winless games; even with such a dismal club, Rick remained a marginal big-leaguer. But he carried assets which caught the attention of Winnipeg general manager John Ferguson — heart and savvy. After 173 NHL games — during which he scored 18 goals and 37 assists — Bowness left the majors to become a minor league coach with the Jets' American League affiliate in Sherbrooke, Quebec.

Unfortunately, Rick's mentor, Ferguson, became the focal point of front office turmoil during the 1988-89 season. Ferguson was fired and, shortly thereafter, Jets coach Dan Maloney got the heave-ho. Management promoted Bowness, who won but eight games with a ramshackle team.

Many NHL observers believe that Bowness rated another full season behind the Jets bench , but he was dismissed and replaced by Bob Murdoch. By this time Rick had developed a positive reputation in pro circles and was hired by the Boston Bruins to run their AHL team in Portland, Maine. After two successful seasons with the Mariners, Rick once again got the NHL call, this time to succeed Mike Milbury — who had been moved up to assistant general manager — as Bruins coach.

Superficially, at least, Bowness appeared to be doing a commendable job. Without his star scorer, Cam Neely, for most of the season, Rick nevertheless kept the Bruins playoff-competitive throughout the 1991-92 season. Less passionate than Milbury, Rick nevertheless jumped all over malingerers and captured headlines when he dispatched Bob Sweeney and Craig Janney to the showers during a desultory loss to Les Nordiques in Quebec.

A second-place finish in the Adams Division was nothing to sneeze at, nor was the Bruins' playoff effort. They edged the Buffalo Sabres in a sparkling seven-game series and upset the Montreal Canadiens in four straight, a feat that almost inspired a civic holiday in Boston. The Bruins parade ended in the semi-finals when the defending Stanley Cup champion Pittsburgh Penguins routed Boston in four straight games.

This should not have been particularly surprising — since Mario Lemieux was in his scoring prime for Pittsburgh — and certainly not cause for dismissal. But somewhere along the way, Bowness rankled the Harry Sinden-Mike Milbury high command, although Rick certainly was favored by the media and fans.

The chute was pulled on Bowness as soon as Brian Sutter quietly informed Sinden that he would be available to coach Boston. Rick was fired and Brian was hired. Bowness was at liberty and disillusioned. But in this case, he was fired at precisely the right time, because the brand-new Ottawa Senators were coach-hunting. John Ferguson, now a Senators aide, pushed for Rick and he was instantly hired.

Bowness knew that it would be a challenge but it seems doubtful that he realized how traumatic Ottawa's first season as an NHL franchise would be. After 18 games his club had a horrendous 1-16-1 record. After a particularly galling 7-2 loss to Philadelphia, Bowness finally erupted.

"The players on this team for the most part are giving their best effort," he said, "but there have been a few exceptions. We simply have been unable to score goals."

Try as he might, Bowness could not coax more than victories out of the Senators, who finished dead last (10-70-4) in the 24 team league. During the off-season, they added promising youngsters Alexandre Daigle and Alexei Yashin to the roster and opened the season with some promise.

But Daigle began fading by mid-season and Yashin, who looked like a rookie-of-the-year candidate, suffered when linemate Bob Kudelski was traded to the Florida Panthers. Some of the additions, like Czech veteran Vladimir Ruzicka, drove Bowness to distraction.

During a practice session, Bowness noticed that Ruzicka was loafing. The coach blew his whistle and withered the forward. "Get off the (bleeping) ice! If you're going to drag your feet, get the (bleep) off the ice."

Ruzicka left and an hour later, after the scrimmage was complete, Bowness explained his move. "If somebody is not going to work, he's not going to practice. I didn't like what I saw so I addressed it. Tomorrow is another day."

Within days, Ruzicka was given his release. Still, Bowness was frustrated with defeat and ineptitude. Whenever possible, he demonstrated to his players that he was behind them and, once, erupted when Buffalo Sabres defenseman Craig Muni delivered a cheap-shot to one of the Senators. Bowness broke a stick and threw the pieces on the ice and then waved a white towel of surrender at referee Dan Marouelli.

Montreal Gazette *columnist Pat Hickey observed, "There's no room for tantrums like that. You have to wonder how the Senators are expected to keep their cool when their coach is losing his."*

Later in the 1993-94 season, as the Senators again were secured last place, Ottawa Sun *columnist Earl McRae suggested that the club fire Bowness to "put the man out of his misery."*

McRae concluded, "How can the NHL allow Bones Bowness to be treated this way? How can the Ottawa Senators brass allow it? Where is the Canadian Mental Health Association? Where is the Canadian Psychiatrists Association? Where is God? Bones Bowness must be fired. Right now. Not a moment later."

But Bowness finished the season and the Senators, with some late additions, actually played some respectable games down the stretch. When it was over, there was conjecture as to whether Rick would do it again — or even get the opportunity. Nevertheless, he departed Ottawa in the spring of 1994 with many supporters, and secure in the knowledge that he extracted the most he could out of a motley crew.

In an interview with reporter Rick Middleton, Bowness spelled out his thoughts on coaching and his life in hockey.

When I was a kid, growing up in Sydney, Nova Scotia, I began playing serious minor level hockey and after the family moved to Halifax, I continued until I reached the Junior B level. My father had played minor pro hockey and I can remember going to watch dad play. He loved hockey and he got the love for the game started within me. No question about it, hockey was in my blood, starting very, very early in my life. Pretty soon, I was good enough to start thinking about high-class clubs and had my eyes on the Quebec Junior League.

In those days, Junior clubs couldn't draft Maritime kids like me, but I had offers from both the Quebec League as well as the Ontario Hockey League. I was attracted to Quebec because their Junior team, the Remparts, had won the Memorial Cup and they were drawing 10,000 people every night. At that point in time, Quebec had the best Junior franchise in Canada and, besides, it was the closest to Halifax.

As everyone knows, Quebec is an almost totally French-speaking community and even though I didn't speak the language at that point, I learned it. At first I really enjoyed it there, but then things developed that I didn't like, so I requested a trade to the Montreal Junior Canadiens and they agreed, so I finished my Junior career in Montreal.

In 1975, there were a lot of openings in the pro hockey market. The World Hockey Association was in its third year of existence and the NHL had expanded to Atlanta and Long Island and was looking to go elsewhere. I got drafted by the Flames in 1975 (2nd pick, 26th overall) and played with guys like Jacques Richard, Dan Bouchard and Eric Vail. Fred Creighton was our coach.

Naturally, I thought I was going to have a long, illustrious career with Atlanta, but the bottom line was that I wasn't good enough to crack the lineup on a regular basis. I wound up moving up and down and eventually the Flames sold me to the Red Wings and I spent a year with Detroit, then they sold me to St. Louis. I was up and down until the Blues dealt me to Winnipeg, but I still couldn't quite hang in there and be a regular in the NHL.

By the time I was 25- or 26-years old, I was back in the minors and I realized that it was pretty much over for me playing in the National Hockey League. Still, I wanted to stay in the game so there were a couple of choices to make. On the one hand, I could have played in the minors for as long as I had wanted, but that was not exactly what I wanted to do. What I had my eyes on was coaching and, with that in mind, I negotiated my last Winnipeg contract with a clause that said at some point I would like to be a coach. In other words, there was a salary for playing and another clause that had a salary for coaching.

If I played, I got one salary and if I retired and went into coaching, I got the other. In 1982 Winnipeg sent me to Sherbrooke as a player-assistant coach and that's when I began learning the profession.

It didn't take me very long to realize that you can learn something from everybody. You absorb what the others do and then apply it to your own way of doing things. But I learned right away that it's important to always be yourself — there's no sense trying to do what someone else does, or be what somebody else is, because that's not going to work. You've got to be yourself.

In the meantime, I studied the coaches around me: Tommy Watt, Tom McVie; I learned a lot from Orland Kurtenbach, who was one of my first coaches. I took their knowledge and applied it to my beliefs and the way I do things, then I ran with it.

You don't have to be Albert Einstein to realize that you coach differently if you're handling an established club like the Boston Bruins than if you were coaching a brand-new team like the Ottawa Senators. In Boston, the work ethic had long ago been established and passed down from decade to decade. In Ottawa, the work ethic had to be established from Day One in 1992, when the club began operation.

One thing is certain: you don't win in the NHL without working hard. I realize that "work" is a very wide and general term, but the specifics of it break down into different things and different areas. That was what we were trying to bring to the Senators organization: the backchecking part, playing tough defense. That's all hard work. It's not just going up and down the ice and working hard and getting nothing done; it's working hard and accomplishing something with that work.

I go back to my own performance as a player. I wasn't very talented, so I worked hard and played pretty good defense. I expect all of my players to play like that too, but I also have to appreciate when artistic players have that creativity and that offensive genius that we didn't have. You have to let them play it; you don't tell them how to play offense. You have to have them learn how to play defense, but you let them do what comes naturally to them on the offense. You don't change every player to fit your mold. That would be a huge mistake. It's ridiculous for me to take a goal scorer and try to make him into an up-and-down winger.

Every team has to have its share of checkers and its share of scorers, and your scorers have to know how to check. You have to analyze your players and their strengths and weaknesses — allow them to play to their strengths and help them with their weaknesses.

It was no secret that the Senators were not the most talented team in the league, so my challenge was trying to stay competitive with the cards I was dealt. I made them work hard; taught them to work hard; taught them how to do little things well so that when they're working hard, they are actually getting something done.

I pick up information about coaching from whomever I can. I never played for Al Arbour or Glen Sather, but I talked to them whenever I could and I learned something from chatting with them. When the late Bob Johnson was coaching Pittsburgh, I talked to him and learned something about the game. There are plenty of coaches out there who will sit down and talk to you and help you learn. I'm always ready to learn, ready to improve, although I would never try to get trade secrets from them; it's all fraternal in its nature.

Coaching in many ways is an instinctive process. My instincts are different from my competitors'. My feel for the mood of the team is different than it would be for another coach. Someone else might walk in and get a completely different feel than I would in the same situation. I really have to trust my instincts and have to make tough decisions. I have to think them out and live with them. You can't second-guess yourself over every little incident, because not everything you do is right. That would be impossible. So, I trust my instincts, live with them and go on.

This business is very consuming. Some guys talk about "leaving the game at the rink" but that doesn't happen with me. The game stays with Rick Bowness 24 hours a day. It's only during the off-season that I can get away from it. During the winter it's 24 hours a day.

When I go home to the family, I'm not talking, I'm thinking. I'm off in another world, walking the floor and saying, "Okay, that's it, I'm spending time here." So, I take an hour or half-an-hour, whatever, and all of a sudden I find myself thinking about the game again, the team, or something hockey-related. The game consumes you and it's the only way to do it. If you're going to do something, you've got to give it one hundred per cent. You get behind it, stay behind it and keep involved with it. You can't do anything half-assed.

Fortunately for me, I have a wife who is very understanding about my profession. She has put up with tons of moods and mood swings, trades, getting fired, sold, you name it. It all has happened to me and she's been behind her husband one hundred per cent all the way through. Our kids know and they're now old enough to know when dad is in a good mood and when dad is in a bad mood.

Preparing for a game involves several elements, especially the use of video. Let's say we have a game coming up against the Bruins and Boston has just played the Islanders. Well, out comes the video of that game; we take notes and apply what we've learned. I also lean heavily on my assistant coaches and I have a lot of faith in their judgment. We're a group and we make group decisions, although the ultimate decision is mine after we all discuss the subject. A coach has to be willing to try anything. Granted, it doesn't always work, but what the hell, you've got to try.

We want to improve in every area and we want to continue to improve until we win the Stanley Cup; that's the ultimate icon. Then, the day after you win the Stanley Cup, you'd better try to improve again. You never sit still.

13

Pat Quinn

FROM PRESIDENT TO COACH

"If there's one thing I've learned, it's that you don't create a winner by snapping your fingers. It takes time because you're drafting kids who are 18 years old and who aren't yet ready to play in the NHL."

It isn't often that the president of a hockey club decides to move behind the bench and coach his team while retaining his executive position, but Pat Quinn is one of the few exceptions to the rule.

During the 1990-91 season, Bob McCammon was into his fourth campaign behind the Vancouver Canucks bench. In 1988-89 the popular McCammon had helped the Canucks to a 33-39-8 record and into the playoffs for the first time in three years. The Canucks went seven games before being eliminated; all in all, a commendable feat.

But the club floundered the following year, missed the playoffs and was on a treadmill to oblivion in 1990-91. After 54 games, Vancouver owned a horrendous 19-30-5 record and it was then that Quinn fired McCammon and took the unusual step of naming himself coach along with his other functions as general manager and president of the club. Despite suggestions that a president and general manager cannot also function as a coach, Quinn rebuilt the Canucks through a series of judicious trades. In 1993-94, he did an unusual job, piloting his club all the way to the Stanley Cup finals before losing to the Rangers in seven games. He finally turned the head coaching reins over to his aide, Rick Ley, for the 1994-95 season.

In an interview with Stan Fischler, Quinn explained his thinking in firing McCammon and making the transition, as well as other matters related to coaching.

I had believed that the club was heading in the right direction although we anticipated an up-and-down year. One reason for that was the fact that we had infused a lot of young faces into our lineup. When you do that, you know you'll have some troubled times.

Our organization had established a five-year program and this was Year Three and in some ways we had made good progress. In fact, just a week before [the firing] we beat Los Angeles, Edmonton and Calgary in short order; and we played well doing it. So, I believed that the direction of our club was strong.

But I had also detected trouble. We started to lose our focus on the defensive part of the game; we wanted to get more goals and the emphasis shifted to goal-scoring. That constantly was a sore point with our media and fans — that we weren't scoring enough goals.

Some of our young, offense-oriented people tried to open up but instead of opening up out of a solid defensive posture — the transition game — we became a gambling hockey club. We gambled for the offensive opportunities; gave up too many of those opportunities going the other way and then we tried to get order restored, but it didn't seem to be out there for us.

I don't know if Bob McCammon was necessarily part of the problem. Bob had been a good coach and was a good coach at the time. What mattered was that we needed a wake-up call for our players and sometimes, in cases like that, a drastic move is taken. As I said, McCammon was a good hockey man.

When I made the move a lot of people pointed fingers, suggesting that McCammon was the scapegoat in the affair, but I don't think so. We had gone in with a plan and Bob was part of the plan. The idea was that he would be our coach for two or three years and then would move into management duties with me and then we would go with a teaching style of coach — not that he wasn't. But I wanted someone with a more fundamental style to help the kids through.

You have to remember that our franchise had undergone a lot of hardship, losing over the years. People used travel as an excuse, or they pointed to the weather or the owners and that [losing] attitude was something we were trying to get away from for a long time.

The bottom line was that a drastic measure was needed to get the team on the right track and I felt it was important that I put myself in the breach and answer my own critics. The time had come to put my money — or my body, or my mind — where my mouth was. All the criticism was being directed at myself, so I wanted to step in there and I felt it would have been unfair to bring someone else into that situation.

My hope was to ride out the year [which he did] and get the players' focus back where it belonged and get each player to be better and improve the hockey club as a whole, as a result.

When did I realize that there was something wrong? The club was playing out of control and forgetting the fundamentals and failing to live by them on a day-to-day basis. Teams that play out of control don't win many hockey games, and we were playing out of control. The idea was to give shock treatment to the team and see if we could regain our focus.

It didn't happen overnight. I finished the regular season's 26 games with nine wins and 13 losses and four ties. Then, we went six games in the playoffs before being eliminated.

One of the interesting aspects of the turnover was the events leading up to Bob's leaving. We played the Rangers on the night before the coaching change. For about a week there had been a lot of speculation about the possibility that something might happen, but we tried to give no indication that it would. What we really wanted to do was ride through to see if there was any semblance of a positive change, but what we saw was the wrong direction. I don't think any of the players knew that we were going to make a move on the night we played the Rangers, but that night we threw a remarkable number of pucks at their goalie, Mike Richter.

When I took over we were in Los Angeles and I felt as if I had 14 years of rust on me, and plenty of butterflies in my stomach. What I tried to do was emphasize the defensive scheme of things and talk to the players about intangibles. Panic had become part of our game plan and panic wins nothing.

Once I had had a few games under my belt, I realized that I had done the right thing and had no regrets at all. I knew I had to work on the players because they had become immobile in their approach to the game.

Players react on the basis of what they learn through their practices and discipline themselves as part of their system. Hockey is not a game where you stop to think, "Where am I supposed to be?" That's what our team was doing when I took over. They were wasting a second of reaction time. It escaped them and that second was necessary for them to play the game well.

I had also made a couple of deals, bringing Gerald Diduck and Tom Kurvers to our defense. Unfortunately, they joined the team in the midst of its turmoil and they had to learn along with the rest of the guys and become assimilated into the framework of the team. Teamwork became a priority because, quite frankly, it had been sorely lacking before.

And speaking of teamwork, one of the more interesting elements of running an NHL club at the start of the 1990s was the infusion of Russian players in the various lineups. In the case of the Canucks it was Vladimir Krutov and Igor Larionov.

A lot had been said about that move and, naturally, there was criticism. But my mandate as part of management was to bring in the most talented people available and if they happen to be Russians, so be it. Unfortunately, the rest of our team didn't accept them as well as we had hoped. On top of that, one of the two athletes [Krutov] came in with an attitude that wasn't team-oriented. His conditioning was poor and the players came to believe that he didn't care about the team.

All of this eroded the level of belief in each other that we had established the year before. So, one might say that I made a mistake in bringing him in, but my intention was to produce a better team and these two players should have been able to make a difference on our hockey club.

In cases such as those, the media has a lot to say and it's no secret that the press has a great deal of influence on our business. However, I try not to be influenced by them. I know that some of the things done by the Canucks organization in the past were the result of reaction to [media] criticism. Myself, I try not to be rabbit-eared, making changes based on what's said in the paper or on the air. I make changes because I think they are the correct ones.

That's not to say that I don't react to what's written. I'm human, too, and I'm affected by criticism. I can be influenced and that [the media] may have been one reason why I changed the coach.

But if there's one thing I've learned, it's that you don't create a winner by snapping your fingers. It takes time because you're drafting kids who are 18 years old and who aren't yet ready to play in the NHL. We had to impress that on our fans as well. I told them that it would take time to build a winner and patience is required to get us out of the rut. We had to stick with our program, building from within and making trades whenever we thought they might be helpful.

The process of developing promising youngsters is difficult. Our classic case was Petr Nedved who had a lot of raw talent but, in the eyes of some, might have been too young to crash the NHL. Some critics said we should have let him stay in Junior hockey for at least another year, but I don't believe that that was the way to go.

We had a formula of games for Nedved: an X-amount of time that we wanted him to play and we left that to the coach as far as whether he played or not. Bob chose to play him enough so that it met the criteria we had set and we were happy with his progress.

Nedved was a victim of the publicity that goes with high draft choices. People expected big things of him right away and when he didn't produce they began to figure that something was wrong; he's not getting his points; he's not doing this or that. What they didn't consider was that he didn't figure to be a star right away; he was merely the best of the [draft] bunch who might have been able to play but not necessarily be a star.

POSTSCRIPT: Although many Canucks-watchers believed that Quinn's stewardship behind the bench would be relatively brief, Pat continued to hold the positions of president, general manager and coach through the 1993-94 season.

Meanwhile, his Canucks continued to improve. In 1991-92 they finished with a record of 42 wins, 26 losses and 12 ties and Quinn was named NHL Coach of the Year. A year later he upped the win total to 46 and the club's winning percentage to an all-time high .601.

While pressure mounted for him to forsake coaching, Quinn resisted and in 1993-94 the Canucks concluded the season on a positive note. They met Calgary in the first playoff round and then toppled Dallas and Toronto before reaching the finals, and losing to New York.

14

Brian Kilrea

THE KILLER COACH

"One thing I learned about coaching is that you can't let a prima donna rule the roost. You can't avoid giving it to a star, just because he's a star. You have to let him know he's no better than the rest of the team even though he may be the fellow to lead you on the ice."

That Brian "Killer" Kilrea never attained the position of head coach in the NHL is one of the more unfortunate might-have-beens in modern hockey annals.

Those who watched and studied Kilrea during his long stint as a highly successful junior coach had long been convinced that Brian could have ranked with the Scotty Bowmans and Al Arbours of major league hockey had he only been given a chance.

Kilrea's lone opportunity to make it in the NHL occurred during the 1984-85 season when he was imported to Long Island as Arbour's assistant. "I never got to play under Brian in Ottawa," said Hall of Fame defenseman Denis Potvin, "but when he came to the Islanders, I got to know what they were talking about. He was a great coach. The best."

Those close to the Islanders assumed that Kilrea was heir apparent to Arbour, but Brian's ascension to the throne never took place and eventually Islanders President Bill Torrey signed Terry Simpson instead, much to the dismay of those who had grown to respect Kilrea.

Undaunted, Brian returned to Ottawa although in 1989 he rejected an offer to coach the Toronto Maple Leafs. By this time Kilrea had become an institution in Ottawa and preferred coaching the Junior 67s until his retirement at the end of the 1993-94 season.

Kilrea's hockey career began on the neighborhood rinks of Ottawa. When it became apparent he had enough talent to be a professional, he moved on to Springfield in the American Hockey League where he played under the infamous owner Eddie Shore.

He eventually made it to Los Angeles of the NHL and Denver of the old Western Hockey League where he concluded his player career. Among the many friends he made along the trail was Don "Grapes" Cherry, a teammate on the Springfield Indians, and one who disagreed with Kilrea about Shore.

"We all hated playing for Shore because of the way he treated the players, but Brian loved the game," Cherry recalled. "We almost got into a fight at the bar about a week after he arrived because Kilrea actually liked Shore. I couldn't believe it."

Nevertheless, Kilrea and Cherry became the best of friends and now Grapes unabashedly declares that Brian "was the best coach in hockey."

Like so many others, Cherry was disappointed that Kilrea never attained the head coaching job on Long Island. "Brian phoned me up the day before he took the job," Cherry remembered. "He wanted to know what I thought about it. I said, 'Brian, don't take it.' He said, 'Why?' I said, 'Because you're a head coach, not an assistant coach. Some guys are born to be assistants, some are born to be head coaches.'" Cherry was right.

When Kilrea began his coaching career in 1974, replacing former NHL defenseman Leo Boivin, Jim Roberts and Bruce Baker led his Ottawa club to a 9-5 win over the Toronto Marlboros. Brian was 39 years old at the time, and at 59 and some 1,200 regular season games later he retired.

"I never set out to do this," Kilrea said. "One day the owners asked if I was interested. I said yes. And that's how it happened. The thing was I never took this job hoping it would lead to something else. When I took it, I wanted to be here in Ottawa. I wanted to try it. And, like my father always said, everything works out for the best."

In an interview with Ottawa reporter Rick Middleton, Kilrea spelled out his thoughts on playing, coaching and life in hockey.

How did I get into coaching? It was the tail end of my playing career and I was in Tulsa. Johnny McLellan, who would be the next coach of the Toronto Maple Leafs, was there, and one day he asked me straight out whether I'd ever be interested in going behind the bench.

"Geez," I said, "I never thought about that; I'm just a player." Then, McLellan told me that after he goes to Toronto, they may be looking for a coach. But I had to have spinal fusion done so nothing materialized and I finished my playing career in Denver.

When I was in Colorado, we registered our son, Billy, in a hockey league and it turned out that they were short of coaches. I told my wife not to nominate me as a volunteer coach. I figured if I started getting involved with hockey again, there'd be an urge to return again as a player after my injury healed. I told my wife, "I don't want to get the itch to go back."

My wife didn't volunteer me as a coach after all but rather as an assistant. But it turned out that the head coach told me, "I don't know anything about hockey and you've got to help me." And that's how I got started. I began by helping him and after a while I took over the coaching.

This was the Tyke level; kids play like bowling pins and it was fun, the way hockey should be. From there I eventually came back to Ottawa and was asked to coach a Midget team that was affiliated with Ottawa's Junior B club. I enjoyed this except that I only lasted a year because I ran into a problem with the parents.

As it happened we had three players on our club who I figured could help the Junior B team so I sent them up, thinking it was best for the kids to have better competition. Our team [West Ottawa] was shorthanded the three players and the parents were mad that we weren't doing better in the tournaments. What they did was fire me at a banquet while they were introducing a new coach. That's how I found out I wasn't coming back the following year.

It didn't take long for me to hook up with another club, the South Ottawa Midgets. That was the year the powerful Russian Midget touring club was going across Canada, demolishing everyone. We put a team together to play them and I coached us to a 4-4 tie.

This was weird because all of the officials seemed to want to pacify the Russians, and after the game the officials rushed down to their dressing room to console them for not winning. Only one person came to our dressing room and that was Murray Costello, the head of the CAHA.

Then, there was a banquet honoring the visitors. Every one of the Russians got a prize and they were told how great they were. After we had clapped for the 21 recipients of these awards, they told us we could leave and never even introduced our players or gave them any token gift as they did for the Russians. That was an event I'll never forget.

Nevertheless, that particular 4-4 tie with the Russians brought my name to prominence and a year later the Ottawa 67s asked if I would be interested in coaching on the Junior A level. I accepted and from then on it was just a matter of adjusting.

No matter how you look at it, my getting into coaching was more an accident than anything else. I had fully intended to go into the business world, running a restaurant, when the coaching intervened.

I learned a lot over the years from a variety of people. When I left Ottawa to go to work for the New York Islanders, Al Arbour was the head coach and he was a big help. Of course, during my playing years in Springfield, I learned from Eddie Shore who was the owner of the Indians and also had a lot of great coaching ideas. Red Kelly was a good instructor — patient and understanding — as was Johnny McLellan.

One of the points that came across to me was that everyone is different and you can't simply go around patting guys on the back, saying, "You're wonderful." Especially if you have a bad team. It can't be wonderful if you're losing all the time. It's nice to say that a coach should always be positive, but every once in a while I'll get a kid who will take advantage and he'll require a boot in the ass because that particular kid happens to be spoiled. A lot of them are spoiled and they have to be made aware of the need for hard work and dedication.

It would be nice to be able to treat all of them the same but you can't. There are some kids who, if you give them shit, will pout and be dejected. What I tried to do was hit the best guy in the room; the one who could accept my criticism and hope that everyone else would fall in line. By hitting guys One and Two, I might actually reach the ones I want to get — guys Three and Four. Then, what I said should be accepted because the best players got shit from me.

One thing I learned about coaching is that you can't let a prima donna rule the roost. You can't avoid giving it to a star, just because he's a star. You have to let him know he's no better than the rest of the team even though he may be the fellow to lead you on the ice. If I were to give it to everyone else, my players would say, "But that guy [the star] never gets shit."

I did the same thing with my son when he practiced with us. I would always give him shit right off the bat to let everyone else know that I wasn't going to give him any special privilege. My other players realized that if I gave it to my boy, I would give it to anybody.

Times have changed in coaching, even on the Junior level. For example, education is stressed more so now than ever before. On the 67s we had two guidance counselors reporting to me. We figured that if families entrusted their sons to us, it was up to us to follow through and be sure that they got a good education. What we tried to do was prepare them to join the work force, hopefully after a pro career.

I've been asked what impact I may have had on some of our boys — like Doug Wilson or Bobby Smith — who went on to distinguished NHL careers. I don't think I had that much impact, although I tried hard to get them prepared off the ice. Their talents are what got them there, but I wanted to let them know what they were going to face when they became professionals and not to set themselves above their fellow players. I wanted them to be the humble persons they were then.

I stressed that friendships were the most important thing in life. Your name and your friendships. That was stressed along with the fact that they earned what they got; they have had great successes — and it beats working.

Of course, Springfield might have been an exception because with Eddie Shore we were treated like dogs. It was the reason we banded together. Every day everyone took his turn to bark. But that taught us unity and the need to be loyal to each other.

Shore has taken a lot of heat over the years, but what's been forgotten is that Eddie also happened to be a great teacher. Unfortunately, in today's hockey a lot of Shore's methods wouldn't work because you no longer can suspend a player for no reason or fine him for no reason because the Players' Association would jump right in and stop it. To be honest, everyone in hockey should have been required to have a year with Eddie Shore because, after that, he'd appreciate anywhere else he might have gone that much more.

A year under Shore and today's players wouldn't get involved in constant bickering, little complaints about meaningless things. That's what happens when you're spoiled. But if everyone had a year with Shore they would appreciate wherever they were and there wouldn't be squabbling going on.

I spent eight years with Shore and we won three Calder Cups [American Hockey League championship] in those times, but even though we won, Eddie was still tough on us. Still, we won in spite of him because the players stayed together and we had tremendous talent. The toughest time was when he kept suspending guys and doing different things for no reason. Overall, though, the good outweighed the bad in Springfield.

But there were some lulus with Eddie, who thought he was a chiropractor. We had a defenseman named Bob McCord whose back was so bad one time you couldn't straighten him out. We had to put him in Shore's car laying him down sideways just to get him to a chiropractor uptown. Even if you had a cold, Shore would get you. He said he could get rid of the cold by cracking your back and making the nerves straighten up.

Wherever you go in hockey, you'll find characters and Springfield had its quota. One of the best of all was Bill Sweeney, who at the time, was one of the best players in the American League but who didn't exactly follow Shore's rules to a T.

Sometimes Eddie would try to embarrass his players and tell us that we had to be in our homes by 9 p.m. or we would be fined. Well, 9 p.m. is ridiculous because we're not going to go to sleep at 9 p.m. anyway. But that was Shore's way of letting us know he was the boss; not that we didn't know it.

Sweeney was different. He would just say, "I'll see you when I'm tired." It didn't matter whether he came in at nine in the morning or nine at night, he was still the best player on the ice. Shore would fine him and fine him and fine him, and the next year he wouldn't give him a raise but give him back his fine money instead. That was Bill's way and that was Shore's way.

Then there was the year the Springfield players got so fed up, we actually went on strike. That season he was suspending everybody. We would go on a road trip and we'd have to sit in a bus for three hours before it would move, going down the highway 15 miles an hour on the Interstate because he didn't want to get into town too early for fear that the bars would be open and everyone would go out for a beer.

His practices were something else. We'd play on Wednesday, Friday, Saturday and Sunday, then have to be at the rink at eight a.m. Monday morning because we lost a game. Then, he'd have us practice twice a day for a week. We'd go from eight in the morning until ten and then from noon until two. Then some guys would have to come back at five and run around the track.

Shore was hoping that somebody on the team would get mad so that he could suspend him. Our trick was not to get mad and beat him at his own game. We'd keep repeating: "Hold on. Hold on. Stay together." That was the big thing; learning how to stay together.

In some practices Shore wouldn't use a puck at all. It was just skating and positional play. Then, he'd put ropes around some guys; tie them up and put laces around their knee pads or elbows to keep their elbows in or keep them from taking a long stride around their knees. He'd tie the goaltender to the crossbar and warn him, "Don't fall!" Shore liked standup goalies.

Even when we were winning, he was tough. Three days in a row he'd have us at the rink at eight in the morning and then go twelve til two in the afternoon and then we weren't allowed to go home until four. He would say that that was "working man's hours." We had to stay there and do nothing, like punching a clock.

He was able to get away with it because we were in the American League and we weren't organized. Besides, Eddie ran the league and he was a very intimidating man, even at the age of 70.

Shore wasn't the only interesting guy I dealt with over my career. There were many including the ones during my two years in the NHL with the Islanders. The deal there was that after I got the assistant coaching job, Al Arbour was supposed to retire after a year. But then he changed his mind and decided to stay on and that created some confusion. They didn't know whether they were going to replace Al or whether he was going to remain on the Island. As it turned out, during the two years that I was with the Islanders, Al continued to be head coach and I remained his assistant.

For the most part, I enjoyed my stay but there were clashes of philosophy between myself and management. My feeling has always been that it's important to get to know my players while their philosophy was that they didn't want that. It just didn't work out, but as far as I'm concerned it was a break for me because I learned a lot under Arbour and met some of the greatest guys in hockey. The Islanders had some of the best — it was a tremendous group — and I'm still in touch with quite a few of them today.

I also was lucky in that when I decided to leave Long Island, the folks in Ottawa were ready for a coaching change and I happened to arrive at the right time. Immediately, I realized how much easier it is to coach in your own home town.

When I got back, I was asked about the difference between coaching Juniors compared with the NHL. Actually, there's not that great a difference. Players all want the same thing; they want to win no matter what level they're on, but the big difference is that more teaching is required by the Junior coach than the one in the NHL.

The toughest thing about working in the big-league is having to deal with the player agents. They stick their noses into our business a lot more in the NHL than they do in Juniors and that creates problems. Every agent wants his player to be a star so the player gets more money and, of course, his rep gets a bigger cut. I could never adjust to listening to an agent and I don't think Al Arbour ever listened to one, although Bill Torrey certainly had to listen to a lot of them.

Another difference between working with a Junior and NHL team is the planning. In Juniors the kids are all in their teens and when I'd have a club loaded with 19-year-olds, I'd know damn well that the next year I'd have a lot of openings on my club because those kids would be moving out. As a result, the most I could have in Ottawa was a three-year plan, whereas in the NHL they could afford to have a five- or six-year plan.

The trick in Juniors is to try and arrange it so that you put yourself into position to win a championship by getting as many experienced good kids in your lineup as you can. If you put yourself in that position, it's possible to make a run for the title. If in that particular season you feel you've got a legitimate chance to go all the way, you go for it with your older kids, and then the following season, you try your best to patch and repair the lineup.

Junior teams run in cycles. If somebody's strong one year, you have to figure that that club will weaken once its older stars move up to the pros. Every three years there's a cycle change so if you're drafting near the bottom one year, then you know you have a chance to catch up later on. Teams generally have seven 17-year-olds, seven 18-year-olds and seven 19-year-olds. Then, you keep that progression but when it comes time to make a run at it, you may end up with having to trade a couple of promising players for a couple of proven players. You have to see when it is the right time to jump.

Over the years I've had quite a few wonderful characters play for me. One of the best was Jimmy Ralph, the goalie who became a broadcaster. Jimmy came to Ottawa and was funny from Day One and, besides being good for laughs, he also played great goal for us. A lot of goalies have this reputation for being flakes. I don't know if you'd call Ralph a flake, but he sure knew how to keep the dressing room loose and the bus rides as well.

During my two years in the NHL, I was associated with some great ones. I can't remember any defenseman being as dominant in my time other than Doug Wilson, who could do everything. He could shoot, skate, pass the puck and play tough. Denis Potvin also had those qualities, and they were the two best defensemen I ever saw in an Ottawa 67s uniform.

Up front, I'd go with Bobby Smith because he did so much for the 67s. Over the years, we had an awful lot of big players but Bobby was a touch better than anyone else I had. Maybe it was because Bobby was so serious about the game and so ready that it didn't matter where we played, on the road or at home. Bobby was tremendously ready and played every game from start to finish. He never had a relaxed game, nor a relaxed moment. Bobby Smith was all business.

Smith and Wilson had greatness in them before I met them and it's just nice that they still call me their friend, which is the important thing. When they get in touch with me, it's not because I was their coach, but it's because they regard me as a friend, which is really what it's all about. When players leave, you hope they leave knowing that what you did was the best thing for them and I'm sure all coaches feel the same. They take tremendous pride in what they've accomplished and I take tremendous pride in the friendships that I've made.

When I started in Ottawa I never thought about how many years I'd be with the 67s but, luckily, I managed to be around for 19 years and even now that I'm no longer coaching, I'll still be connected to management, handling player personnel or scouting.

In those 19 years I made lots of mistakes, whether it be a bad trade or a bad decision in scouting but I've always put those behind me. After all, no one is perfect and all I tried to do was my best. I never second-guess myself. Once, I drafted an 18-year-old named Randy Pierce. As far as I was concerned, Pierce was destined to be on our fourth line which I didn't think was fair to him so I traded him which, of course, got Randy good and mad. So, what happens? Randy scored 40 goals two years in a row. For Randy's sake, I did the right thing. For the Ottawa 67s sake, maybe I didn't.

Every year in Ottawa has not been a bang-up success, but ownership over the years has been very patient and understanding. But as I approached the age of 60, I felt that I had been coaching long enough. I want the kids coming in to the team to have fun and I didn't want someone coming in and saying, "I'm coached by an old man."

15

Ted Sator

THE HIDDEN GENIUS

"To get to the pinnacle, you have to keep working at it every single day and also have the passion for the business. You watch other coaches and pirate every bit of material you can, using it with a flavor of your own while being true to yourself and your ideals in terms of what makes you tick."

There are some who believe that Ted Sator could have emerged as one of the finest coaches of the past decade were he not a victim of hockey's politics.

Twice — after successful stints in New York and Buffalo — Sator was axed despite commendable work behind the bench. And even today, in his latest job as St. Louis Blues assistant coach, Ted is regarded as one of the brightest minds in the coaching business.

Sator originally made headlines during the 1985-86 season, his rookie year as Rangers head coach. Having reached the Stanley Cup finals as assistant coach to Mike Keenan in Philadelphia the previous spring, Sator was hired by New York general manager Craig Patrick on June 19, 1985.

Employing an old-fashioned work ethic, Sator guided the Broadway Blueshirts to resounding playoff victories over both Philadelphia and Washington before being eliminated by the future Stanley Cup Champion Montreal Canadiens.

The dramatic coming-together of the Rangers at season's end was a clear victory for Sator's coaching disciplines. His defense-oriented philosophies helped the club cut its goal against from an all-time Rangers' high of 345 in the 1984-85 season to 276 under Sator.

That Sator succeeded so quickly hardly came as a surprise to those who knew the Utica, New York native. After playing hockey for Bowling Green University, where he graduated Magna Cum Laude in 1972 with a degree in health and physical education, Sator went on to play one season with the New York Raiders of the World Hockey Association in 1973. He then returned to his alma mater to pursue his master's degree while he served as assistant coach on the hockey team.

Sator then travelled to Sweden where he coached his teams to championships in each of his five seasons, three with Vaxjo HC and two with Rogle BK. He returned to North America where he was signed as Keenan's assistant in Philadelphia.

Among Sator's areas of expertise — power skating being one of them — one of the most important was his knowledge of European and Russian training techniques. He was one of ten American coaches selected to attend a three-week Canadian-USSR training clinic in Moscow, and in April 1984 he became the first American to be invited to attend the Czechoslovak National Team Symposium on training techniques.

Based on his 1985-86 success, Sator should have enjoyed a lengthy career with the Rangers but politics intervened. Sator's original boss, Craig Patrick, was replaced by Phil Esposito on July 14, 1986 and it was apparent, even before the season's opener, that the flamboyant Esposito and the studious Sator would have difficulty co-existing.

Less than two months into the new season, Sator was dismissed but, within weeks, was named head coach of the Buffalo Sabres on December 22, 1986. From that point, Buffalo was only one game under the .500 mark through the end of the season. The Sabres dramatically chased Quebec in the second half of the season for the last playoff spot, only to fall short partially because of a rash of injuries.

Once again, Sator's head coaching career came to an abrupt halt after so much promise. The Sabres dropped him whereupon Sator moved on to the Boston Bruins for a brief stint as assistant coach. He then returned to Europe, coaching a Milanese team to several titles. But the lure of the NHL was too strong to resist and in 1993 he was signed by the St. Louis Blues as an aide to head coach Bob Berry. When Mike Keenan moved to St. Louis in the summer of 1994, he made sure that Ted remained as his sidekick.

In an interview with reporter Jim Ramsey, Sator expounded on the whys and wherefores of hockey coaching.

I grew up in a little place in Upstate New York called New Hartford. It's close to the city of Utica and a town called Clinton. It's really cold country there in the winter and what you would call a hockey community.

Clinton has long been known as a top hockey town dating back to the pro team that played in the old Eastern League. They were called the Clinton Comets and had a lot of good minor league players. Mike Nardello, who once belonged to the New York Rangers, played for the Comets after World War II as did Lenny Speck, a really good defenseman who also was Rangers' property for a while.

They had a neat arena in Clinton — real old-style but cozy — and the games there were very competitive and fun to watch. The movie "Slapshot" was based on the old Eastern League and reminded me a lot of some of the guys who played for the Comets.

Since it was so cold in winters, it was easy for me to find ice on which to skate. When I was eight years old, I began skating on a section of the old Erie Canal that went from Buffalo to the Hudson River. We'd play pickup hockey and that's when I learned the raw fundamentals.

As a youth, you find that certain individuals have a profound effect on your future. In my case it was a high school teacher, Oliver Simonson. He ingrained a strong work ethic in us, not only as far as sports was concerned but how we conducted ourselves as young boys. He had a significant impact on Ted Sator. Of course, my mom and dad were just as important.

Up where I lived it was very easy to get the Montreal Canadiens games on the radio and, listening to them, I became a dyed-in-the-wool Canadiens fan. But even though Montreal was my favorite team, I also liked the Bruins because Bobby Orr once spoke at our high school banquet and made an immediate impact on me. I also liked baseball a great deal and might have gone on to a pro career but I suffered an arm injury, and when I learned that I wasn't going to be able to throw anymore, I put all my energies into playing ice hockey.

It didn't take long for me to get to love the game and the next thing I knew, I was playing high school hockey. I was good enough to get a scholarship to Bowling Green State University in Ohio. Playing Junior hockey was another possibility, but it would have been very hard for me, coming out of an itty-bitty high school in Upstate New York to crack a Junior lineup. In those days the trend of an American going up north wasn't nearly as established as it is today.

In terms of getting into college, I have to thank Jack Vivian of Bowling Green, who was my university mentor. Jack was the one who gave me the opportunity to get into Bowling Green and without that chance, I don't know where I would be today.

My grades were fairly good so college was an advantageous route for me. One thing the university does is give you a chance at a four-year program where you not only become educated, but also get a chance to physically mature rather than jumping into Junior or pro ranks.

I've always said that people would die of old age if they could go back and write down what they should have done by the time they were doing them. All I know is that the decision was right for Ted Sator at the time and I have no regrets about it.

One of the things you realize when you get into coaching is how short your career can be, whether it's decided by fate, quirks or opportunities.

That's one of the refreshing aspects of having an education behind you. It doesn't necessarily pigeonhole you or make you uni-dimensional if and when you choose to get out of your sport or vocation. But I had decided that I wanted to pursue a hockey career, and at the start of the 1970s there was plenty of action on a lot of fronts.

That was at the time of huge hockey expansion. The NHL had just added the Islanders and Flames in Atlanta and the World Hockey Association has just been born. The WHA had a team in New York City called the Raiders and I managed to get a spot on their roster.

It was the first year of the WHA and nobody was quite sure whether it would take off or not although there were some pretty good names on the rosters. Winnipeg had Bobby Hull, the Whalers had Ted Green and Cleveland had Gerry Cheevers, among other former NHL players who were there.

The WHA had a lot longer life than Ted Sator as a WHA player. I sustained a knee injury in New York and was told that it would require surgery and a long convalescent period. I decided that I didn't want to just stay on the fence so I applied for graduate school at Bowling Green.

That was when Ron Mason was coming in as coach and I became his first graduate assistant, from a coaching point of view. Ron Mason became my mentor in the coaching world. He molded my career and my outlook on hockey. He taught me what it was like to be a career coach and for that I am eternally grateful.

But my actual coaching began in a little, itty-bitty program in Wisconsin at Stevens Point. It was at the club stage and the program lasted only one year but it was a good weaning point for Ted Sator. Not only was I recruiting, I was folding programs, driving the Zamboni machine, fixing up locker rooms — anything that needed to be done on the ground floor. And it certainly was a very good lesson in humility.

From there I was selected as one of ten Americans to go on an exchange program to the Soviet Union in 1976. In 1977 they selected two of us to go back to Sweden. I also did a stint coaching high school hockey in Findlay, Ohio, which was the first year of a state-sanctioned tournament. I was able to implement some of the European techniques I had learned with a group of kids I had become very fond of and wanted very much to teach the overseas ideas I had learned.

This was a key launching point for my career because I had the opportunity to work with a group of kids who were eager and willing to learn. At that point in my career, I needed them more than they needed me.

My learning process continued on several fronts. I had gone to Czechoslovakia as one of the international advisors for the Czech

National Team and I had gone to the Soviet Union with Ron Mason. As a coach, you are really a teacher and part of becoming a teacher is making sure you are an eternal student. When those opportunities arose, I simply couldn't say no to them.

Another big break came in 1978 when the Swedish coaching opportunity came and I moved into the professional ranks. I was given carte blanche to set up a program with Vaxjo from the time the kids entered their program until they played pro.

In 1981 I moved to Rogle, which was allowed two import players. At the time, I kept my eyes on the Central Collegiate Hockey Association because they played a similar style of game, with a lot of emphasis on play away from the puck. I contacted Ron Mason and told him I was looking for a centerman and he threw the name Dave Poulin at me.

Dave had just graduated from Notre Dame University and was just getting married. He and his wife, Kim, were both career people and I decided to take a chance and invite him. He accepted and, as the season progressed, I became more and more convinced that Poulin could indeed play in the NHL.

Eventually, I wound up in Philadelphia as assistant to first Bob McCammon and then Mike Keenan. Over the years Mike and I have grown to be very, very good friends. Keenan is demanding but he is as demanding on himself as he is on others. I like Mike Keenan as a friend to Ted Sator. I admire his attention to detail and his relentless drive for success.

There's no question but that when Mike goes into a new city, the fur flies and a few hedges get uprooted. When I worked for Mike, I learned all about being a stickler for detail and organization. Mike always was searching for that competitive edge. He has good bench demeanor and good preparation skills. I enjoyed my association with Mike but that doesn't necessarily make me a clone of his.

I finally got my big, head-coaching break in 1985 when I was hired by the Rangers. Needless to say, it wasn't the easiest of situations for a rookie and I made rookie mistakes. I was coming to a team that had finished 16th out of 21 teams and I knew very, very little about the team.

I had to make decisions based on what I had seen in training camp — decisions that wouldn't have been made in previous regimes. For me not to have broken the script would have put the Rangers right back into the place they were in before I had come to New York.

The Rangers were in a state of mediocrity and I wasn't hired to keep the status quo. I told the players from Day One to do something that was going to make an impression on the coaching staff; something that would benefit the Rangers that year.

In that rookie NHL year of mine, one of the biggest sources of controversy was my decision to send popular forward Pierre Larouche to the minors. Pierre had come off a 65-game season during which he had scored 24 goals and 36 assists for 60 points. But I decided that he should start the year in the minors, with Hershey of the American League.

Naturally, the story made headlines and there were those who argued that I had made a big mistake. Some said I didn't like Pierre, which really wasn't the case. As a rule, coaches in any sport like their players. I can count on one hand the players I've met in hockey that I don't like personally.

Sure, the Larouche episode caused a lot of talk but when a player goes down to the minors, it's due to the player's performance. In this case, it was not a personality conflict and I wouldn't have cared if it was Pierre Larouche or Pierre Trudeau; I was just trying to put the parts together that would give us a successful hockey machine.

The way it turned out, we recalled Larouche on January 25, 1986. I put him at right wing on a line with Bob Brooke and Ron Greschner. Pierre didn't score in his first four games but then he went on a rampage starting with a goal on February 5th in St. Louis. Then, he had at least a goal in seven straight games (ten goals during this stretch) which was the longest goal-scoring streak for a Ranger in almost ten years.

Larouche gave us a spark at the end of the season and I wish I would have been smart enough to see that in the earlier days. Pierre was a big reason we were successful and made the playoffs but him going down to Hershey had nothing to do with a personality clash.

Larouche became our leading scorer in the playoffs with eight goals and nine assists in seventeen games, which was great fodder for the New York media. Hey, New York is a demanding city and one of the things I came to realize was that the media there is under as much competition as the athletes in terms of getting their story to the public.

New York is a city that demands the best. It's The Big Apple and it's The Big Apple for a reason. Whether it's baseball, football, hockey or whatever, people want a winner. And since we're in an era of instant gratification, no city magnifies that more than New York. It's both a boon and a hindrance and something that myself, as coach, had to deal with, for better or worse.

After the wonderful playoff finish I had in the spring of 1986, I had high hopes for my future in New York. But that spring, Phil Esposito was hired as general manager. When a new GM comes into office, it's just like a new president moving into The White House; he's allowed to choose his own cabinet.

Phil had a direction and philosophy that he wanted for the New York

Rangers and I had one as well from our playoff team. It was a clash of ideologies and I became a square peg in a round hole. Obviously, Phil was under a great deal of pressure to produce results and in that situation he had to be comfortable with the people working with him. Phil and I had great rapport and he is still one of my personal friends. It was just the fact that we didn't work well together — and that doesn't mean there was a right or wrong. That's just how it works in professional sports.

After the Rangers let me go, I needed to get back on track in the NHL and Gerry Meehan was good enough to afford me the opportunity to coach the Sabres. The difference in winning and losing in the NHL isn't astronomical, there aren't a lot of 8-1 or 9-1 games. When I took over, Buffalo led the league in number of one-goal losses. When you go through that, night after night, the confidence factor becomes rather fragile.

So, we began to play very close attention to the little things that we had to do right consistently. All of a sudden, we began seeing results and there was almost a feeding frenzy mentality in the room. The only problem down the homestretch was that we started running out of bodies. We had a whole host of injuries — part of the sprint mentality — and we ran out of gas at the finish line.

That spring, the Sabres had the number one draft pick and we chose Pierre Turgeon. Interestingly, from a coaching viewpoint — and this may be a shock to some — coaches have very little to do with seeing the prospects who are out there. It's simply a function of the demands of our season. Our attention is focused on the here and now with the active players.

The scouts do a thankless job; they're in the arenas from September until draft day. The consensus from our people — and I trusted them — was that Turgeon was the best player available in the draft. And when you're in a position where you're picking number one, there is no stone left unturned in terms of character, head-to-head competition, whatever. You're going for what is going to be one of the cornerstones of your franchise. Pierre was certainly a player who came with all the raw materials but it would take an adjustment period for him to become a finished product.

When you consider the impact player that Turgeon became, you'd be hard-pressed to say the Sabres made anything but the right choice at the right time, and that's important when you're drafting number one.

Anyhow, the Sabres had improved dramatically under my coaching. We took over a team that had finished in 21st place and left with them in sixth place overall. But there were factors that militated against me. To begin with, Buffalo is hampered by being a small NHL market. Then there was the fact that we wanted the club to advance to the second playoff round but our nemesis was the Boston Bruins. We wanted not only to compete with the Bruins, but to beat them. Unfortunately, the ideal situations and the realistic solutions don't always come together and we didn't get past Boston in the first round which meant that the fans were clamoring. They wanted a team that was going north and we were laying the foundation for that, but we were one round short of the next plateau.

After leaving Buffalo I went to Boston — only this time as an assistant coach. My work as an assistant was no different than as a head coach. There was the same type of quality control, the same type of drive to assure that the athletes would be successful. I wanted our guys to arrive in the winner's circle. How they got there and in which area of the foundation I was a part of was inconsequential to me.

As an assistant coach, I got to do a little more of the strategy planning; the practice diagrams and the Xs and Os — things I really enjoy. As a head coach, so much of your time is diverted to selling the game — the media, radio and television exposure. In many ways the survival of the head coach depends a lot on the quality of work being done by his assistants.

In the years since I came into the NHL there has been a marked change in the hockey market and that has been reflected in coaching changes. Now, it's a players' market and people don't come to see coaches coach; they come to watch the players play. Our job as coaches is to get the players to play their best. One of the things we try to do — and it's a never-ending battle — is to try to guarantee consistency of effort. All the North American public wants is to see the players playing hard night in and night out. You do that as a coach, whether it's by befriending them or disciplining them and you have to be flexible enough to adapt to these demands.

When I decided to go to Italy and become a head coach and general manager, it was because I wanted an opportunity to really control my destiny. Here was an opportunity to make a plan, put it into action and watch it take shape. Was there apprehension and fear? Sure. Was it a challenge? Absolutely. Was it worth it and rewarding? Without question. The reward was being a part of the process that watched this team evolve into back-to-back champions.

Doing both jobs was a good thing for me since administration and organization are two of my fortés. I'm fairly good with time management and I discipline myself for that. The two roles presented no problems at all and were more of a help than a hindrance.

Over a period of two years, I had plenty of kicks. Our record was 92-

8. We won the Italian League championship two years in a row and were the Alpine League regular season champions. But what I was most proud of was that we made the final four of the European Cup for all the champions of Europe. We competed against the Soviets, Swedes, Czechs and the Finns. It was quite an accomplishment.

The eventual overall champion beat us, 3-2, in a game in which we hit three goal posts. We were very proud, having stepped in from being a kind of half-brother to a dog that was fighting for a piece of the bone. We accomplished that in two years, which doesn't mean it was because of the coaching staff's expertise but because of players and personnel. We had Tom Tilley, Gates Orlando, Mark Napier, Roberto Romano, Bill Stewart, Mike Richard — a wonderful group of guys, a coach's dream. It didn't last forever, but I did enjoy it.

On a competitive level, our team could have played in the lower echelon of the Swedish Elite League on a night-in, night-out basis. Our brand of hockey would have been middle-of-the-pack American Hockey League brand. We didn't have the dominant superstar because he was playing on the other side of the Atlantic Ocean in the greatest league in the world.

Having coached in Europe for so long, I was able to get an appreciation of the difference in the two cultures. In America, we have a society that is success-oriented and that's what makes this such a great country. We have a competitive drive that is innate to our sport and business culture. People like to be around those who are successful and the sports world is no different. It's not based on name or city but rather based on people. As a coach, you want to make sure that your people are successful. Nobody gravitates toward failure. When your team doesn't win, whether you like it or not, as a coach you take it personally.

The personal angle is always with a coach. I can't imagine a coach being able to walk away from a loss and not take it home with him. Any coach who says he can do that should send me his magic elixir. The euphoria you get from winning and the emptiness you get from losing, I've never found in any other walk of life.

I hope that doesn't make me unique and I hope people aren't thinking that Ted Sator ought to get a life. This is my life and I enjoy doing what I'm doing.

Which is not to say that it's easy. Take the travel aspect; first you start with the calendar; there's always going to be 365 days to a year, but the number of NHL games have increased and the travel has increased. What remains the same is the number of days into which they are compacted.

With an 84-game schedule, you have an every other day game scenario. Players develop fatigue, which becomes a mind-set, which must be played through to be successful. It's a real problem which needs addressing and is a concern for all of us: trying to keep players fresh and avoiding injuries.

One possible solution is cutting down the exhibition schedule and starting the regular season a little earlier. You don't need a four-week training camp to determine jobs because nowadays some jobs are etched in stone before camp even begins.

A lot of ideas have been knocked around in relation to making the long schedule easier to take. Some teams believe that having their own plane gives them an advantage. I know the Los Angeles Kings tried that and a few other clubs. Personally, I don't think it gives a clear-cut advantage in terms of a club's win-loss record. At the same time, the teams have to consider the cost of having its own plane. Let's face it: hockey is a big business, not just entertainment. Owners and management have to be conscious of the dollar and one of the things that remains a constant is travel and lodging costs. Chartering is expensive although some teams, like the Red Wings who have a captive audience, can afford it. But I'd have to check their road record to see if it really pays off.

Where you get rewarded in the NHL is not the regular season but rather in the Stanley Cup playoffs. There's only room for one winner in the playoffs so you have one telling the truth in the end and 25 liars.

Dealing with the youngsters is one of the most sensitive aspects of coaching and it can be very tough, especially if we have to tell a player he has to go back to the minors. Unfortunately, in the coaching profession we don't always get to be the bearer of good news. When a player comes into this league at 18, you have to be realistic. The NHL is the best league in the world. Players are experienced, talented, big and strong. Kids have a period of acclimatization and we, the coaches, have to have patience. But we also have to have the best interests of the athlete at heart and the kids must learn that sometimes it's best to take a half-step backward before taking two steps forward.

Then comes the matter of teaching the kids and that's not always that easy because any coach will tell you that he doesn't have enough practice time. We have this scenario where it often seems most important to simply keep the team fresh and ready for games. More and more, we're using video as a teaching aid while practicing when the schedule allows. My personal belief is that it's more important to have quality practices than quantity workouts.

The player of the 1990s has to be a reaction player and grounded in fundamentals. He has to be able to skate, pass and shoot; that all has to be there. After that, it's important to be able to react to situations that are presented on the ice. The game has become so fast that we try and remove the thought process in getting the players to react in sync.

Hockey people talk about role players and skill players but I can tell you that the role players are every bit as skilled as the skill players. They are extremely good at the roles they perform. It takes a lot of components to make a team successful. You have to have people who score when they should and people who check when they should and people who play tough when they should. We're now in the age of specialization, and without the role players, you don't get the Stanley Cup.

In this regard, one of the more interesting questions is whether or not a team can have too many skill players. For starters, no coach will lament the addition of talent, but there's only room for five players on the ice at one time. So, when you have a lot of talent it comes down to the utilization of talent that becomes the biggest problem.

There has been more emphasis on talent since I entered the NHL and the game is faster. The enforcement of rules has eliminated some of the clutching and grabbing which, in turn, has allowed skilled players to play the game so it's a more exciting endeavor than ever before. There's more parity and just about every team has five or six very good players.

Not that the game is perfect. Talking as a purist, I'd say that fighting should come out of hockey. Fisticuffs has held back hockey in terms of its marketability. Without fighting, we can have an even more saleable entertainment package. I'm not saying that I want to see hockey played with a no-hit scenario but with the way the players shoot the puck and the speed at which they skate, a player is extremely courageous just going on the ice. We don't need another badge of courage with fighting.

Another change is in attitudes players have for each other nowadays compared with 10, 20 and 30 years ago when players had an intense hate for those on the opposition. Free agency has changed that; players move around now. You only see most of the teams twice instead of six or seven times. It's an out-of-sight, out-of-mind scenario.

When you talk about change on the coaching front, one obvious point is the increase in salaries. You have a Scotty Bowman and Mike Keenan going into Detroit and New York, and then St. Louis, respectively, with hefty deals. Those are teams that were demanding success. When a coach gets those kinds of dollars, the owner, in effect, is telling the players, "We brought them in for a lot of money and we're going to back them!" As a result, some of the onus is shifted back to the players but not to the point where any coach can say, "I don't have to worry about being replaced." We learned in this hockey business that if they can trade a Wayne Gretzky, they can eat a coach's contract as well.

You hear a lot about how difficult it is being coach but I've said it before, it's the greatest job in the world, and if someone ever told me I had to take a nine to five job, I'd probably commit suicide. You see, coaching isn't a job to me, it's a passion. I'm very fortunate to have a job that doesn't require a clock. It requires a passion and it is all-consuming. I'll be the first to admit that there will come a time when that passion will wane and, when that happens, I no longer will be affiliated with the NHL. But I still enjoy life in the sprint lane and I plan to enjoy it for as long as I can.

In the meantime I'll continue to work at coaching. I like to win and I like to be organized and, for me, they go hand in hand. If I'm organized, then I can organize the thought process of my players on the ice and steer them on a course to be successful. My job is laying out a foundation for success. I ask the players to do two things: be on time and play hard.

With the salaries some of the players are making, there's a perception that some of them don't fear coaches the way they might have in the past. But I don't operate on a basis of fear but rather on a respect basis. And that's regardless of how much the player may be earning. But there's no question that, with the escalation of salaries, it has become a player's market with costs passed along to the paying public.

As coaches, we have to ensure that the fans see their star players play. With star players, right across the board, you monitor their ice time and keep them fresh for games. Where you really do the nuts and bolts of coaching is from the supporting cast underneath.

Lots of techniques are used. One of them is video tape. It's part of the competitive edge. In and of itself, video will not get you into the winner's circle, but it is a support vehicle to getting the work done on the ice. It has to be put into meaningful information that the players can use.

The toughest part of coaching is the organization of time. We're in the entertainment business and our time is consumed by getting our team ready to play and having to deal with the media every day. The only time you get to relax as coach is when you're out on the ice practicing with your team or when you're in the games themselves.

Just what separates a good coach from a great coach is a good question. There are intangibles. Sometimes it's timing and opportunity. At the NHL level, there isn't a coach who isn't extremely gifted at what he does and who isn't extremely good. To become an NHL coach persistence is necessary, same as if you were in medicine or law. You're going to get knocked down and you're going to get lessons in humility along the way. You have to realize that you have to pick yourself up and continue on the quest for excellence. To get to the pinnacle, you have to keep working at it every single day and also have the passion for the business. You watch other coaches and pirate every bit of material you can, using it with a flavor of your own while being true to yourself and your ideals in terms of what makes you tick.

One of the wackiest things I ever did as a coach was when I coached in Sweden. I was trying to make a point to the team about the forwards playing a little harder. I put on a Hawaiian shirt and sunglasses, put a camera around my neck, got a Thermos with coffee and a director's chair and sat at center ice during practice and had them do whistle stops for an hour.

There are down times for a coach and up times. As for the emotional part of the job, the up times are those when you feel euphoria. I had that experience when I coached the Rangers and we advanced out of the Patrick Division finals. We had planted a seed of hope at Madison Square Garden during training camp and it grew and grew until the playoffs when we upset Washington and rose to the cream of the crop. To see the team blossom and bear fruit is a special time for a coach.

Another time I was with the Sabres when we played the Soviet Team in the Challenge Cup. We beat the Red Army team, 6-5, in overtime and I remember NHL Players' Association executive director Alan Eagleson running down and hugging our coaching staff, Barry Smith and myself after it was over.

The lowest point for a coach is rejection. Being let go by the Rangers was tough and it was difficult dealing with the emotion that went with being fired. It's the toughest human emotion in any realm, whether you're talking personal or job relationships. You get that rejection complex and it's hard to get your head above water again.

If I had to pick an All-Star Team, I'd start with John Vanbiesbrouck in the nets alongside Tom Barrasso. My defense would have Ray Bourque with Mike Ramsey and Phil Housley — as well as Alexei Kasatonov, when he was in his heyday. My centers would be Pierre Turgeon, Dave Poulin and Mike Ridley. Wingers would be Tomas Sandstrom, Pierre Larouche, Cam Neely, Brendan Shanahan and Brett Hull. I rate Hull as the most pure natural sniper I have ever seen.

When I walk away from the game I'd like to be remembered as a persistent and loyal worker whose friendships mean a lot. I would want them to know that Ted Sator was a pretty square shooter who sometimes wasn't the bearer of good news, but who never shirked his responsibility in doing his job. He wanted his teams to play hard and play smart.

Lester Patrick, shown here between sons Lynn (left) and Muzz (right).

Eddie Shore, near the end of his active playing career. Known as the toughest player in a tough era, Shore's renowned nastiness was less effective from behind the bench.

Don Cherry, known affectionately as "Grapes" to millions of hockey fans. His achievements as a coach have been overshadowed by the success of his "Coach's Corner" an analysis segment of the CBC's "Hockey Night in Canada" broadcasts.

Scotty Bowman, the most successful coach (most wins) in the history of professional hockey.

Vancouver's Pat Quinn. As coach, general manager and president of the Canucks, he took the team to a seventh game against the New York Rangers in 1993-94.

Al Arbour. The Sudbury, Ontario native became a coaching legend in Long Island.

Below: Darryl Sutter, seen here with the author. He has succeeded in transferring the renowned Sutter family grit to a position behind the bench.

Devilish Duo: New Jersey head coach Jacques Lemaire (left) in action. Lemaire took the Devils to the conference finals in his first season behind their bench. He won the Jack Adams Award as the NHL's Best Coach for his efforts. (Above) Jacques Caron, the New Jersey Devils' ace groomer of goalies.

Iron Mike: Mike Keenan, shown here in the uniform of his former team, the New York Rangers. A master motivator, Keenan has been described as among the most complicated individuals in professional sports.

Toronto head coach Pat Burns. His previous career as a cop gives him an edge in toughness.

16

THE SUTTER

"It would not be an exaggeration to say that how a team plays tells you something about the coach."

It would not be stretching it to say that Darryl Sutter's coaching career actually began in the loft of a barn at the family farm in Viking, Alberta. In that setting, Darryl developed the leadership qualities that would become invaluable when he became head coach of the Chicago Black Hawks nearly three decades later.

Darryl, along with brothers Brian, Duane, Brent, Rich, Ron and Gary, developed a work ethic which was reinforced by their parents, Grace and Louis Sutter. Originally, they had to make do in the most primitive conditions imaginable in the 1950s.

The original Sutter farmhouse had neither electricity nor running water. There were four rooms and no toilet, and when the boys had to relieve themselves, it was the outhouse or nothing. During the sub-zero Canadian winters, a night trip to the outhouse ranked among the least-desirable walks in the world.

Darryl's "bathtub" was a galvanized washtub which, during the winter, was filled with melted snow heated on a potbellied stove. The big advance in their lifestyle came in 1967 when Grace and Louis bought a new farm with a big kitchen, three bedrooms and an indoor bathroom.

Each of the Sutter boys had a chore, but Darryl was the early-bird. He would be up before his brothers and help Grace prepare the boys' lunches for school. He also became the one Sutter boy who could be counted on to weed his mother's extensive garden.

Hay-baling was a standard family chore. According to their biographer Dean Spiros, author of Six Shooters, "The boys loaded 20,000 bales a year."

When they weren't attending to farm chores or schoolwork, the Sutters were playing baseball — Darryl was a superb shortstop — football or hockey. They even devised an offbeat form of hockey that could be played in the hayloft and another on the slough where the cattle cavorted during the summer. There would be weekend nights during the winter when the boys would be playing "slough-hockey" until midnight.

Interestingly, both Darryl and Duane were Chicago Blackhawks fans when they were kids. Brent rooted for the Bruins, Brian liked the Red Wings and Gary favored the Maple Leafs. Darryl idolized Bobby Hull, then the Black Hawks superstar, and kept a scrapbook of Hull clippings which he titled "Sixteen Years of Bobby Hull."

An early influence on Darryl's career was Clem Loughlin, a former NHL player with the Red Wings and Black Hawks and later Chicago coach, who lived in Viking. At the tender age of 80, Loughlin coached the Viking midget team of which Darryl was one of the better players. One of Loughlin's messages remained with young Sutter for the rest of his life: "The player who will make the most sacrifices will have as much a chance to reach the top as the one with the most talent."

Eventually, Darryl made it up to the Red Deer Rustlers, following brother Brian, who would be the first Sutter to make an imprint on the NHL. For Darryl, the trip would be longer and more circuitous. Selected as Chicago's 11th and last pick in the 1978 draft, Darryl was so disillusioned by his inability to be better recognized, he seized a rare opportunity to play professional hockey in Japan.

"They were paying decent money," said Darryl, "and, at that time, I really didn't think I had a shot at playing in the NHL."

He accepted the Japanese offer and emplaned for Sapporo which would be his home during this unusual hockey stint. The quality of hockey approximated that of a Canadian senior league and, not surprisingly, Darryl was the club's best player.

"In a lot of ways, the atmosphere was terrific," Sutter recalled. "In some rinks, there were crowds of up to 15,000 fans and I became something of a hero there."

When the Japanese hockey season ended, Darryl returned home and immediately was contacted by the Blackhawks who asked him to sign up for some minor league playoff games. He skated for Chicago's AHL farm team in New Brunswick and, after it was eliminated, he also played for Flint in the IHL. The Hawks invited him to training camp the following fall and, although he performed well, management assigned him to the New Brunswick club where he starred and finished the season as AHL rookie-of-the-year.

"By that time," said Sutter, "I felt good enough to play in the NHL."

He was rewarded in September 1980 with a Blackhawks jersey and responded with a 40-goal season. It appeared that Darryl was heading for a spectacular career but injuries intervened and he never reached the 40-goal-level again. But his talents extended beyond goal-scoring. Management soon realized that he had extensive leadership qualities and in his third campaign was awarded the captain's "C."

Darryl served with the intensity one would expect from a Sutter and his captaincy was marked by notable triumphs although no Stanley Cup. During the 1985 playoffs, he totalled 12 goals and seven assists in 15 games, his finest post-season effort, but the following season, his chronically injured knee limited him to only 50 games. A year later, Darryl knew that the wheels had become too creaky to enable him to continue as a full-timer.

He retired at age 29 and became assistant Blackhawks coach, working with head coach Bob Murdoch. The taste of coaching appealed to Darryl so general manager Bob Pulford named him head coach of the IHL's Indianapolis Ice in 1989-90. Sutter delivered a Turner Cup, emblematic of the IHL playoff championship, and was invited back to Chicago as assistant to then-Blackhawks coach Mike Keenan.

When Keenan was moved into the general managers slot in 1992, Darryl achieved his oft-stated goal of becoming an NHL head coach. "It was no secret," Sutter revealed, "that I wanted to become a head coach and bring the Stanley Cup to Chicago."

His two years were marked by frustration although he did guide Chicago into a playoff berth. In 1993-94, the Blackhawks finished fifth in their division and met Toronto in the opening round. After Chicago dropped the first two games at Maple Leaf Gardens, one Chicago columnist called for Darryl's firing.

Down two games to none, the Hawks rallied to tie the series at two apiece but then fell apart losing to the Leafs in six games. Fortunately, Sutter survived demands for his scalp and returned to coach for 1994-95.

During an interview at Chicago Stadium with reporter Rick Sorci, Sutter revealed his thoughts on the events that led him to a major league coaching career.

My father was the first coach I can remember. Dad had been interested in sports all his life but especially hockey, although he was a pretty good ball player. He was a shortstop, which is what I wound up playing as well.

Dad's philosophy about sports was very simple: make sure you play hard and play to win. That's always been my theme and that of my brothers as well. We weren't always the best players on our teams, but we always found a way to maybe be better than the best players. As a result, the Sutters became role models for the other players. Everybody expected us to be the hardest working guys.

Competition came naturally to us. Remember, we were so close in age that we always were playing some game or other around the farm. Sometimes we'd play makeshift hockey up in the loft or the barn or bang a puck around the slough or whack the baseball in the summertime.

Since we came from such a small town, some of us would wind up playing on the same team. For example, Brian and Gary — the oldest — would be playing on the town club and would be short a player from time to time so they might ask me or Brent to join them on their club. There always were two or three of us on a team, whether we were supposed to be or not. There was very little difference between the oldest and youngest Sutter brother.

They say that sibling rivalry is very intense and, in our case, it was when we played against each other at home. We always tried to better each other but when we weren't on opposite sides, we pulled hard for one another. In the NHL it was a little odd playing against them at first, but I got used to it pretty quick.

As a player, I learned a lot about coaching, just by observation. One of the most interesting was Orval Tessier who became Blackhawks coach in 1983. He had been an NHL player in the 1950s and later coached Junior hockey. In Tessier's first season behind the Chicago bench, we had a really good season, finishing with 47 wins, 10 ties and 23 losses for 104 points. That put us in first place in the Norris Division.

Everything was going well in the playoffs until we went up against the Edmonton Oilers in the semi-finals. That was the time that Edmonton's dynasty was taking shape with Wayne Gretzky in his prime along with Mark Messier, Grant Fuhr, Jari Kurri and Paul Coffey. They proved their worth by knocking us off in four straight games.

During the series, Tessier got upset with us and made a statement that the Blackhawks needed 18 heart transplants. The story caused a lot of controversy and some of the guys on our club really were upset over what Orval had said. They never played the same level of hockey for him again. My contention is that it's not imperative for a player to be buddies with a coach in order to skate for him but, obviously, others didn't think that way.

Orval didn't have much luck the following season. Our three left wingers — all among the best in the league — Al Secord, Curt Fraser and myself — were out a whole bunch of games with injuries and the team went to pot. We finished with only 68 points and eventually Tessier was replaced behind the bench by Bob Pulford, our general manager.

One of the things I learned was that there's a big difference between playing and coaching. A player can go to the rink, sweat it out and then basically leave the rink. When I became a coach, I realized that it never leaves you and you're always thinking about your team. ALWAYS. It doesn't matter what you're doing, there's always something in the back of your mind that keeps you thinking about the games, the team and the individuals.

For me, the transition from player to [assistant] coach was very difficult because I made the move from being on the ice to being on the bench immediately. One minute I was playing alongside these guys — and they were my pals — and the next minute I was coaching the fellows I had been playing with, which wasn't a comfortable feeling. It was very hard for me that first year, which was why it was a relief to get an opportunity to coach our farm team in Indianapolis.

Coaching in the minors can be very gratifying and it certainly was for me. The teaching experience, in that sense, is at its best when I can see my instruction paying dividends with some of the youngsters who eventually make a name for themselves in the business. There aren't many feelings more satisfying than seeing a kid, who may be lacking top skills, succeeding on desire.

Once I got my feet wet, the adjustments to coaching were not that tough. To be a good coach, the instincts have to be there and I had those instincts. Just because you want to be a coach doesn't mean you can be a coach. I was fortunate since my roots went back to Viking and our big Sutter family which, in effect, was a team. I learned about teamwork at home and now I was applying those principles to coaching a group of hockey professionals.

The art of coaching has changed considerably in this era of high-technology. In the old days of the six-team NHL, there was almost no advance scouting because none was necessary. Each team played the other so many times that their individual and collective styles were known from one team to another. But as the NHL expanded from six to 12 teams (in 1967-68) and on up to 26 teams today, the techniques of preparing for games became drastically altered.

For example, we pre-scout every team we play either by satellite or by sending a pro scout or a coach to watch that team in a previous game. Then, we evaluate what we feel we have to do to beat that team, without making any drastic changes in our own system. What I tried to do in Chicago was make the other team adjust to us more than us adjusting to them.

I learned a lot from Pulford as well as from Bob Murdoch, who was replaced by Mike Keenan. Murdoch, who we called "Mud," for short, was an easier-going guy than Keenan and the feeling then was that the players took advantage of Mud, which was not the case with Mike.

Being Keenan's assistant was not hard for me and no adjustment was necessary since Mike and I are a lot alike in terms of our expectations of players and our expectations of ourselves. On more than one occasion, Mike told me that he's a lot like the Sutters. His intensity and passion are very similar to our own. When Mike and I discussed a game, I knew exactly what he was going to say.

If we have a difference it's in the way we're demonstrative. I've said it all along — I don't think for a minute that I need that attention or that I'm the main person there. My responsibility is to give the players direction and make sure that they're responsible for their actions. And I'm ready to take the heat because that's what it's all about. The players get paid to play and I get paid to tell them how to play.

In that capacity, I frequently tell my players about my expectations. I put a lot into coaching and I expect that intensity out of them, too. The players are all different and I've learned that you can't put a square peg into a round hole. So, whatever the players do, I want them to do it with their very best and do it with respect. And because each player is different, I can't handle them all the same way. Sometimes I speak with them as a group; other times I find it better to deal with them individually.

The key to it all is that they're grown men playing a boy's game. For them to do that, it has to be a whole lot of fun. But in order for it to be fun, there has to be some success in it, too. And success is winning. In order to win, you have to work extremely hard. The top players in the game are also the hardest workers, and that can filter down to the rest of them.

In terms of coaching, the biggest challenge is the day-to-day motivation of the players. Hockey has changed so dramatically in terms of a season. They once played a 50-game schedule, then 60 games and now it's up to 84 games with training camp starting in September and the playoffs ending in mid-June. That's a long drive and an awfully long stretch for a coach searching for a different angle on an opponent or a game to maximize its importance.

The key is to coach with the team you have. If you look at the teams who win the Stanley Cup, you see that it starts with the goaltender and a hell of a team defense. The team with the best goals-against in the playoffs is often the team that wins the Cup.

Everybody used to talk about the Islanders dynasty or the Oilers dynasty and the Montreal dynasty and they all had great defense. Sure, they had a tremendous amount of talent, but a coach doesn't control the talent on a team — he controls the talented players. So, if you're not the most talented, you have to find a way to win.

More and more, the coach has to have more input with the front office. That's because there are so many more teams and the talent is more evenly spread than ever before. A coach has to have more input to see what's available out there and whether he wants some of those available players on his team or not. I've had a good working relationship with the Blackhawks front office.

One of the hardest aspects of coaching is having to tell a player that he has to go down to the minors. It's easier to do it with a first or second-year player because, in the long run, that's usually for his own good. But for someone who's been knocked three or four times and still hasn't made it, that's tough.

There's always a kind of sadness when it comes to players who are at the end of their careers. But for the older player, the reality is that at some point everybody has to leave. At some point, somebody is going to tell you that you're done; that your services aren't needed anymore as a player. That's hockey; that's the business part of it. A lot of times the player himself knows that it's time to move on. It happened to me and it happened to my brother Brian.

With him coaching the Bruins, the question has come up from time to time as to whether we talk about coaching philosophy. Actually, we talk a lot because we're in separate conferences but we don't discuss coaching philosophy. In a way, we help each other out and since we only play each other twice a year, we don't divulge anything. On the other hand, he can help me with information about teams in his conference and vice versa.

Brotherly help has always been an aspect of our family life, but there's a difference in attitude when one or two of my brothers are playing for me as it has been in Chicago where Brent and Rich have been Blackhawks.

To some it would seem as if it was difficult for me having two Sutters on my team, but actually the opposite was the case. The hardest thing about coaching your brothers is that I tend to be harder on them than anyone else on my team. The public's perception is different, of course, thinking that I would favor them, being my brothers, but the fact is that I expect more out of them than anybody else on the Blackhawks.

It's no secret that none of the Sutter boys had the kind of talent that made a Mario Lemieux or a Wayne Gretzky what they are today, so we had to compensate with intangibles like hustle and brainwork. And if there's one thing that disappoints me as a coach it's when I see a player with God-given ability who doesn't apply himself and get the most out of his potential.

When I see a player who should be a top player — or should be making more of an impact than his ability shows — I view it as a waste and find that the most frustrating aspect of coaching. So often we see players in the NHL who we know could be playing at a certain level yet we can't figure out why he's not playing better, or playing our way. Usually, I conclude that he's an underachiever; he's not willing to sweat, pay the price and go the extra mile. Bobby Hull used to put it another way: players used to sit on their wallets.

Motivating players such as these is the supreme challenge for a coach. First and foremost, at some point the players have to be able to motivate themselves. There's a continual process of a coach motivating this player or another player, but eventually that wears out and the player is done.

That explains why certain players move around a lot. It's usually a case of that player not producing to his ability so his team finally gives up on him and trades him to another club. In the end, it usually turns out that that individual is not a very motivated player.

Since I became involved in organized hockey, the game has changed and so have the attitudes. Big-league hockey is more of a business for the players than it ever was before. Almost every single player has his own agent, and the agents have a bigger impact than they did, say, in 1980.

Beyond that, the diversity in salaries has had a tremendous impact on the game. You've got one guy on your team making $3 million and then you've got some kid making only $150,000. In that sense hockey has become similar to baseball where the different players come to the rink, play and don't have a whole lot in common.

That common bond is something we Sutter brothers have always shared and it was evident during a very difficult time in my family's life when my son was born. It was one of the few times during a hockey season that we've ever put the hockey aside; probably the only time that we've done so. It was important. We had a lot of people there for us, but it's not the same as it is when you have your brothers.

But once the game is on and I have brothers on the other side — like Ron playing for the Islanders — I don't see them as brothers. I see Ron as someone with a responsibility and, to tell you the truth, I don't really think much about it. I've always maintained that if I compete against my brother, I want to beat him, but if we won, 4-3, I'd want him to get all three goals.

As for my own future, coaching is something that I really want to do — not managing or other front office work. But if I ever lose my edge in terms of the love for coaching, then it would be time to move on.

In my career, I've taken something from every coach I've had, good or bad, easy or tough. The toughest one I played for was Joe Crozier and maybe he appeared so rough to me because I was still a kid at the time and he was a tough little guy. Crozier didn't do a whole lot of talking, but he was very demanding. Bob Pulford was too, when I first came to Chicago. I mean I was scared of him because of his intensity but, by the same token, I liked him. Pulford made me a better player.

As a matter of fact, I liked every coach that I played for because every one of them was committed. To me, it didn't really matter who the coach was because I played hard. Still, a player needs direction and I always got that.

The coach must be sure of what he is doing because if he isn't, that feeling of uncertainty seeps down to the players. Then there are cliques on teams which can make life difficult for the coach. When I came to Chicago, the Blackhawks were a team in transition. There was a group of older guys who were close and who didn't want us younger guys in their circle, so it was like two teams in one, which wasn't easy on the coach.

Of all the coaches who were in the NHL during my playing years, the one who I really wanted to play for — and didn't — was Al Arbour. I respected him because he started right at the bottom with the Islanders and won four Stanley Cups with them, then turned the team over and weathered the storm.

It would not be an exaggeration to say that how a team plays tells you something about the coach.

17

Jacques Caron

THE GOALIE COACH

"A big danger in goaltending is anticipation. When you start to anticipate, you become a spectator. Once you become a spectator there's no reaction."

Prior to the 1993-94 season, the New Jersey Devils were given only a 50-50 chance to gain a playoff berth. One of the primary problems, it was said, was the space between the goal posts.

The Devils had lost goalie Peter Sidorkowicz — obtained in a deal with Ottawa — because of a serious shoulder injury and were left with only Chris Terreri in the nets. A second goaltender was needed and it was decided to gamble on inexperienced Martin Brodeur as backup for Terreri.

At the time, the prevailing opinion was that Brodeur simply was not ready for big-league action on a regular basis and that New Jersey was bringing him up to the varsity simply as a desperation measure.

Enter Jacques Caron.

Hired by Devils president Lou Lamoriello as the club's goaltending coach in 1993, the angular Caron immediately began tutoring Brodeur. By season's start, head coach Jacques Lemaire decided to gamble on the rookie and Brodeur responded.

Caron continued to work with Martin and, to the astonishment of many, Brodeur became the Devils number one goaltender and, eventually, the agile rookie won the Calder Trophy as NHL rookie-of-the-year. Clearly, Brodeur's ascendency was as much a tribute to the youngster's natural talent as it was a credit to his professor-of-puckstopping, Caron.

For Jacques, this was but another in a long line of goaltending successes which began when he turned pro and soon reached the NHL. A native of Noranda, Quebec, Caron played 72 regular season NHL games, sprinkled among the Los Angeles Kings, St. Louis Blues and Vancouver Canucks between 1967-68 and 1973-74.

His big-league career record — spent entirely with weaker expansion clubs — was 24-29-11 including two shutouts and a 3.29 goals against average. Caron's best season was 1971-72 when he posted a 2.52 goals-against average in 28 games.

Prior to that Caron paid his dues, rubber-stopping for Eddie Shore's legendary Springfield Indians, beginning in 1961-62 when the autocratic American League boss traumatized players and executives alike. Caron became a central figure in the Indians player uprising against Shore which, in time, led to a players' strike and ultimately creation of the National Hockey League Players' Association.

Jacques completed his active goaltending career with the World Hockey Association's Cincinnati Stingers in 1976-77 and then turned to the off-ice aspects of hockey. He began his post-playing career in 1977-78 as general manager of the Binghamton Broomdusters. When the club was taken over by the Hartford Whalers, he remained with their organization through the 1991-92 season as a member of the coaching staff at both the NHL and AHL levels.

When the Devils reorganized their high command, first with head coach Jacques Lemaire and then assistant coach Larry Robinson, Caron was asked to join the triumvirate and soon came aboard.

Caron's expertise not only was translated into Brodeur's rise but also the ability of Terreri to maintain a high level of competency working as the Devils alternate goaltender.

Despite dire pre-season predictions, New Jersey finished 1993-94 with the NHL's second-best record, due in part to the behind-the-scenes work of Jacques Caron. In an interview with reporter David Levy, Jacques recalled his early life as a goalie and discussed goaltending in the big leagues today.

When I started playing goal I was an eight-year-old kid, growing up in Noranda, Quebec, which is up north and shares a border with an Ontario town called Rouyn. A lot of hockey players who made it in the pros have come from that area including Dave Keon, a Hall of Famer who starred with the Toronto Maple Leafs when they won all those Stanley Cups in the 1960s.

Ice hockey was a way of life in Noranda because the winters were so long and ice was available all over the place. We were a French-Canadian community, 400 miles north of Montreal, which is pretty much in the direction of the North Pole, no matter how you shake it.

There were eight kids in our family and life was fairly primitive in our house. Nobody had a television set so if we wanted to know what was happening in pro hockey, we had to listen to the radio. In those days, the NHL was only a six-team league — Montreal, Toronto, Boston, Chicago, Detroit and New York — so it was much easier for a kid like me to follow it than it is now.

By the time I was eight I was already infatuated with hockey and I knew what I was going to be, a goaltender. How did I know? As kids, we used to shoot pucks at each other after making a four by six-foot net out of the snow banks. We'd shoot pucks at each other across the road.

At first I loved to shoot more than anything and beat the goalie but soon I found that I liked to stop pucks more than actually shoot them. It didn't take very long for me to figure out that the thrill of stopping the puck was greater than scoring a goal. Right then and there I knew I wanted to be a professional goaltender.

The next challenge was learning how to skate and finding equipment, but I got lucky; one of our neighbors — I used to shovel snow off his walkway — had a sporting goods shop in town and he used to give me some of the used equipment that customers would bring in to exchange.

Like all kids, I had my dreams and, with us, the National Hockey League was like heaven. We'd listen to the games on radio and imagine anything we wanted and then make it come before our eyes. We'd read about the stars in the newspapers and, occasionally, even get posters of them.

There were a lot of great goalies around in those days. Toronto had Turk Broda, Montreal had Gerry McNeil and Detroit had Terry Sawchuk. Sawchuk was my idol.

I played hockey wherever I could, be it on the high school team or the local clubs. Sometimes I played for two or even three teams at once and, after a while, I got to be pretty good. By the time I had reached the Midget level, I was being scouted as were other guys from our area. One of them was Dave Keon, a fast little center who eventually made it all the way to the Toronto Maple Leafs. Every once in a while Dave and I would be teammates and one day, a Toronto scout by the name of Bob Davidson — he played on Toronto's Cup-winning team in 1942 — came up to see us; liked what he saw and put us on what they called a "C" form.

Remember, those were the days before the draft, and in the 1940s and 1950s teams could permanently latch on to a player simply by putting his name on a "C" form. In any event, that's how Keon and I became property of the Maple Leafs.

It meant leaving home and playing Junior [amateur] hockey in Toronto which, as you can imagine, was quite a thing for a French-Canadian kid from a small town up north. We left home by train on a Friday night and arrived in Toronto on Saturday morning. The train pulled into Union Station, the big terminal downtown, and when I walked out on to the street, we were right next to the huge Royal York Hotel with the Toronto skyline right there in front of me. When I looked at the streetcars, the skyscrapers and all the people, I did a double-take. It was scary and exciting at the same time.

Davidson, who was like a chaperone, had me in hand, leading me to Maple Leaf Gardens, which is like Canada's hockey shrine. "You're going to meet The King today," Davidson said.

My English wasn't very good at the time, but I could understand enough to realize what he meant by The King. Canada was ruled more intensively by England in those days so I assumed he meant that King George was in town and that Jacques Caron was going to meet His Majesty.

We walked up Yonge Street, the main drag, and Davidson took me to a hotel where the Maple Leafs boarded their young players. As we approached the hotel, Davidson pointed to a smallish man who was standing on the corner. "There's The King," he said.

That was not my impression of what King George looked like, nor was it Britain's leader at all. The fellow in question was Francis Michael "King" Clancy, who had been a great Toronto defenseman for years and later an NHL referee. Now he was working for the hockey club.

Davidson politely introduced me to The King and then checked me into my hotel. I was 400 miles from Noranda and very homesick. That state of unpleasantness would last about two months until I got used to life in a big, English-speaking metropolis like Toronto. But the more I got to know the place, the more I got to like it and after a while, I knew it was better to be there than in Noranda where the temperature was 45 degrees below zero.

Howie Meeker, who had been a star right wing with the Maple Leafs when they won Stanley Cups in 1947, 1948, 1949 and 1951, was now coach of the club and in those days they carried only one goaltender. One day Meeker asked me if I wanted to hang around and work out with the big team and, naturally, I said I would. Our Junior club would practice at the Gardens at 9:30 a.m. and then the Leafs would come on the ice at 11 a.m. so I'd stay out with them. At the age of 16, I had the thrill of practicing with a National Hockey League club.

Better than that, when they played their actual games, I would be dressed in uniform and would sit on the end of the bench in case of an emergency. They paid me $25 a game just to sit and watch a hockey game from the bench. I was there as an emergency replacement in case anyone got hurt but, fortunately, nobody ever came out, so I collected my money and enjoyed the games.

At first I played for the Toronto Marlboros, which was the Leafs' farm club in the Ontario Hockey Association's Junior A Division. When I was 18, I was traded to Peterborough which was the first time I really got the feeling that hockey was a business. I knew then that it didn't matter who you liked — you had to survive because it was a job. That's when I knew that if I was to make a career out of hockey, I couldn't harbor any special emotion for anyone. You just have to do the job and realize that it's going to be a long, challenging life.

The best part of my working out with the Leafs was that I got used to the hard, major league, shots while I still was underage to play in the NHL, so I was ahead of the pack, so to speak. Any fear I had had of the puck went away after working out against the pros. I wasn't afraid and I knew that I could play pros. I had a lot of natural talent; it was just the matter of getting a chance to play there. Nobody could question my determination, nor did they.

My first significant coach was Walter "Turk" Broda, who handled the Marlboros when I played for them. Turk had been around hockey a long time, all of it with the Toronto organization. He had played on five Cup-winning teams in 1942, 1947, 1948, 1949 and 1951. Broda knew everything there was to know about goaltending. At first, I was a bit hyper and wanted to do so well that I tried too hard and created problems for myself. Turk settled me down and got me into the right groove.

Much as I liked Turk, he wasn't my idol. I loved to watch Terry Sawchuk, who broke in with the Detroit Red Wings in the early 1950s and then moved over to the Boston Bruins. He had a terrific style and was the best in the NHL at the time. Jacques Plante of the Canadiens was the best angle goaltender to know the game than anybody I've ever seen. He could do anything. A reflex goaltender like Glenn Hall of Chicago was great because he could see the puck anywhere and find a way to stop it.

Once I finished with Junior hockey, I was picked up by Eddie Shore's Springfield Indians of the American League. That was quite an experience, let me tell you, because Shore was one of the strangest men in our business and certainly the most unusual.

As a player in the 1920s and 1930s, Shore was one of the best defensemen in NHL history with the Bruins. He finished his career in New York with the old Americans and then bought the Springfield AHL franchise. We used to play in an old barn of an arena called the Eastern States Coliseum in West Springfield, Massachusetts and Shore ran the show, from top to bottom. Even though he had a coach, it was Shore who dictated everything.

The thing that set Eddie apart from others is that he was full of radical theories about hockey and health and he insisted that his players follow through on them, whether the player liked it or not. And even though he was not a goalie, himself, he had specific ideas about stopping a puck and how the crease should be played.

There are stories that in some cases, Shore would diagnose and treat illnesses with his own medications! Or he would tie the goalies to the goalposts, but thankfully, he never tied me up. Shore did however, put a big steel rim on the goal post and you had to skate around it, never in it, which was his way to have me learn to move around the net without falling. He made the team tap dance for agility and now I'm a pretty good tap dancer. And if you could believe this, he once tied my knees up so I wouldn't sprawl to make a split save since you'd have to walk or jump around on your skates. He called this "drill" the "chop-chop" and would have you chopping and skating close together. But I was the goalie in Springfield for seven years, so I must've done something right.

Springfield was a great hockey town and I met many friends there. I was fortunate to play with a very good team which won its third straight Calder Cup in my first season with the team in 1961. But playing for Eddie Shore was a real tough experience. There were even times when he told us we couldn't have sex the night before a game, especially for me. He called me into his office one time and told me it would be bad for me. He even called a meeting with the wives and told them for their husbands' careers, for the sake of their husbands, especially during playoffs, we could not abuse sex. It was kind of silly, but funny in retrospect.

What wasn't funny was the abuse heaped on us by Shore, which is why the team revolted. We had had enough of not getting paid on time and around Christmas time it was even more difficult. Shore was fining players for absolutely no reason but alibied that it was for indifferent play. We not only didn't understand it, we didn't have a place to turn to like now where you have an agent or you can go to arbitration in disputes. The only thing we could do was go to the American League commissioner, Jack Butterfield, and protest. But Butterfield was Shore's puppet and Jack did pretty much what Shore wanted. We just got fed up with not being paid on time and never knowing how much we were going to be paid when we were paid.

We felt that as players, we were doing everything we could do right, but it was never good enough for Shore so, finally, we went on strike and that's when he decided to sell the club. That was the main objective during the strike — to get him out of there, get him out of hockey. This was hard because in the eyes of some AHL people he was Mr. Hockey. But we finally got the rest of the players to understand that it's better not to play than to play under his brutal conditions.

How did the strike actually come about? Well, it all started when I was suspended for "indifferent play." Shore claimed that my feet would go down too often so then he'd bench me and fine me. You could never argue the point with him and that was the hard part for me because sometimes he'd just make a statement with no explanation. And I could never understand what he was trying to tell me. The worst thing about my years with Shore was that he took away my natural ability. I had to leave there after seven years and it took me two years to regain my normal form because of what he preached — his idea of stand-up goaltending.

Getting back to the strike, he suspended me, abused others so we finally decided to do something about it. We had meeting by ourselves and decided to call Alan Eagleson, a Toronto lawyer at the time.

Eagleson had been friendly with Bob Pulford and Carl Brewer of the Toronto Maple Leafs and, eventually would become Bobby Orr's agent. We liked Eagleson because he was a fighter and he suggested that we go on strike. Our main objective was for us to survive the year and standing up to Shore was a matter of pride.

The strike worked because it brought Shore to his knees and finally forced him to sell the Indians and get out of hockey as a owner. This was quite a breakthrough for hockey players in general and me in particular, not to mention my wife, whom I had known since my Junior days. I met her when I was playing for the Toronto Marlies. At first it was a tough life for her but she adjusted very well to my constant travel, the moods I'd get in when we lost, my not wanting to be disturbed during the day and goalie things like that. I really took a lot of time for concentration and staying positive. If people distracted me, I felt it was taking more energy for me to concentrate. I'm the type of guy who requires lots of sleep because I was a nervous goaltender, so I had to get more sleep after the game. But my wife put up with me. I guess, in a way, she had to.

We have a daughter, Marjorie, who has twin boys. I often see myself as a goaltender in one of her boys, but I want to make sure he doesn't repeat the same mistakes I did. He has a totally different character than I did. He's a little bit like Martin Brodeur, with good awareness and a relaxed and confident style. That helps when you're a goalie. If you're too uptight it's hell out there in goal. But goalies are a different breed. Take my identical twin grandsons, for example. One is a goalie and the other a forward. But their temperaments are so different. You have to have a temperament and be a little different to be a goaltender. It's an awareness to know what you want to be so early in life. A forward can be a defenseman, but a goaltender knows exactly what he wants to do. It's the instinct, and the feeling that you like the competition.

I've worked with many goaltenders in my career and I feel they're all a little different but, on the other hand, basically all the same. The way each approaches the game is different. Some get too hard on themselves when they lose and get too high when they win. You can tell a lot by a goaltender's character because they feel the club depends too much on them. They take it real high and then real low if they feel that they let the club down. That's why I feel that the goaltending coach is very important to a club because of the communication element. It's the seemingly small things to keep them confident and polish them up.

A goaltender will progress at a lower level a lot faster if a coach is around to let him know exactly what he's doing. With a coach, he doesn't learn by trial and tribulation. A coach enables him to keep his confidence and allows him to get back on track faster.

One regret I have in my career is that I didn't take care of myself during the summer months. I was married young at 18 and I had to work all the time — even in the off-season — to make ends meet. I'm a machinist by trade, so I worked very hard in the summer, seven days a week, because we didn't make much money from hockey. I earned about $4200 a year as a goalie. It was a time when you had to work hard in the summer and didn't get the proper conditioning and rest. Then you'd go to training camp just to get in shape. Now, if you're not in shape by training camp, you don't have a job. In the old days, they'd give you a month to get in shape because every one of the hockey players had to work in the summer.

I got into my post-career job by a sheer coincidence. After I had retired, I was working on my farm one summer when I got a call from someone who wanted me to run a team. I didn't even know the man! The call was a blessing because the farm wasn't doing too well. Here I was trying to think what I would do to make my farm survive when this man asked me if I wanted to be his general manager in the AHL. I asked him where he got my name from and he said, "I've been inquiring about you from different people and you're very loyal and you know the game." He got the AHL Syracuse franchise and moved it to Binghamton where I worked for five years. It was quite successful and eventually the franchise was bought by Hartford. I stayed with them for 11 years.

The biggest challenge I found as a new general manager was signing players and getting an affiliation with the NHL because we came in relatively late. We bought the club in late October and had to put the program together, in a very short time, which I did by myself with just common sense. It was very difficult that first year. What I had to do was get the best players at the cheapest prices, of course. Thank God for Barry Fraser, the assistant general manager of the Edmonton Oilers. He had been with the Houston Aeros of the World Hockey Association and loaned me about eight players, and I only had to sign ten.

You learn to do things very fast when you have to. Fortunately, I didn't have to be head coach. I'm too demanding and impatient with the players, just as I was never patient with myself and very demanding as a player. I guess its true when they say: you can't change a leopard's spots. Same thing with a coach and his players. What I've found with all the coaches that I worked with was how frustrating their job could be. It's hard on them because the players don't do what you tell them or they don't seem to try when you tell them and you end up repeating yourself. I never had any desire to be head coach because I knew I couldn't take it. As a matter of fact, I got sick one year. I got a stress attack when I was coaching in Hartford. I know my limits which is why I stick to being a goaltending coach.

My favorite coaches were quite different than myself. For starters, there was Red Kelly from Toronto and Terry Slater, who coached me in the WHA and was a good goaltending coach. Also, Al Arbour was an excellent and effective guy when I played with the St. Louis Blues. He gave us a lot of hope and he would never put pressure on you. He built confidence and knew what made you tick. He's the best coach I ever had.

What makes me happy as a goaltending coach is when I see my pupils play well and stay in control through the whole game. That's an accomplishment— 60 minutes of concentration and total control. You don't see that very often. They'll have it for 10 minutes, lose it, get it back. It's when you see it for a full 60 minutes that you know your instruction is working.

It's easy to tell when a goalie is losing concentration because he'll move for nothing, take stupid chances, maybe go out of the net for no reason. After that happens is when I talk with them. Take Chris Terreri, for example. I didn't really change anything in his style except settle him down a little bit. Chris is very, very fast. Not hyper, but upbeat. He wants to do so well that sometimes he puts a little bit of pressure on himself. What we did was settle him down, move him after the puck with the stick and not have him jump, just let the puck come to him. If Chris is patient, he'll stop all the pucks. I stressed early settling, watching the puck, letting it come to you, don't try to beat the guy, let the guy try and beat you. These are things we worked on.

Also, Chris is making the game look a lot easier. He used to make the game awfully hard jumping around. In the past year he settled down very nicely. It's easy to say "less is more", but to do it is another thing. As a goalie, you have to stay very confident. You can't second guess yourself. Chris Terreri is the fastest goalie in the NHL. I know this for a fact because we do different drills each day and he does them effortlessly. He's like a figure skater. If he uses these assets to his advantage and is patient and doesn't jump around, then he'll be great. And that's what he's doing now.

Unfortunately, while I still was a goalie coach in Hartford I didn't get to work with Sean Burke because I was hurt in a car accident. I wish I had had the opportunity to instruct him because I think I could've really helped him, on mobility especially. He creates a lot of holes and seems to lean back more than most goalies. Big goalies, such as Burke, count on their size more than they really should. A big danger in goaltending is anticipation. When you start to anticipate, you become a spectator. Once you become a spectator there's no reaction. You try to get them to the right angle as early as possible, but as soon as the puck crosses the red line I like to see them at the proper angle. They start to watch and try to challenge early and that's a problem because it's hard to follow the puck that way.

My prime project for 1993-94 was Martin Brodeur. This man uses his stick quite a bit and the secret of goaltending is leading with your stick. If you can lead with your stick and you can see the puck on top and feel it, you're square with your puck, then your stick is going to be there when you need it. That's the hardest thing for goalies and yet half of them don't know that they should do this. That's what I teach in hockey school. I stress this and five or six different things that are very, very important. If you learn to do this at a young age then you'll place yourself and square the puck all the time.

I work on all these things in the off-season at my goaltending school, which I've run for 27 years in Noranda, Quebec, near my hometown of Rouyn. I've worked with a lot of goaltenders in the NHL when they were young and now I'm working with my grandson. That shows you how long I've been doing it.

Teaching hockey school is a whole different aspect than coaching pro because the pressure of the NHL and the pressures of a hockey school are different. Hockey school is a place where you don't see immediate results like winning. It's a different level with different ages. With all the problems I had with Eddie Shore, there were things he did teach me and all my hockey knowledge as a teacher comes from him listening to him during all his practices — the skating drills, how to shoot the puck, how to be a goaltender and so on. That's why I like to put what he taught me in practice. It stays fresh in my mind if I do it every year.

Of course, the game has changed and it's now a game of speed more than ever but skating has always been the big part of the game and Shore had the best skaters. The advent of the goaltending coach is relatively recent and probably started when an older goaltender was still being paid by his club, wasn't playing that much and was under contract to help out the other goaltender. When I was 39 years old and was still playing, there was still no goaltending coach around. In those days the goalies didn't talk with each other because they were afraid the other guy would take their job away. So nobody would say anything and nobody would learn anything from anybody. But I was not afraid to ask questions and I played with some great goaltenders like Terry Sawchuk of Los Angeles, Glenn Hall in St. Louis. That's why I can relate to different goalies with different styles.

My style as a goalie coach is to talk to my goaltenders after a game where they had a bad goal. I say, "Forget it and go on with the next game." It's easier said than done, but they feel I understand their situation. I don't want them to get used to giving up bad goals but, by the same token, they are part of the game. Goalies have to know they're not that bad just because they gave up a "weak" goal. I've seen the best goaltenders get pulled, even Jacques Plante. They should feel that if they get pulled it's not a big deal because it could happen to anybody.

That's part of the game. You're only a human being. A goalie can't feel good every night because that would be impossible.

18

Don Cherry

THE OUTRAGEOUS COACH

"I don't mind people calling me names —
racist, pig, cretin, redneck — but to call me
a wimp, never!"

If it's possible for anyone to be a Don Rickles-Rush Limbaugh-Howard Stern of hockey, Don Cherry is that man. Affectionately known as "Grapes" to millions of Canadians (and some Americans as well), Cherry is at once the wittiest, most conservative and wildly irreverent personality this side of the blue line.

And if you believe some critics, a full-blooded racist as well. That matter is open for dispute, but this much is certain: the one-time NHL coach-turned-broadcaster is *the* most popular character in hockey, which is either a sad commentary on ice dullards or a raving endorsement of the Cherry persona.

Novelist-hockey nut Mordechai Richler calls Cherry "an appropriate role model for cretins," while *The Globe and Mail* labels him "rude, overbearing, pompous and arrogant." In any event Cherry's "Coach's Corner" segment on the Canadian Broadcasting Corporation's *Hockey Night in Canada* telecasts is merely the most popular show in the dominion to the extent that Don has been dubbed "the Prime Minister of Saturday Night."

It is from this pulpit that Grapes spins his tales and spews his venom, usually against foreigners such as Alexei Kovalev. After the Rangers forward dispatched Washington's Dale Hunter to the hospital with torn knee ligaments, Cherry did what Cherry does best of all: he verbally drew and quartered Kovalev, not so much for his indelicate knee job but more for his birthplace.

"Never turn your back on a backstabbing Russian," barked Grapes. Canadian sociologist-author Allan Turowetz is hardly surprised at Cherry cutting up Kovalev. "Sure it's racist," says Turowetz, who co-wrote a history of the Montreal Canadiens, *The Lions of Winter*. "Don is incredibly contemptuous of Europeans and this is his example of vile, left-handed humor."

While Cherry may sound racist to some politically correct intellectuals, such oratory draws standing Os in bars across Canada where fans have grown accustomed to the NHL's Mister Bluster.

"Don is the most recognizable man in Canada," says Islanders broadcaster Jiggs McDonald. "If you're in a bar on a Saturday night, it can be the noisiest place in town, but when Don comes on, they shut up and listen. Then, someone will yell, 'Atta boy! Way to tell 'em, Grapes.' And another will say, 'Aw, Jeez, where is he coming from?' But they listen because he's the mouthpiece for a large segment of the Canadian hockey-viewing audience."

Besides, Kovalev is in good company. Ask Ulf Samuelsson, defenseman for two Pittsburgh Stanley Cup-winners. In the finest Murder Inc. tradition, Cherry went on the air suggesting that some NHLer break Ulf's arm between the wrist and elbow.

He has been no less kind to Tomas Sandstrom of the Pittsburgh Penguins ("the dirtiest guy in hockey") and Pavel Bure of the Vancouver Canucks, who escaped with merely being called "a weasel."

"I'm the Anglo redneck of all time," boasts Cherry, from his Mississauga, Ontario home outside of Toronto. "When Patrick Roy joined the Canadiens and they called him 'Roo-ah', I said, 'What's this? Who ever heard of Roo-ah Rogers?'"

When Cherry filibusters, it always is in a high-decibel Edward G. Robinson, "All right, you guys!" bulldog bark that commands attention, if not respect, and sometimes produces temporary lockjaw. New Yorkers, who remember Jimmy The Greek getting the boot for indelicate oratory, gagged on Grapes' Kovalev putdown.

"It was a blatantly bigoted comment that brings to mind The Greek," says Madison Square Garden Network commentator Al Trautwig. "It deserved an immediate apology. There's a certain responsibility that comes when you carry a microphone that is heard by many. And Don Cherry has to answer that responsibility."

Typically, Grapes responds with all guns blazing. He does not suffer critics gladly, especially when they side with Russians. Cherry opens by deliberately mis-naming Trautwig as Al Airwick; then come the real insults.

"Here's a guy who works for Madison Square Garden, the same outfit that owns the Rangers," snaps Grapes. "Which makes what he says ridiculously self-serving. He sounds like he's worried about his job and he *should* be worried about his job."

Not that Cherry's critics are limited to Manhattan. *Ottawa Citizen* columnist Roy MacGregor reamed Grapes in his book *Road Games*. MacGregor charges Cherry with a conflict of interest. On the one hand Don makes a bundle marketing "Rock 'em Sock 'em Hockey" videos while on the other, Grapes promotes violence in the NHL.

"Fisticuffs," argues MacGregor, "is money in Cherry's pocket." Mention MacGregor to Grapes and his voice lowers as if mourning a lost friend. He admits that at one time, MacGregor "was a good guy," but then Roy wrote this book and blasted Don.

"It looked like the criticism of me was thrown in to spice up the book," laments Cherry. "It's a sad situation when you sell your soul for a book. He knows that if he mentions my name, it will sell books because people want to read about me."

Others, such as *Winnipeg Sun* sports columnist Pat Doyle, claim it's even sadder that Cherry's act is stale and that Don "hasn't found a new scriptwriter."

Grapes chuckles. "Like Popeye says, 'I yam what I yam what I yam.' And if the day comes when *Hockey Night In Canada* people say, 'Don, you gotta change your style,' then I'll say fine and get off the air because I'm not going to a new tack just to entertain people."

Judging by his ratings, Cherry should remain right where he is, at the top of the heap. Wearing his Wilfrid Laurier collars and Runyonesque suits, Don cuts an imposing figure when he moves to center stage with his straight man, Ron MacLean.

Although their gears mesh as smoothly on-air as Beavis and Butthead, the partners have been known to clash. Once during a playoff series, Grapes suggested that Ron was being partial to the Flames.

Cherry: "I said to him, 'You're cheering so much for Calgary, why don't you take my red jacket?' He went bananas after we went off the air. He said, 'You're gone. You won't be on TV.' Ron likes to act professionally, like he isn't cheering for anyone, but he was really cheering for Calgary."

Grapes obviously survived MacLean's tantrum as he has innumerable outrageous Cherryisms that have shaken the CBC boardrooms. In 1987, he raised eyebrows, defending the Canadian Junior hockey team for brawling with the Soviets at the 1987 World Junior Championships.

"Everybody was hiding after I made the remarks and I said to myself, 'Boy, oh boy, you could be finished forever on television.' The left-wing pinkos were ripping me to shreds and I hate left-wing liberals. I go out of my way to antagonize them."

Limbaugh-like, he rails against homosexuals and peaceniks. During the 1993 playoffs, he caused a stir when CBC switched from the Serbian-Bosnian conflict to live hockey, prompting Don to suggest that fans were uninterested in "Lower Slobovia attacking Slimea."

Cherry: "The worst was during the Gulf War when I went on in Chicago with a big six-by-eight-foot Canadian flag behind me and ripped all those creeps and kooks back home burning the flag. They said it was not right to talk politics on a hockey show. Then they said, 'Was what you did premeditated?' I said, 'Premeditated? Of course not. Like I always carry a six-by-eight-foot Canadian flag around with me in my travels. My father always said, 'If you're gonna get shot, get shot for being a wolf, not a lamb.'"

Peter McNab, who studied Grapes as a player with the Bruins and more recently as a broadcaster, says, "Things he says on Canadian TV couldn't be accepted down here."

Cherry has survived his critics because of the bottom line. His popularity outweighs his indiscretions in the eyes of the CBC high command which finds it fiscally incorrect to fire him.

"On the air, I find him offensive and racist," says *Toronto Sun* columnist Steve Simmons, "and the CBC is appalled by him. But they're also deathly afraid and terrified by his popularity."

One might add that his players were astonished by Cherry's popularity when he coached the Bruins (1974-1979) and later the Colorado Rockies (1979-80), although opponents such as Ed Westfall were less amused by his tactics.

"After I left the Bruins in '72," Westfall recalls, "I came into Boston with the Islanders and Cherry resented the fact that I was getting all this ink. One night in Boston he had Stan Jonathan chase me but I hammered Jonathan in front of the Bruins bench. Then, I turned to Don and said, 'Cherry, you keep sending these guys after me, why don't you try me? You've got 16 guys sitting on the bench and not one of them likes you.'"

Naturally, Grapes offers another version. "In my first NHL coaching year Eddie told the papers, 'The Bruins don't look like they're in shape.' I, of course, was the guy responsible for putting them in shape. It made me look bad. Next season I had Jonathan and John Wensink chase him around. There was a time-out with the face-off in front of our bench. I leaned over and said, 'What kind of bleeping shape are we in now, Eddie?' I don't mind people calling me names — racist, pig, cretin, redneck — but to call me a wimp, never!"

Cherry's last NHL stint in Denver took a turn for the worse after

Grapes had a disagreement with Mike McEwen and settled it by grabbing the defenseman by the neck.

"Right after that," Westfall remembers, "the Rockies came to Long Island and the word was out that Don would soon be fired. I ran into him in the corridor and he put his hand out and said, 'Eddie, I got to talk to you. Remember all that bullshit we went through in Boston? Well, I would like to bury it. As you probably realize, I need all the friends I can get.' I said, 'You got that right!'"

Hockey purists resent Cherry's act because of its contradictions. He seems to play both sides of the fence as in the case of spring 1993 when Washington's mini-goon Dale Hunter injured Pierre Turgeon with a cheap-shot from behind in the Isles-Caps playoff.

"What I did," Cherry explains, "is stick by a friend. I told Dale, 'You were totally wrong, but I'm sticking with you.' I told him it was absolutely a cheap shot but I also said that Turgeon was not hurt bad and that he would be back and he was back. That really upset Don Maloney."

If there's one New Yorker who reveres Cherry more than most it is Mark Topaz, a TV statsman who doubles as publisher and editor of *The Aggressive Hockey Report* — the international hockey fight paper.

"Grapes is the lone media representative who expresses the majority opinion," Topaz asserts. "Fans want rough, tough physical hockey played by North Americans, which is why we love Don."

That Cherry's pro-fighting schtick could play Stateside was evident in the spring of 1993 when he was offered a lucrative deal to become a commentator on Pittsburgh Penguins telecasts.

"I could have gotten five times what I get in Canada," he says, "but I said no because I've got too much on my plate up here. They even said they'd have a private jet meet me in Toronto at 5:45 on game nights, fly me to Pittsburgh, limo me to the games, limo me back to the airport afterwards, and jet back to Toronto. I still said no."

Perhaps Cherry got some advice from his pet dog Blue II, just as he would accept Don-imagined tips from Blue I, who, according to Grapes, would correctly tell him which Bruins goalie to play, Gerry Cheevers or Gilles Gilbert, on any given game night.

"Original Blue was the first feminist," Cherry insists. "Now I've got Baby Blue but he's like a Swede. He likes everybody. He's showing a lot of promise, but following Original Blue is like trying to replace Bobby Orr."

And following Cherry is about as easy as coming on after Rickles, Limbaugh and Stern.

DON CHERRY SPEAKS OUT...

° **ON WHAT HE HAS AGAINST RUSSIANS:** "I resent the fact that they come over here and get a free ride. They don't earn their way on the power play. They never come through in the playoffs. There are Russians in Moncton making more money than the captain of the Winnipeg Jets."

° **ON A RUSSIAN HE LIKES:** "That Sergei Zubov of the Rangers doesn't wear a mask and blocks shots. I like guys who pay a price, but a lot of the Russians won't pay the price."

° **ON HIS 10-YEAR WAR WITH HARRY SINDEN:** "He said he'd like to poke me in the jaw. I say he'd have to use a stool to reach my jaw."

° **ON WHO SAVED HIS JOB IN HIS FIRST MONTH OF BROADCASTING**: "As soon as I started out, the CBC wanted me fired for a lot of reasons, starting with the way I acted. But [*Hockey Night In Canada* producer] Ralph Mellanby, who got me started in TV, said, 'If he goes, I go!' So, I stayed."

° **ON THE NHL'S PARANOIA ABOUT FIGHTING TALK:** "The [NHL] brass shudders when you say 'fights' on TV, so now I say 'tussle.' One or two tussles a game is alright with me. I don't like three or four."

° **ON HIS WEALTH**: "I don't even know where my bank is or how to write a check. My wife, Rose, runs my life. I don't even know where the money is."

° **ON ROSE AS A CRITIC:** "Fortunately or unfortunately, she does not like me on television and can hardly wait until they say, 'We don't want you anymore, Grapes.' Rose does not like the way I act on 'Coach's Corner'. She never, ever, says I do a good show. She's a little Italian girl who is so sensitive about other people's feelings. I think she'd rather upset me than upset other people."

° **ON HIS EXPERTISE:** "To be an expert you have to be in the game for 40 years, you have to play for 16, you have to be Coach of the Year in the NHL, AHL, and coach Team Canada in the Canada Cup, and then coach kids to a championship in a high school when I was in Rochester. So if I'm not an expert, and I watch at least 10 games a week, and if I'm not an expert, I don't know who is."

° **DON CHERRY'S BEST FIGHTS — FIGHT WITH BRYAN WATSON:** "We were in Quebec. I wasn't playing much. I was sort of like the fifth or sixth defenseman. They were winning 5-2 and Bugsy Watson was running around hitting all our younger guys. Joe Crozier [the coach] took Al Arbour off the ice and put me on, so I know he didn't put me on to score a million goals. I went up and stood in front of the Quebec net and sure enough Bugsy came across and checked me. Well, that was my chance. We had a real donnybrook. In those days the players sat in the same penalty box. As he was stepping into the penalty box I reached over the policeman and gave him a shot between the eyes, and a real donnybrook broke out. I remember I was being held by two policemen and [Jean] Guy Gendron came around the crowd and hit me over the head with a stick. It went on for about a half hour. Jack Riley [AHL president] had left ten minutes early to go to mass, and he hears on the radio, riot in Quebec. I think I got fined seventy-five dollars."

19

COACH GRAVEL-VOICE

"I try to get every player who's playing that night to give a total effort. I believe that as long as you play smart, the rest will look after itself."

Job security has long eluded Boston Bruins assistant coach Tom McVie but his survival instincts are second to none in the NHL. The gravel-voiced McVie was a head coach for 22 years before becoming top aide to Brian Sutter in 1992-93. "Tommy has forgotten more hockey than any of us will ever know," said Sutter.

McVie's precise age is a matter of some debate but his deportment suggests a perpetual teenager. "Tommy is 60-something," noted Boston Globe columnist Bob Ryan, "but the face is right out of the Little Rascals and the heart is eternally young. If Brian Sutter is the conscience of the Boston Bruins, Tommy McVie is the spirit. Sutter smolders. McVie soothes. Bad Cop/Good Cop? Yup, they'll admit to that juxtaposition."

How good a head coach Tommy actually was is a moot point. Under McVie, New Jersey pushed the eventual Stanley Cup champion Pittsburgh Penguins to the seven-game limit in 1991. A year later he lost a seven-game series to the Rangers before being fired. After Herb Brooks replaced him in New Jersey, McVie moved on to Boston, where he found himself working for an old adversary, Sutter. At one time Brian had skated for the St. Louis Blues while McVie coached the Washington Capitals. Each remembers an irksome encounter.

"One night Brian skated by our bench and said something like 'C'mon, let's get something [expletive] going!' to his teammates, McVie recalled. "I turned to our team and said, 'Hey, we're not going to let that [expletive]

145

guy get his team going!' And we didn't."   Later Sutter was coaching the Blues at the time when McVie was behind the Devils bench. It was opening night of the season at Byrne Arena. "We thought we had prepared our team well and he thought he had prepared his team well," McVie said. "We just killed them that night and when the game was over, Brian looked at me and I looked at him and nothing was said, but there was a connection. Later that season, we went to St. Louis and they just killed us. When the game was over, I looked at him and he looked at me, and still nothing was said. But there was a tremendous amount of respect in his eyes that night."

Respect has not come easy to McVie, partly because he has been aligned with so many weak teams and partly because of his vocal personality. But Tom is proud of a record that includes coaching stints with two of the worst teams in NHL history, the Washington Capitals and Winnipeg Jets, and resents the lack of reverence accorded somebody of his experience.

He is not surprised, though.

McVie is nothing if not realistic. "Somebody once told me," he says, "that if you really want to be a good coach, get some good players. Now that's what I call good advice."

Tommy has no end of advice and thoughts about coaching as revealed in an interview with Stan Fischler.

SF: Describe yourself as a coach..

TM: I'm a stand-up-and-call-it-type of guy. I can be serious and I can also control the room with humor.

SF: Did you always apply humor in coaching?

TM: No. For the first three years as coach, I was a miserable sonuvabitch. All the coaches I played for were like that. I can remember walking down a hotel hallway and I would see the coach up ahead, and when I got to that spot, he was gone. He'd just disappear. And when you did walk by the guy, he wouldn't even look at you, wouldn't say, "Good morning." That's the way it was and that's the way I was. I would turn and walk away rather than encounter a player.

SF: What made you change?

TM: A player I had skated with for years knew me as an off-the-wall guy but now he saw I was different. We went for lunch one day and he said, "What's the matter with you? You're the most miserable sonuvabitch I've ever seen." When he asked me why, I said, "Because I'm the coach. That's why! You have to be that way when you're the coach." He couldn't believe it. "Tommy," he said, "that's not you. Keep it up and you're not going to last long." From that point on, little by little, my true personality came out.

SF: Some coaches are very private and aloof with their players. Are you that way?

TM: I never close my door. I don't like the players to see it closed all the time. It's like talking with your wife. As soon as the communication breaks down, the marriage is in trouble. Same with the team. Some guys come in and say they want to play more. I say, "Okay, play better!" That's all there is to it.

Young guys coming out of junior or college not only need the direction, they need someone to talk to. If you've got a coach who doesn't want to do these things, you could lose those young guys. When things are going bad for these kids, they think the world is going to end so they need to talk. In all these years I've never had a discussion with a player where some good didn't come out of it. Nothing but bad comes of silence.

SF: Players often beef about lack of communication. How do you handle that?

TM: I do a lot of 1-on-1 stuff. Every time I talk to a player, a player feels better about himself and he always plays better after that happens. But you can't keep 20 guys happy all the time. I always say, that of the 20 guys on the team, you have four or five who don't like you and you try to keep them away from the other 15 who hate your guts.

SF: Do you care about your players?

TM: If I didn't care about these guys, life would be easy. I could go into the rink for a 10 o'clock practice at about 9:50 and when practice was over at 11:30, I'd be out of there by 11:40. Why do I go to the rink every morning about six or seven in the morning and then stay there all day? Because I love hockey. And when I'm tough with young guys they know that whenever they have a problem, either personal or financial, they can come right to my office and they'll find me. One of my ex-players recently wrote me a letter. He said, "Tommy, you taught me a lot about hockey but you taught me more about life." I think that's great.

SF: What are your theories on motivation?

TM: There are three great motivators. The first is fear because if someone jumps you, you want to give it right back. Hunger is the next greatest motivator, but few hockey players are very hungry these days. The last motivator I have to work on is pride.

SF: How do you handle big-money players?

TM: When I first came to New Jersey to coach the Devils, all anyone was talking about was money, money, money. No one was talking about hockey so I went through the room and said, "Don't any of you guys ever talk about hockey? If I catch you talking about money, I'm going to kick you outta the dressing room."

SF: How difficult was it coaching a United Nations-type team like New Jersey as compared with one stocked with just Canadians?

TM: I've coached all-Canadian teams and they understand what you're saying but they may not do what you're telling them. When I had this melting pot with the Devils, I decided to do the very best because those were the cards I was dealt. I'm a simple coach and a simple guy. All I do is hang around the rink. If the players don't understand what I'm doing, they should get a job some place else because this is as basic and fundamental as you get. So it doesn't matter if they're from Russia, Sweden or Panama; if they can play hockey, they can play for me. All I want is a tough, driving, forechecking game, making sure that everyone doesn't get nailed in the other end. It really isn't that complicated.

SF: How do you make sure you get the players to play your style?

TM: I'll tell you a story; after coaching for three years, I thought I could make all my guys play that tough, driving, forechecking game because when the Islanders won four Stanley Cups, they won that way. I worked on trying to get my guys to play that way but after three years I said I must be doing something wrong because I couldn't get my guys to finish their checks. So, one year I'm at the draft and I met Freddie Shero and I asked him how I could get every one of them to finish their checks.

He said, "C'mon, Tommy, that's simple." I said, "Simple! I've been trying for years. How do you do it?" He said, "It's easy. You take the ten guys who do it and eliminate the eight who won't. Then, get a new bunch of eight, and then everyone will finish their checks." What he was getting at is that no matter what you'd do with the original eight, no matter how hard you teach, they come out of the crib not being able to finish checks. They either do it or they don't. And size has nothing to do with it.

SF: What about the European influence?

TM: There was an influx of Europeans who were trying to complicate hockey but let me tell you, I've played the game and coached a long time and hockey really isn't that tough. The blue lines are still 60 feet from the net. There's a net at each end and you try to put the puck in one and keep it out of the other.

SF: Tell me about your background.

TM: Let me tell you something; I started coaching in the lowest league, the Eastern League and eventually I moved to Dayton and I learned the business. I went to Washington and they fired me there. I went to Winnipeg and we won the championship. I went to an expansion team and I got fired there. Eventually, I wound up in Oklahoma which is a great place for a rodeo but not for hockey.

I coached all over and then they had some problems in New Jersey so I come in during the homestretch and we make the playoffs and then give Pittsburgh a hell of a run. Then, the season is over and, all of a sudden, they don't know who the coach is going to be. They give me the job but the papers say the other guy's going to have the job. That doesn't make me mad but what does is the trip I've taken around. Do the people writing this stuff know who I am?

Am I chopped liver? Why wouldn't I have the job? I mean I worked and earned that job. When other guys coach in the NHL they say they're never going to coach in a lower league. It's almost as if I just rode into town on a turnip truck or came drifting down the river on a bale of hay. I've been doing this all my life. What I'm saying is that I know what I'm doing.

SF: You seem to be a hard-luck guy.

TM: Well, I've been fired more times than Clint Eastwood's Magnum. When I worked for the Flyers in Maine, they sold the whole franchise just to get rid of me. No wonder they call me the Rodney Dangerfield of hockey.

SF: Do you like anything besides hockey?

TM: If you talk to me about anything else, I would sort of be out of it but if you want to talk about hockey, that's what I do and what I'm comfortable with. I'm wrong sometimes but when it comes to hockey, it's almost like I'm Karnac the Magnificent. It's scary, some of the things I say about certain players. I see the way these guys act and I'll say something to somebody and say what's going to happen and a month later, it happens. In Jersey, my assistant coaches Robbie [Ftorek] and Doug [Sulliman], would say, "Tommy, how the hell did you know that?" I know. I just know.

SF: Of the NHL coaches, who is tops on your list?

TM: Al Arbour sure rings a bell. He became a better coach than when he won four Stanley Cups. When he came back [from a two-year absence] he didn't have the horses. For him it was like trying to win the Kentucky Derby with a bloody mule. You can whip that sonuvabitch forever but Man-O-War is going by. What does Arbour do? He takes that losing team and stays in there and brings them around. But he had had an advantage over a lot of us because on Long Island he was the man. You didn't screw with Arbour over there.

SF: What goes through your head during a game?

TM: You're pretty well set with a game plan when you start but things change along the way. I never yell negative stuff at a player. What I try to do — and I've heard players say it — is really get inside them. They're not always going to be on top of their games, so I try to explain to them how badly the team needs them. I'm more of a cheerleader back there. I try to get every player who's playing that night to give a total effort. I believe that as long as you play smart, the rest will look after itself. If you made a mistake when I was playing, the coach would come in and in front of everyone and would just tear a strip right off you.

SF: You once rejected a Devils' coaching job, didn't you?

TM: I'd been called up from the farm team in Maine to coach the Devils for the rest of the 1983-84 season. That summer I told Mr. Mac [owner John McMullen] his team didn't have any talent. I said it was so bad that if I stayed, it wouldn't be long before he'd have to fire me. I said I'd rather develop young players for the organization in the AHL. Mr. Mac just looked at me and said, "You mean you'd rather go back to Maine, earn half as much money and ride the buses for 20,000 miles?" When I said, "Yes," he shook his head and said, "Tommy, you may be a good hockey man, but you're not very smart."

SF: What has been your low point as an NHL coach?

TM: It was in Washington where I had my first NHL job. I gave my soul to that team. I put the team ahead of my family and health. We came back from a road trip one day and the organization tells me I'm done. You've got to remember that I was a guy going to the rink and spending 16 hours a day there. Now I've got 16 hours a day with nothing to do but stand on the front porch like an idiot waving at cars.

SF: Any other memories of that year?

TM: Once we were beaten bad by the Kings in L.A. We didn't have any assistant coaches in those days and I was going up the ramp at The Forum, all alone, after the game. I looked down at the street and I could see the players laughing and jostling while they're piling into cabs for a night in L.A. and I'm not sure a tear didn't roll down my cheek. But I get to my hotel near the racetrack and on one side of the wall is a huge window. I'm standing there, looking out and the thought actually occurs to me that I should go back to the wall, take a run and dive right through the window.

It's so scary that I said to myself, "Hey, man, you ought to get out of here." So I go down to the lobby and I see our equipment manager, Keith Parker. I tell him how I was thinking about jumping and he looks at me and said, "The way you're going, you'd have landed in the swimming pool and ruined your new suit."

SF: You have a reputation for hanging out at rinks till all hours and much more than other coaches. How do you figure that bond between you and the ice came about?

TM: All I can remember is that when I was a kid and it was the middle of the summer, I still wanted to be at the rink.

SF: How difficult was it switching from being a head coach in New Jersey, and so many other places, to being an assistant to Brian Sutter in Boston?

TM: At first, it was tough. What I found out is that there's a big difference between a suggestion and a decision and I'm not sure I could've done it for anyone but Brian because of his principles and loyalty.

SF: What's the interplay like between you and Sutter?

TM: When I first got here in Boston, *(laughs)* he called me "Mr. McVie." Then he changed that to "Sir."

SF: Which players do you associate with the most?

TM: I like to hang out with the ordinary guys. Like when we're traveling, I'll sit on the plane with a fellow like Cam Stewart or Brent Hughes. You won't find me staying around an Adam Oates or a Ray Bourque. The second and third stringers are the ones who I should be with. They know I'll be at the rink when they get there and won't leave till they go home.

Part Three:

A TALE OF THREE COACHES

A TALE OF THREE COACHES - AL ARBOUR, MIKE KEENAN AND JACQUES LEMAIRE

Never before in hockey history has there been a situation where three dramatically different — yet equally fascinating — coaches operated within a 25-mile radius of each other as happened in the 1993-94 season.

On Long Island, there was the professorial Al Arbour, coaching the New York Islanders, after a dramatic 1993 playoffs during which his club upset Washington and the Stanley Cup champion Pittsburgh Penguins to reach the semi-finals.

In Manhattan, there was mercurial Mike Keenan, hired at great expense to bring the New York Rangers their first Stanley Cup since 1940. Keenan had been out of work since the Chicago Blackhawks bid him adieu in 1992.

Finally, there was the Inspector Clouseau of National Hockey League coaches, the witty and wily Jacques Lemaire. Hired by the New Jersey Devils in June 1993, Lemaire would attempt to bring stability to a franchise which had gone through five coaches in five years.

Based on their energetic spring playoff run in 1992-93, the Islanders were expected to do even better in the new season. Some experts predicted that they could lead the Atlantic Division, although they had barely slipped into a playoff berth the previous year.

Arbour, who had coached the Islanders for 19 years over two separate tours of duty, was best remembered for leading his club to four consecutive Stanley Cup championships from 1980 through 1983. After relinquishing the coaching job in 1987 for a front office position, Al returned behind the bench after his replacement, Terry Simpson, was fired in 1989.

Each spring, Arbour would consider retirement but then change his mind and take another run for the top. Following his unexpectedly successful 1993 run to the semi-finals with Montreal, Arbour decided to come back one more time to continue molding his young team into a Cup challenger.

But the ever-so-promising season began to crumble before the first puck was dropped. Arbour's general manager, Don Maloney, traded for goalie Ron Hextall and, in the process, lost both 1992-93 goalies Glenn Healy and Mark Fitzpatrick, each a hero on Long Island.

Playoff ace Tom Fitzgerald was lost in the expansion draft to the Florida Panthers and then another horrendous blow was dealt when the multi-talented Brian Mullen suffered a stroke which hospitalized him and ended his career for 1993-94 at the very least.

Mullen's replacement, Claude Loiselle, suffered a season-ending knee injury at the very start of the new season and Loiselle's replacement, David Volek, soon went out with a back problem. "It was one thing after another," lamented Arbour who struggled to get his club on track in the opening months of the campaign.

Disaster piled atop disaster at Nassau Coliseum. Hextall, who came to the Island with good credentials, turned into a thoroughly undependable puck-stopper. His backup, Tom Draper, was so bad that Maloney finally dropped him and elevated inexperienced Jamie McLennan to be backup goalie.

In spite of all the misfortune, Arbour managed to maintain some semblance of sanity and, for brief periods, the Isles appeared capable of a playoff run, only to slip into the slough of despondency once more.

By the time his club headed for the homestretch, still trailing the Florida Panthers and Philadelphia Flyers, Arbour had lost his most reliable hitting defenseman, Rich Pilon, and captain Patrick Flatley.

Yet, somehow, he rallied his troops and in the final two weeks of the season, the Islanders pulled off an amazing comeback and nailed down a playoff berth on the next-to-last night of the regular season.

Arbour's arch-rival in New York City was Keenan who had arrived on Seventh Avenue with more fanfare than any coach in Rangers annals and certainly with more money.

Controversial to a fault, Keenan took command of a club that had dismally finished out of a playoff berth in 1992-93. With an intensity rarely matched in New York coaching circles, Iron Mike guided his Rangers to first place and kept them there throughout the season.

Days before the March trade deadline, he demanded that his general manager Neil Smith trade for size, so Smith — just as he had done earlier in the season in unloading Darren Turcotte and James Patrick — obliged by dealing Mike Gartner and Tony Amonte while obtaining bigger, better checkers Brian Noonan and Stephane Matteau.

When the Rangers' hold on first place was challenged by the New Jersey Devils late in the season, the New Yorkers defeated the challengers and won the President's Trophy. Keenan appeared well-poised to deliver the first Stanley Cup to The Big Apple in 54 years.

Although Jacques Lemaire hardly attracted as much media attention as Keenan, the French-Canadian Hall of Famer nevertheless orchestrated a symphony of beautiful hockey across the Hudson River in East Rutherford, New Jersey.

Along with sidekicks Larry Robinson and Jacques Caron, Lemaire gained instant respect from his players and quickly won them over to his disciplined system that accentuated defensive play and quick counterthrusts.

By mid-year the Devils had won league-wide acclaim for their steady, disciplined play although some skeptics wondered how they managed to remain afloat without a single notable center while employing a rookie goaltender, Martin Brodeur, as a first-stringer.

Lemaire's answer was victories. By early April the Devils owned the second-best overall record in the league and, at one point, had actually tied the Rangers for first. But New York defeated the Devils in their final regular season match-up at Byrne Meadowlands Arena to clinch the top spot. Nevertheless, Lemaire had crafted an arresting group which accented the team over the individual.

He admitted uncertainty over whether his skaters could advance very far into the playoffs but also added that they just might fool many critics, such as Boston's general manager Harry Sinden who mocked them as one of the worst of the Cup contenders.

In this section, the author attempts to compare each of the three coaches from an assortment of angles. Arbour, who was chronicled first-hand from opening game to the finish, is studied from the third-person.

Lemaire, who was interviewed before each New Jersey home game by the author, is treated in chronological fashion.

Keenan, who spent two hours with the interviewer, is examined both through the question-and-answer method as well as in a month-by-month survey.

Remarkably, Keenan faced Arbour in the first playoff round and then Lemaire in the third round Battle of the Hudson.

The East Conference semi-final between the Rangers and Devils was a contemporary playoff classic which was as gripping because of the respective coaches — and their styles and strategies — as it was for the players.

Because of the plots and sub-plots, the Lemaire vs. Keenan playoff confrontation is being treated as an entity all its own.

ARBOUR'S LAST HURRAH

"A lot of people thought we were dead in March but we kept fighting and fighting," said Hextall. "The key was Al. He wouldn't let us believe that we were dead."

It was May 1993 in the cramped visitors' dressing room of Pittsburgh's Civic Center, well past midnight. A couple of hours earlier, David Volek of the Islanders had accepted a pass from Ray Ferraro and one-timed the puck over Penguins goalie Tom Barrasso to seal New York's stupendous overtime victory over the defending Stanley Cup champions.

Arbour and his aides, Lorne Henning and Rick Green, were sipping beers and pressing hands of well-wishers as the equipment men packed the last of the sticks and pads into the long canvas bags. Exhausted as he was, Arbour was secure in the knowledge that his coaching wisdom had outfoxed that of his one-time mentor, Scott Bowman.

For Arbour, the upset victory over Mario Lemieux and the defending champions would be his last major triumph in a coaching career that began in St. Louis shortly after the NHL expanded from six to 12 teams in 1967. In the spring of 1993, Arbour's Islanders advanced against the Montreal Canadiens and, but for a bad break here or there, could very well have made it to the final round.

Al — known to his players and friends as Radar — couldn't have been better poised to fulfill his coaching destiny in 1993-94. With promising youngsters such as defensemen Darius Kasparaitis, Vladimir Malakhov and Scott Lachance as well as gifted forward Marty McInnis, the veteran coach seemed correct in his assessment that he needed one more year to hone the youngsters.

Apart from dealing with the traumatic stroke and hospitalization of Brian Mullen, Arbour realized that his team could come to training camp believing the lofty 1993-94 predictions made about them and filled with overconfidence because of the glorious playoff run during the previous spring.

Right from the start, Arbour was tested. Kasparaitis, who had become the most exciting of his rookies, ran afoul of the law — he was arrested for speeding — during the summer of 1993 and then ran afoul of his coach. Darius came to camp significantly overweight and Arbour went public with his anger.

"If he doesn't get those pounds off," Arbour barked, "he'll wind up in a pine box."

By nature a rebel, Kasparaitis grumbled about the admonition, knocked off a few pounds but failed to regain the sharpness which had made him so effective in his rookie season. Darius' inability to attain mint condition would prove to be one of Arbour's primary liabilities.

Malakhov brought with him the talent of which coaches dream. Tall and maneuverable, the Russian defenseman was armed with a blazing shot, superior skating strides and an extraordinary reach which enabled him to make poke-checks that others could never attempt. During an exhibition game with the Rangers, Vladimir unhesitatingly traded punches with Rangers goon Joe Kocur and bloodied the New Yorker. In the opinion of some Islanders-watchers, Malakhov had now completely rounded out his game. This, however, would be a deception and Malakhov, as good as he was, would be a constant challenge for Arbour all season.

A former U.S. Olympian, Lachance was a Connecticut product and the Islanders top draft pick (4th overall in 1991). He had shown enough promise in 1992-93 to project an effective season in 1993-94 — if not actual stardom. In time, though, Lachance would rank among Arbour's keenest disappointments.

Perhaps the most striking and most discouraging of all of Arbour's players was his one and only superstar, Pierre Turgeon. Winner of the 1993 Lady Byng Trophy, Turgeon was signed to the highest-paid contract in Islanders history and was believed capable of surpassing his extraordinary 132-point season.

Instead, Turgeon suffered a serious arm injury in training camp that carried over into the regular season. When the club needed a catalyst in the first month, he was either out of action or severely below par. Another Turgeon injury, later in the season, would cripple the club just as it appeared ready for a dynamic run.

None of these factors alone would have torpedoed Arbour's voyage to a playoff berth, but one unexpected element turned out to be a killer.

Although his goaltending never was of All-Star calibre, Glenn Healy had become a Long Island favorite because of his ebullient personality and his occasionally extraordinary performances. When the Islanders lost him, along with Mark Fitzpatrick, Arbour was presented with goalie Ron Hextall whose fiery disposition and track record for competence seemed ideal for the 1993-94 edition.

Arbour believed he was getting a clutch goalie with exceptional leadership qualities and one who would add spice to the dressing room.

The latter was true. Hextall was a total team player and an off-ice leader. On the ice, it was another story; a disastrous one. In fact, the first home game summed up Hextall's season.

Following a sensational pre-game light show which had the capacity crowd in a frenzy, the Islanders then faced-off against the New Jersey Devils. Within minutes a questionable goal went past Hextall, then another and another. The final score was 6-3.

Arbour kept hoping that Hextall would get back on track and, for brief periods, he seemed to have regained his form of yesteryear. But he then would revert to his imbalanced, confidence-shaking mode.

In the previous season Arbour could go to his second goalie, Fitzpatrick, and the youngster, invariably, would come to the rescue. This time, the alternate goalie was Tom Draper, a Buffalo Sabres cast-off who provided less support than Fitzpatrick and inspired even less confidence.

Bedevilled by these minuses, Arbour struggled to keep his club within striking distance of a playoff berth. After 19 regular season games, they finally came up with a big win, defeating the Canadiens, 5-1, in a neutral site game at Hamilton.

"It was a very good team effort," said Arbour who saw his team win two in a row for the first time in the season. "It was what we needed; the second effort, the third effort, from the goaltending right on out. And (Pierre) Turgeon was starting to do his magic."

But team-wise, the magic was still not there. By early December, the Isles had a 9-15-1 record, one of the worst in the NHL. Arbour's frustration was evident and becoming more public.

"I'm tired of excuses," he declared. "There hasn't been any chemistry."

Actually, there was and there wasn't. The club momentarily righted itself and ran off a six-game winning streak that became the talk of the league. Instead of capitalizing on the momentum, the Isles went into another funk.

Draper had become so patently useless that Arbour now employed Hextall — and only Hextall — who was heading for his 20th straight game on January 4, 1994 against the Devils at Byrne Arena. It was evident before the match that Draper was history but nobody quite knew how long Hextall could stand the game-after-game strain. Just to make matters worse, the Isles learned before game time that their star shooter, Steve Thomas, would be out of action.

Visibly strained, Arbour nevertheless submitted to this interview with the author:

SF: Just about a year ago the Isles came into Byrne Arena and we found out an hour before game time that Benoit Hogue was not going to play and now we find out that Steve Thomas is out. What's the story?

AA: He's had a sore neck the last couple of days and been getting treatments on it. This morning he had several muscle spasms in his neck and we took him over to the city to see our doctor. He's under medication. He was in real pain this morning when we left.

SF: Interestingly, a year ago in the game I mentioned, the Islanders did win the game. Mark Fitzpatrick was in the nets and played very well. Who's in nets tonight?

AA: The same goaltender who has been playing most of the games. Hexy's in goal tonight. He's played a lot of games. Our schedule hasn't been very tough on a goaltender. But it becomes very, very tough after the All-Star break. We are going to do something the next couple of days. Switch things around here. Get our goaltenders really geared up and we'll see what happens later on.

SF: Are you saying Tom Draper will be going in the next game or so?

AA: I'm not saying that. We're going to rearrange things in the next couple of days. Our other goaltenders are going to get some work also. After the All-Star break we'll have somebody to share the goaltending duties.

SF: Now do I read it right, Al, that someone is coming up from Salt Lake?

AA: It's a good possibility, Stan.

SF: The team was going great guns. You won six in a row. And then all of a sudden, there was the flip-flop against the Anaheim Mighty Ducks. How do you explain the turnaround?

AA: It's very easy to explain. It really started in the Pittsburgh game. We lost Dennis Vaske and Uwe Krupp. Those are two big people back there. With defenseman Richie Pilon out of the lineup, we played Montreal and Buffalo after. We didn't really play well. And it catches up to you. We lost Malakhov. The big thing is that you can get away with missing players up front if you have your core back there on defense, but when your core is missing on defense, it's very, very tough.

SF: So that means tonight, guys like Wayne McBean, Chris Luongo, these guys have to lift their game up a notch?

AA: Hopefully, they'll step up and do the job.

They didn't. The Islanders were beaten again and a day later Draper was gone, having played his last game for Arbour. His replacement would be Jamie McLennan, a youthful goalie who until recently hadn't even figured into the club's big-league plans.

Arbour, who had the luxury of two competent goaltenders last season, now had an underconfident, overworked veteran and an inexperienced kid who might not even be ready for the big-time.

Even worse, the coach was in trouble with the league. Arbour was slapped with a five-game suspension after right wing Mick Vukota came off the bench and joined a fight during the 6-3 loss to New Jersey. Vukota was suspended for ten games. "It's a miscarriage of justice," snapped Arbour.

The Islanders playoff crusade became even more discouraging as the club lost to teams they had expected to beat. After Arbour's suspension, the Hartford Whalers walloped them 6-0. They were regularly beaten by the Florida Panthers and the Anaheim Mighty Ducks. Just prior to the All-Star break in mid-January, they visited Tampa Bay for a game against the Lightning. The result said much about Arbour's dilemma.

New York led the game, 3-1, going into the second period but, characteristically, began playing a defensive game. The Lightning scored another against McLennan in the second, but still Arbour's skaters nursed a one goal lead through nine minutes of the third.

At that point Tampa's Brian Bradley took the puck in his own zone and went end-to-end. His last defensive obstacle was Malakhov who tried a futile stick-check as Bradley went around him and beat McLennan, sending the game into overtime. And just when it appeared that the Isles would escape with a tie, rookie Chris Gratton beat McLennan with 40 seconds left.

The furious coach chewed out his players one by one before meeting the media for the post-game chat. His indictment of them was unsparing. "We've got a number of players whose work ethic isn't there for the whole game," said Arbour. "That shows a lack of commitment and a lack of concentration. We had a great first period and then everybody reverted to doing individual things. The selection of our plays is not very good offensively and defensively, and it's killing us."

Arbour's relationship with General Manager Don Maloney seemed cordial, although every so often the coach issued what appeared to be veiled criticism. On January 21, 1994, Arbour took off the gloves and asserted, "We have to make some moves. Too many players on this team are too soft, and you can put that in big, bold letters."

If this wasn't a challenge to the general manager, what could be?

Maloney responded, "I talked to Al and I certainly don't take it personally. We are all very, very frustrated. It's like you say, 'Ah, let's get rid of them all.'"

Arbour's hope was that Turgeon, somehow, would move to the fore and ignite the offense. To a certain extent, he did, and then IT happened.

During warmups before a game against Toronto at Maple Leaf Gardens, the most freakish of freak accidents downed Turgeon. He wheeled in for a shot, turned away and the puck richocheted off the crossbar, hitting him in the right cheekbone. The fracture would sideline Turgeon for a month and virtually crippled Arbour's playoff hopes. The injury jinx was unprecedented in the club's history.

"First we start off the year and Pierre misses the first game," said Arbour. "Then he plays a few games but he's never really right. Then Derek King's mother passes away. Then Uwe Krupp gets hurt. Then we get on a roll but we lose Dennis Vaske, and then Kruppie again. All at the worst possible times."

Privately, Islanders analysts wondered whether Arbour had lost his dressing-room charisma. After a 3-0 home loss to the Bruins, the coach wistfully observed, "If you wait for something to happen, it's going to happen against you. We didn't have a bad first period; we had some good opportunities and we fluffed them."

Given an opportunity to indict Hextall for questionable goaltending, Arbour rationalized the goals. "Ron had no chance at any of those goals," said the coach. "The rest of the team has got to wake up. They've got to learn you have to battle through the little things. Every shift for us is do or die."

Privately, Arbour continued to complain about his club's lack of physical play. In conversation with a friend, he offhandedly said he wondered who on his club needed a new set of pantyhose. His regular enforcer, Mick Vukota, had lost much of his bite, leaving the hitting to Kasparaitis who finally found his groove in mid-season.

Publically, Arbour avoided criticism from a relatively kind media. The club's chief operating officer, Ralph Palleschi, insisted that the media protection of Al was justified. "Al's reputation earns him that insulation," said Palleschi, "and so does the job he did for us last spring. We think we've got one of the best in the business."

By mid-February the Islanders record was 22-28-6 and they were 11 points away from qualifying for the playoffs. At the same time a year earlier, the Isles were 24-24-6 and finished strong, winding up in third place with a 40-37-7 record.

As the trade deadline approached, Maloney had still failed to negotiate a significant deal although 6'2", 215-pound David Maley was obtained from San Jose to provide some grit up front. Maley, a fringe player at best, helped as a checker but never became a meaningful factor.

Nevertheless, none of the playoff challengers — Hartford, Florida, Tampa Bay, Quebec, Philadelphia and Washington — had pulled out of sight. Arbour knew that a couple of wins could turn the season around and he got them starting with a 4-0 shutout of Ottawa with Hextall suddenly at the top of his game.

"Ron played outstanding," said the coach. "This was wide-open hockey and this was a shutout he richly deserved."

The Capitals were next at Nassau Coliseum and once again Hextall rose to the occasion — another 4-0 win. "Hextall was in total control of this game," added Arbour. "It's a great sign for our team."

So was Turgeon's return to the lineup. Hextall went for his third straight shutout against visiting Quebec. For two periods he held Les Nordiques scoreless but finally was beaten at 2:39 of the third period. His scoreless string, over more than 12 consecutive periods, was 249.39 minutes.

"That's the longest string that I can remember and I've been here a number of years," said Arbour.

The Islanders finished February with a 9-4-1 record and had 58 points, only four behind the Flyers and Panthers who were tied for the final Eastern Conference playoff spot. Ray Ferraro, who had been a major disappointment at center, had revived and Turgeon continued to help since his recuperation.

But The Big Push never materialized and Hextall faltered once more. As the Isles loped through March, it became more and more apparent that rookie Jamie McLennan would become a key element in the goaltending plans. After Hextall had been knocked out of two of four starts, Arbour started McLennan against the Devils who came to Nassau on March 15th with a club record nine-game (7-0-2) unbeaten streak.

New Jersey was beaten, 3-2, and the Isles had pulled themselves within three points of the Flyers and two of the Panthers. Next stop was Detroit and Arbour offered an analysis of his club: "We have to be patient. We can't get carried away looking for the home run. We have to wait for our opportunities and not get caught out on an odd-man situation. We're going to have to be very solid and not take too many gambles, and if we do, they have to be in our favor. We have to play very, very patient and smart. The run for the playoffs is in our hands and we're the ones who have to do something about it."

Unfortunately, they did less than Arbour had hoped while the surprising first-year Panthers remained in a playoff berth and showed no signs of faltering. Beginning on March 22, a few key games would determine whether the Isles would make it or not. The first took place against Tampa Bay at Nassau Coliseum and, in a sense, was the biggest upset of all. The second ranked among the most demoralizing of defeats.

Facing the Lightning, Arbour expected his troops to take the offensive against one of the NHL's weaker teams. Instead, they fell behind by one, two, three and, finally, FOUR GOALS, after 37 minutes had elapsed. For all intents and purposes, they had been written off by the 12,293 fans.

But then the Isles began creeping back into the game. They got a pair of power-play goals from defenseman Tom Kurvers, a goal from Derek King at 11:15 of the third period and another power play score, this one from Steve Thomas at 15:16 to tie the game. As the sudden-death period wound down to a conclusion, Pierre Turgeon intercepted the puck at the Tampa Bay blue line. He skimmed a pass to Vladimir Malakhov who whipped a wicked shot over the catching glove of goalie Daren Puppa. The Isles had won, 5-4!

The elation lasted exactly four days until the Panthers arrived on Long Island for a Saturday afternoon game. Florida had tormented the Isles all season and Arbour was counting upon a rousing performance. Entering the game, New York was four points behind Florida. A win would trim the margin to only two and establish the Isles as a force in the homestretch.

For Arbour, the 3-1 defeat could not have been more depressing. "WIMPS WHEN IT COUNTS" shouted a *Newsday* headline. The coach didn't disagree. "The problem is, you've got to show some character and we exposed a lack of character. When you cut through all the baloney, Florida wanted it more."

The loss dropped New York six points behind the Panthers. A day later the demoralized Islanders moved on to Buffalo and were promptly wiped out 4-1 by the Sabres. Anyone who suggested that the Isles were capable of rebounding at this point would have been viewed very curiously, to say the least. Their next game was at Washington and Arbour struggled to find some way to infuse vigor into a dormant offense. Captain Patrick Flatley, the club's best checking right wing and undisputed inspirational leader, was sidelined for the season with a torn abdominal muscle. Desperation had become the Islanders' middle name and Arbour scrambled for a prescription for all the ailments.

He gambled on two farmhands, Dave Chyzowski and Zigmund Palffy from the Salt Lake City farm club. Remarkably, Chyzowski responded with a goal at 17:35 of the first period to tie the score, 1-1. But Washington had a 2-1 lead entering the third period and appeared to have the visitors well in hand with less than three minutes remaining.

Just when it seemed as if the Islanders would forego any playoff chances, Marty McInnis took his team's 14th shot of the night and shoved the puck under goalie Don Beaupre. The time was 17:15 and the 2-2 score held through the overtime. "At least we got a point," sighed Arbour, hardly overwhelmed by the performance, "which is something we haven't got many of lately."

Barely alive, the Isles next were challenged with a home-and-home series against the Stanley Cup champion Canadiens. They beat Montreal, 5-2, at Nassau and squeezed out a 3-3 tie at The Forum. Hextall was formidable, the Panthers had begun losing and, suddenly, a flicker of hope began growing on Long Island. At 32-35-11, the Isles had six games remaining on their schedule, owned 75 points — as did Philadelphia — and trailed Florida by three for the eighth and final playoff spot.

They returned to US Air Arena on April 5th for another meeting with the Capitals. Florida was in a full-blown slump (1-4-4) and now seemed catchable — if the Isles could keep winning. The character Arbour had derided earlier appeared to have changed. Trailing 0-2 and 2-3, the Islanders rallied after Arbour pulled goalie McLennan in favor of an extra skater in the final minute. Ferraro tied the count with 43 seconds left and Benoit Hogue delivered the winner at 3:34 of overtime. For a change, the Islanders dressing room was filled with hope. An overnight trip to Hartford for a match with the Whalers looked appetizing, especially since Hartford had long since been eliminated from playoff contention.

Alas! Sean Burke was spectacular in the Whalers goal and all the Isles could extract was a 3-3 tie. The coach, who by this time continued to exhort his troops that they WOULD make the playoffs, was not discouraged. "Vladimir Malakhov had an outstanding chance," said Arbour, "but we weren't able to get one to get the two extra points. We were going for it. We wanted it. We're inching our way back and that's the important thing. We were a little tired and lacked that extra zip, that sharpness."

The good news was in Miami. Try as they might, the Panthers couldn't shake their lengthy slump and now held a flimsy one-point lead over the Isles. No less meaningful was the fact that the NHL tiebreaker rule stipulates that wins are the first criteria should the teams end with the same amount of points. The Isles now had two more victories (34-32) than their rivals and were cruising on a five-game unbeaten streak (2-0-3) which began with that apparently doleful tie with Washington.

When Flatley left the lineup, Arbour created a new unit with Ferraro, Hogue and Brad Dalgarno which immediately clicked. "Hogie picked it up since we played in Montreal," explained the coach. "We need him to skate. When he does, he creates room for other people. Brad is mucking and banging. All three of them have blended very well."

Heading into the final weekend of the regular season, the Isles were only one game shy of the .500 mark (32-33-16) but on tap were the hated Rangers, the NHL's most successful team. "It doesn't matter who we play," Arbour insisted. "Points are points and we have the momentum."

The game, which appeared on U.S. network television (ABC), was about as exciting as it could get. Arbour's skaters rallied for a 5-4 victory. "We hung tough," said Arbour, "although we were on our heels at the end." The Isles had finally, climbed ahead of the Panthers who played a tie with the Devils. At long last Arbour had his team positioned to clinch a playoff berth — except that the final two games were on the road, first with Tampa Bay and then with the Panthers.

Even before the Isles were to meet the Lightning, Florida played host to the struggling Quebec Nordiques. If the Panthers were to win that game, they would pull ahead of New York once more. Fortunately, the Nords played their best and took the two points. All Arbour had to do now was orchestrate a victory at The Thunderdome and his club would have concluded one of the most astounding homestretch comebacks in NHL annals.

Their unbeaten streak now had reached 4-0-3 and it was hard to remember how woefully weak they had been in losing to Florida and Buffalo a few weekends ago. However, the match against Tampa Bay would not be easy and, in fact, became even more complicated because of unexpected by pre-game hype ironically generated by ex-Islanders president Bill Torrey who now held the same position in Miami.

To the astonishment of many who knew the man, Torrey insinuated in a newspaper report that the Lightning would surrender the game purely to spoil the playoff bid of its more successful Florida rival. Arbour, who had been a longtime friend and colleague of Torrey, was livid.

"I've been in the business a long time and I've never seen a team quit just because it's not in the playoffs," barked Arbour.

In the hours before the opening face-off, l'affaire Torrey had become the talk of Tampa and members of the Lightning responded just as the Panthers boss had hoped — with the promise that they would take the Isles to the limit.

They weren't kidding. From the opening face-off Tampa had New York on its heels. The Lightning dominated the first period and were unlucky to emerge without scoring. The Islanders attack was nonexistent, but Ron Hextall was at the very top of his game, looking better than he had all year.

"Hexy was in total control," said Arbour. "He made big saves repeatedly."

Just short of the seven-minute mark of the second period, Isles right wing Steve Thomas pulled up on a rush just below the dot in the right circle, faked defenseman Marc Bergevin to the ice and wristed a high shot past Puppa. The time was 6:50 and the Isles were ahead, 1-0. At 12:18 Thomas converted a Pierre Turgeon pass with a 39-foot slapshot to give the Isles and Hextall the cushion they needed.

The Lightning remained unrelenting in their pursuit of the puck, but they simply could not solve Hextall whose puck control was impeccable. "A lot of people thought we were dead in March but we kept fighting and fighting," said Hextall. "The key was Al. He wouldn't let us believe that we were dead. Just 20 games back it looked real bad. But he kept saying, 'Boys, we're going to make it. We're going to make it,' and he made us believe it."

Hextall underlined the point with a 2-0 triumph that sealed the playoff berth. After his troops had celebrated on the ice and then trooped into the dressing room, Arbour wiped the beads of sweat from his brow and told the gathered media that he was grateful for Thomas and Hextall.

"It's a good thing Stevie whipped those two in," said Arbour, "and Ron came up with a perfect game. For me, it's a big sense of relief because there was so much on the line and we didn't want to have to go to Miami having to win that game.

"In the last eight games we played very solid hockey and found ways to win. In the early part of the season we were finding ways to lose."

Then, a pause and a grin: "It doesn't matter when you make the playoffs."

As Arbour began to leave, a friend strode up to him, grabbed his hand and pumped it.

"This," said the friend, "was your finest coaching job — ever!"

And it was. Having lost Brian Mullen, Claude Loiselle, David Volek and Rich Pilon for most or all of the season, his captain Patrick Flatley in the home stretch, his top defensemen, Dennis Vaske and Uwe Krupp for long stretches and his crack scorer, Pierre Turgeon, during critical periods, Arbour was forced to juggle, coax, coddle and admonish a ragtag squad that was further ravaged by undependable, mediocre goaltending. And still, he perservered and pushed his skaters into the final playoff berth on the next-to-last night of the season.

It would be nice to be able to put a happy finish on the end of Al Arbour's career, but hockey reality wrote a different dénouement.

Having returned from their Florida conquest, the Islanders met the first-place New York Rangers in the opening playoff round. Based on the regular season record, it loomed as a classic confrontation. The Isles had actually won the series and seemed capable of keeping the Broadway Blueshirts off their game.

In the first minutes of the first playoff game, the Isles buzzed into the Rangers zone and looked dominant once again. But the Blueshirts eventually counterattacked and, on a power play, defenseman Brian Leetch carried the puck down the left alley over the Islanders blue line. He released a wrist shot that appeared eminently stoppable, but it blooped past Hextall and Arbour's skaters were down, 1-0.

Thomas, Hogue, Ferraro, Turgeon and King returned to the Rangers zone again and again, but to no avail. Early in the second period, Hogue took the puck behind the Rangers net, circled in front and beat goalie Mike Richter with a backhand shot, but the puck rebounded off the far post and skimmed out of danger. Shortly thereafter, the Rangers beat Hextall and the rout was on, big-time.

The Islanders were defeated 6-0 in both games at Madison Square Garden before returning to Nassau. In Game Three, the Arbourmen dominated the Rangers again in the opening minutes before Esa Tikkanen carried down the left wing and fired a rather ordinary shot at Hextall. But the goalie's angle was flawed and the puck sailed into the net. The Isles were doomed. They lost the final two games and were swept in four straight.

In all of Arbour's coaching career he never had been more disappointed in his players' performances. Pierre Turgeon was ineffective; Derek King didn't score a single goal; Vladimir Malakhov disappeared; Ron Hextall was a disaster; and Travis Green, supposedly the top face-off man, couldn't win face-offs.

Arbour hardly could contain his rage and disenchantment when he met the press following the series loss. "I have a lot of things to say but I don't think I should say it right now," said the furious coach. "I know exactly what I'm going to do about my future. You stick around long enough, you're going to feel everything, especially if you're with the same team a number of years.

"There's an empty feeling you can't explain unless you're really involved in sports. There's absolutely nothing there. There's nothing. It's a very sick feeling, regardless of whether you lose, 4-0, or another way. You just can't describe this emptiness.

"Losing is always hard to accept. I'll feel it for a few days or a week. After that, I'll march on. I didn't dwell on winning the Stanley Cup and I'm not going to dwell on this."

On June 1, 1994, Al Arbour resigned as Islanders coach.

Upon completion of career he had become the leader in regular season games coached (1,601) and the runner-up to Scott Bowman in wins (779), playoff games coached (209) and won (123).

Al Arbour was one of the greatest coaches hockey has known.

PLAYERS' COMMENTS

Patrick Flatley:
"He has this gift for talking to a group and making you feel he's talking to you personally. You get the feeling he genuinely cares for his players."

Ray Ferraro:
"Al really understands what each player can bring to the team. Al's always up front with you."

Chico Resch:
"He was as sensitive and considerate as a coach can be. I always thought Al really hated it when people were mad at him. He was always in control of every area of coaching and he never seemed to seek the gratification of external praise. His real strength, though, was that he didn't burn his teams out. You did feel a kind of pressure from him, sure, and sure, I saw him discipline people. But he did it in a way, usually, that let the player keep his dignity.

"He's the best coach of our time. He made you play your best, but he wasn't mean. He didn't have to harass or ridicule you to make you play better. He simply made you a better person and a better player."

Bryan Trottier:
"He's not a father figure, but if you have a problem he cares enough to give you advice and the time to work it out. He's a guy who demands 100% from you. If you don't give it, he's disappointed and expects you to be disappointed, too."

Mick Vukota:
"Al's gift is his feel for the pulse of the team. He yells during and after games and practices, but I don't remember him ever giving a 'Win one for the Gipper' speech. I think he knows we're smart enough that we don't need him to tell us the importance of a Game Seven in Pittsburgh."

21

THE MAGNIFICENCE OF LEMAIRE

"Jacques has turned into a terrific coach," said Robinson. "He comes across well and is kind of a player's coach because the decisions he makes and the way he prepares for a game are the way he'd like to be prepared as a player."

At dinner with friends early in June 1993, New Jersey Devils president Lou Lamoriello allowed that hiring Herb Brooks as head coach was not the best decision of his managerial career. Brooks left the club shortly after the Devils were beaten in the opening 1993 playoff round by the Pittsburgh Penguins.

"I'm going to have a surprise for you," Lamoriello assured over the pasta and vegetables. "This time I'm sure we've made the right move."

On June 28, 1994, Lamoriello called a press conference at Byrne Meadowlands Arena in East Rutherford, New Jersey. Normally, there are news leaks that result in advance word of the coach signing. But now there wasn't a clue — not even a remote hint — as to the choice of Lamoriello and club owner John McMullen.

After the dining room had filled to capacity, Lamoriello strode to the podium. Behind him was a compact, balding man wearing a broad grin. He tapped a veteran hockey reporter on the back of the shoulder as he headed to the microphones. When the reporter realized who had nudged him, the newsman did a double-take.

Jacques Lemaire!

A Canadian hockey legend had somehow been coaxed out of the Montreal Canadiens organization by Lamoriello and asked to bring New Jersey the brand of hockey respectability that had been the Habs birthright for years.

What would evolve into one of the best acquisitions in modern memory actually began a few days after the Canadiens had won the 1993 Stanley Cup. Lemaire had been a trusted aide to Montreal general manager Serge Savard when Lamoriello phoned Savard and requested permission to hire Lemaire.

"The answer is 'yes,'" said Savard, "if you will only wait until after the entry draft. I need Jacques' input at the draft table."

The parties agreed and Lemaire, who had a comfortable position in the Canadiens front office, decided to put his neck on the Devils' chopping block.

"You always have coaching inside of you," Lemaire explained. "I can't say I was frustrated. I just thought I could give more. I thought it was a good challenge." The Canadiens were both flattered and flabbergasted. "It came quickly and caught me by surprise," Savard admitted, "but I did not try to talk Jacques out of it. I had no reason to interfere. He knew what he had in Montreal and he knew the challenge that was in front of him in New Jersey.

"Jacques is a great hockey person. He wasn't fired as a coach with the Canadiens. He just didn't want to coach in Montreal anymore, so I kept him in the organization. He told me that he felt he could coach somewhere else, but not in Montreal. He's a guy I would hire in a minute. He's a great coach and he'll get 100 percent from that team. You'll find out how good that team is."

The words hardly calmed the skeptics who had seen Doug Carpenter, Jim Schoenfeld, John Cunniff, Tom McVie and Herb Brooks go through the New Jersey coach grinder. Lemaire had not coached since 1985 and who was to say that he would be greeted any differently than the mentors who had been Devil-scorned before him?

The answer would come when training camp opened in September 1994. Lemaire and his newly-minted assistants, Larry Robinson and Jacques Caron, made an instant impact on the players who previously had complained about Brooks, Schoenfeld, et. al.

"He gained the instant respect of everyone from the first day of training camp," said goalie Chris Terreri. "Certainly, that had a lot to do with his past and the championships he won and the tradition he brought from Montreal.

"But beyond that, it's his approach. He's upfront with everybody. He's honest. He tells you exactly what he expects of you. And if you don't do it, you don't play. It's not, 'This is the way I want you to play.' It's, 'This is the way we're going to play.' It's that simple."

But training camp wasn't that simple.

The Devils had hoped to open the season with two experienced goaltenders, Terreri and Peter Sidorkiewicz, the latter of whom had been obtained in a deal with Ottawa. But after Sidorkiewicz arrived in New Jersey it was learned that he had not recovered from a shoulder injury and, in fact, was damaged goods. El Sid, as he was known to teammates, might not be available for the entire season.

That left Lemaire with 20-year-old Martin Brodeur as backup to Terreri. Although he was considered promising by Devils scouts, Brodeur had not been ticketed for the NHL at least for another season. But the Sidorkiewicz emergency suddenly changed the timetable and goalie coach Jacques Caron promptly began working with the kid.

Meanwhile, the media focused on Lemaire as well as the players. Newsmen had chronicled the various uprisings in the Devils dressing room and wondered how Jacques would be affected by the potential malcontents.

"We had been through so many coaching changes and so much chaos — and a lot of it had been our responsibility," said Terreri. "I know I came in thinking, 'Enough is enough. We're going to do whatever the coach says and there'll be no talking back.' It came to that point with a lot of veterans."

Still, there was a matter of respect to be earned and that developed quickly because of Lemaire's straightforward personality, his lucid teaching and his clear defense-first philosophy.

"Jacques had us playing a system that plays into our strength," Terreri explained, "and that is defense. That can't be stressed enough."

Lemaire: "I believe that to win, you've got to play pretty good defensively. One of my first steps was to show how to play in our zone and the neutral zone."

Despite the advent of Lemaire, several observers predicted a low finish for New Jersey. They cited the goaltending deficiency and the absence of a power center and game-breaking forward. Small but fast Corey Millen was obtained from Los Angeles while ex-Bruin Bobby Carpenter was offered a free-agent tryout. Both made the team and would have a lasting impact through the regular season.

World-class veterans such as defenseman Slava Fetisov enjoyed instant rapport with Lemaire. "I feel like I know the man for a long time," said the former Soviet Olympic hero. "I liked what he said the first time he spoke. He said a team is the only way to win, not some individual."

When the season opened, the Devils put their actions where their mouths were and translated their enthusiasm for Lemaire into wins. After defeating the New York Islanders 6-3 in the home opener at Nassau Coliseum, the Devils sported five straight wins, giving them the best start since the franchise moved to New Jersey from Colorado for the start of the 1982-83 season. It was also the best start in the history of the 20-year-old franchise which began play as the Kansas City Scouts in 1974.

Nobody was more pleased than Lamoriello, who had personally selected Lemaire. "What happened," said Lamoriello, "was the team responding to what Jacques wanted. What has to happen from here on is not dwell on any kind of success but look to the future. The presence of the coaching staff is a reflection of the way the team is playing. There is a total focus on the end result by all the players. Every person sacrifices for the other. Every player is contributing in various ways. That is what makes a good team."

The Devils were better than good. They won seven consecutive games before playing Montreal at The Meadowlands. A media circus surrounded the match because of Lemaire's past Canadiens connection, not to mention the fact that the Habs were defending Stanley Cup champions.

Although the home club came out flying, the Devils were foiled by acrobatic Patrick Roy in the Canadiens goal. He stopped everything New Jersey threw at him and came away with a win. As was his ritual following every game, Lemaire met the media after the game.

Q: Are you upset over the loss?

JL: I don't think so. I'm very happy about the way we played. The guys came out, played hard and played a great game. We had our chances to score, but Patrick [Roy] played super. It was a matter of getting the goal at the right time that would have lifted our team . . . and we never got it.

Q: What were your emotions when the Canadiens stepped on the ice?

JL: I had chills the first time they stepped on the ice in the warm-up. After that, it was just another game.

Q: What impressed you the most about the streak?

JL: I am really happy with the game we played here. I think that we could have won even though it was 2-0. Like I said before, it was a matter of getting a goal, but I had a great feeling and I really loved the bench tonight. Since I've been here, I've never had a bench like that. The guys wanted to win until the last shift and even on that last shift they were saying "let's get a goal." To me that means a lot.

Q: Has this team established itself as one of the better teams in the league?

JL: A game like tonight will prove this. If we keep playing like that, and the guys have confidence and show up for every game, we can be.

Q: Did you want to win more tonight because you were playing against the Canadiens?

JL: No, not really. It's mostly the challenge you have playing against a good team, a team that is hot. I knew the team was struggling earlier in the season, right after training camp, and I knew the team was getting to their best over the last few games.

Q: Patrick's performance?

JL: He's the best goaltender in the NHL and he proved it again tonight.

Q: Does it help in any way to lose to the defending champions?

JL: It's always the way you lose. It's not who you lose to — it's the way you lose.

Q: Are the Canadiens a model?

JL: In a way, yes. I am teaching the things we went through in Montreal. The things that I supported I brought them in. I don't like to take them as a model, but in my mind, every time I talk about the game it's what I know from the past, which is Montreal.

Q: Let down after the streak?

JL: No. That's why I'm happy with the way we played. That's exactly what I said. The way they played I'm not shocked at all. I'm just happy because I know that in the next game we will play, we will play well. If you break a streak and the guys just quit at a certain time then you start to worry.

The loss to Montreal was regarded as a benchmark for the young season. Some Devils-watchers opined that the club now would find its own level, which was a low one, and slowly slip to the bottom of the Atlantic Division. A listless Halloween night loss to the Rangers in Halifax added to the gloom.

But Lemaire was not one to panic. The Devils next embarked on a 12-hour, two-stop flight to Los Angeles whereupon the coach whisked his players to The Forum and put them through a punishing workout that delivered a clear message that another poor effort would not be tolerated.

"Five nights later," observed John Dellapina of the *New York Daily News*, "he benched big names Stephane Richer, Claude Lemieux and Bernie Nicholls for long stretches of a victory at Anaheim. Sitting third and fourth-liners could not have had the same, attention-grabbing effect — although it would have been the preferred easy way out for many coaches."

Six weeks into the season, Lemaire had won the respect of his entire team and that respect would continue to grow as the season matured.

"The team aspect is the biggest thing with him," said John MacLean.

"The guys sense that Jacques treats players one through 22 the same way. If you're working hard you get rewarded. If not, it doesn't matter if you're the best player on the club, he'll skate you extra or you won't play."

As the Devils won more games, the focus inevitably turned to Lemaire who, in turn, was compared to other notable coaches. One of them was his former mentor, Scott Bowman, now leading the Detroit Red Wings.

"What I remember of Scotty as a coach," said Lemaire, "is that he was the type of guy who was always looking for something new to bring into the game. Also, he was the type of guy who always got the players worried. You never knew what he was coming up with the next game and he kept us on our toes all the time. Which was great at that time.

"With me it's a little different today. I talk more with the guys to make them feel comfortable. I don't know if it's because of the money they're getting, or what, but you have to be more on their side and try to understand them a little more than in the past."

He coached against Bowman on November 20, 1993 at The Meadowlands. Before the game Lemaire was interviewed about two of his contrasting forwards, Corey Millen and Stephane Richer. After the game, he was questioned about a number of things, including the result.

Q: Two guys on your team, Stephane Richer and Corey Millen, form a very interesting combination. Stephane Richer uses one of the longest sticks in hockey; Corey Millen uses one of the shortest. What is the advantage of a long stick? You used one when you played.

JL: (*Comparing the two sticks*) Well, this is a big difference right here. But Corey is 5'8" and Stephane is 6'2" . . . but still, Corey uses a very short stick. The difference is some guys like the short stick because when they go along the boards, it's easier to play there. Other guys like a longer stick to control better the puck.

Q: That short one, he seems to be right on top of the puck. It almost looks too small. Is that possible?

JL: Well, he bends down quite a bit. Richer uses a long stick to go around the net and it's really good to make passes or get shots when you go around the net.

Q: As a coach, would you tell a player like Millen: "Hey, your stick is too short, change it!"

JL: I wouldn't tell him now because he's playing well (*laughs*). But, if I see that he loses the puck a lot, or things like that, maybe I would try to change it. When a guy has a certain problem, you try to change something. And sometimes the stick is a good part of the equipment that a guy could change.

Q: Were the guys ready for the game today?

JL: No, they were not. They were not and I had that feeling right before the game. When I looked at the guys in the dressing room, I told them that they'd better be ready because this team [Detroit] is a good skating team and they'll be coming on pretty fast. And I also told them I don't know what is wrong with them, but they don't look like they are ready to play. It took them a little while before they woke up. When you give a three point lead to a team like Detroit, it's pretty tough to come back. The good part is that we did.

Q: Jacques, when you say that you can foresee that things are not right, what can you do to change that situation?

JL: You try, but it doesn't mean that you will succeed. You can't assume that the second you step on the ice everything will go the right way. You have to prepare yourself to play the game.

Q: Do you try to find out what's wrong? Do you talk to the players?

JL: Yes. Before every game it's different. You come into the dressing room, sometimes the guys are very lively, sometimes they don't say a word and they are thinking about the game. They could be lively and not think about the game. So, it's all different.

Q: Could it have been the early hour on Saturday [1:35 p.m.]?

JL: Well, maybe that too. Maybe they woke up at noon and thought the game was at two!

For the most part, Lemaire betrayed no uneasiness about his job. He was cordial with the media and ever the gentleman. But his calm demeanor would be challenged on December 8, 1994 when the Devils made their first trip to his native Montreal where he enjoyed a 12-year Hall of Fame playing career and 10 years in the Canadiens front office.

Many things had been written and said about Lemaire's coaching stewardship in Montreal. A prevailing theme was that he had to step down as coach after the 1984-85 season because of unfair attacks by the media. Then there was the much-overblown feud with former teammate Guy Lafleur.

Larry Brooks of the *New York Post* was the first journalist to pump Lemaire about the Lafleur dispute. In Georges-Hebert Germain's biography of Lafleur, *Overtime: The Legend of Guy Lafleur*, the player and author depicted Lemaire and GM Serge Savard as villains who plotted and oversaw Lafleur's demise and exit.

One of the most contentious aspects of the book involved Lafleur's last game with the Canadiens when Lemaire was coach. Lafleur insisted that Lemaire had promised him ice time and then broke his word and benched him, and that's when he made up his mind to quit. Lafleur claims that Lemaire forced him out. Now, Lemaire argued that that was *not* the case.

"That is not what happened," Lemaire said, evenly. "I went farther with him than I would have with anyone else because he was Guy Lafleur. But if I had gone any farther, with the rest of the team I would have fallen off a cliff.

"Does he say that I spent hours with him watching tapes, showing him how he stopped getting involved in the play, how he would just be by the boards when he had the puck in the offensive zone?

"I said to him before that last game [November 24, 1984 vs. Detroit at home], 'Guy, you have to go to the front of the net with the defensemen. I understand what it is like when you just do not want to take the punishment of being whacked all of the time by the defenseman. I told him just go to the high slot. But no. He didn't. He wouldn't."

In the book, Lemaire is quoted as saying that Lafleur, who'd scored 50 or more goals in each of the six seasons from 1974-75 through '79-80 but never more than 30 in the following four seasons, had become interested in only trying to score. Lafleur and the author say he had become stifled by the coach's defense-first system.

"No, I never said that," Lemaire said. "Guy was the greatest player I ever played with, and the second-greatest behind the Bobby Orr I never played with or against in the NHL. The talk was that Guy could not play defensive hockey. I wasn't going to make him play defensive hockey or backcheck. He was Guy Lafleur!

"I told him to be the first man on the puck, then he would not have to be back. If not, he would have to come back, but just pick the last defenseman, just pick up the fifth guy, then be ready to break when we get the puck. I would not try to change him. But he didn't want to. He was a different man than the one I played with. He didn't want to play anymore.

"Players on the bench would watch him and shake their heads. I could not use him or I would have lost the team."

Lemaire was fully prepared for the media onslaught once he arrived in Montreal. He asserted that he no longer was at war with Montreal journalists, although he did tweak them once or twice.

"No, I'm not angry," he said. "It's only that I will have to repeat myself 20 times. It seems like you're under pressure of watching what you say to them all the time. And after they get your answer, they go to someone else and try to make something of it. There's too much competition. They have to fill the pages."

There were plenty of pages to fill. Lemaire's Devils not only invaded

The Forum without Bernie Nicholls, Slava Fetisov and Bruce Driver, but Lemaire chose to play rookie Martin Brodeur in goal, right in front of the goalie's father, Denis, who was house photographer for the Canadiens.

The hypnotic effect of The Forum finally got to Lemaire prior to the opening face-off. "During warmups," Lemaire recalled, "I was looking at the players on Montreal and then said, 'Wait, this isn't my team.' It was a strange feeling."

The game itself was terribly exciting and resulted in a Devils victory over the Habs. It featured Brodeur's outstanding goaltending and reinforced the conviction that Lemaire was grooming Martin to become the Devils primary goaltender.

Having built the Eastern Conference's second best record on discipline and team defense, Lemaire and his team were gradually winning attention from the opposition. Teams came away from games with the Devils muttering about New Jersey's overall strength and the coach's fine-tuned handling of his sextet. All, that is, except one club — the Rangers.

After losing three straight games to New York, the Devils skated onto Madison Square Garden ice on December 26, 1994 and were thoroughly mauled, 8-3. Among the frightening aspects of the encounter was the emotionless aspect of the Devils performance.

"It's unreal," Lemaire said after the game. "I talked to the players trying to find out the reasons why we played like that. It seems like they didn't have the answers. Except that they didn't play their game."

On the positive side was the Devils ability to rebound. Though the defeat was disheartening, Lemaire was able to rally his skaters and get them back on track and, by the time 1994 arrived, New Jersey was the talk of the league.

Prior to a game with the Islanders on January 4, 1994, Lemaire talked about his club:

SF: Last September you never would have imagined that your club would be second best in the NHL on this date, would you?

JL: Not at all. Especially when you start a new season, you don't know the players, you don't know how they'll respond to you.

SF: Well, it's interesting because I've been talking and reading. None of the players have said anything critical about you, at least publicly. What do you think they are saying privately? Is there anything about your coaching you think that they don't like, like the tough practices of the other day?

JL: I know why — because we're second overall (*laughs*). If we were lower, maybe it would be different. The other day, it wasn't too hard. The practice is hard only when I see the guys don't put the effort in at the practices. Then, I make them skate after. Usually they don't skate if they have good practices.

SF: Bernie Nicholls certainly is deserving to play. He got a hat trick against Ottawa. Tell me how Bernie is looking here.

JL: Bernie, as everyone knows, has good moves and can shoot the puck. He's a guy that scored many goals when he was younger. He's just not scoring as much anymore. It's nice to see him in that Ottawa game, to get those goals that he got.

SF: Nice subtle play there.

JL: Yeah, he lifted the guy's stick there and got the puck.

SF: He reminds me of you when you were playing — those subtle plays. Guy Lafleur got all the attention while you were making all those subtle plays.

JL: He was (*laughs*)!

SF: About Bernie, you're putting him in a defensive role more than he's ever been. How has he accepted that?

JL: I think he loves it. I'm trying not to put pressure on anybody to score goals. I think the players feel more comfortable in it. Playing Bernie in a defensive role, he concentrated on doing a great job defensively. There's no doubt at times I would ask him to get shots or get chances to score, which he's working on. But he doesn't feel the pressure that a goal scorer feels every game.

SF: Coach, you've put a lot on pressure on me! I come to the game and I'm expecting Chris Terreri to be in goal and I found out that you are going with younger Martin Brodeur. How come?

JL: I know that there's a lot of coaches that are getting their lineup ready. I think it's a matter of knowing who we are going to play next. I want this kid against that team and I want Chris against Florida and so on. I'm just trying to get a guy that will get maybe two, three games and to win them.

For the most part, Lemaire avoided controversy through the first half of the season. One nasty episode erupted at Byrne Arena late in a game which resulted in a Devils win over the Islanders. Mick Vukota of the Isles became an extra man on the ice in a brawl that featured Randy McKay of New Jersey and Darius Kasparaitis of the visitors. As a result of the brawl, both Vukota and Islanders coach Al Arbour were suspended.

Surprisingly, Lemaire pleaded guilty and in a one-on-one interview explained why.

SF: You say if you had known that there was bad blood between Randy McKay and Darius Kasparaitis you might not have let McKay on the ice. Now tell me exactly what was behind your thinking on that.

JL: Well, if you are at the end of the game I don't think it's good to send a guy to get another one to settle what they have among each other. If something happened, it would have happened in the game and that's fine with me. At the end when you see the game is gone or you won the game, you don't send guys to settle other guys.

SF: You're not blaming yourself, are you?

JL: No. I didn't blame myself. The only thing is that I didn't know about that — that Randy would get him. I wanted to give him the chance to play on the power play more than he's been used to.

SF: An article in the *Bergen Record* says you're leaning towards Martin Brodeur, but you're going with Terreri tonight. What's the story?

JL: He's been playing the same amount of games so far. Maybe one or two difference. I'm looking forward to giving Chris two games in a row at certain times that I feel that he'll be playing at his best.

SF: Are you leaning towards Brodeur?

JL: I'm not leaning towards anyone. I'm looking at the one I figure is the most ready goaltender to play that game.

SF: A guy who has impressed me against the Islanders was Scott Stevens, because he's playing more than his usual well-rounded game. On the power play he seems so important. Tell me about this play.

JL: What I like about Scott is that he has a great shot and puts it mostly on net. He's the type of defenseman to make the play — he's the guy going to the net.

SF: We're also looking at Bernie Nicholls and his effectiveness in the last game. Now tell me what you see in Bernie's role. Tell me about this play.

JL: When he has the chance, when he has the puck, he knows what to do with it. He's got good hands. Right here he gets a shot, it hits his arm, and still goes in. A goal scorer will do that! A guy that doesn't score too many goals, the puck will hit his arm and not go in.

SF: Another guy who we don't hear enough about is Jaroslav Modry, who is quietly working his way into the lineup. Tell me a little about this guy.

JL: Modry is a guy that has a lot of skills. He's really good on his skates, has good mobility and has a very good sense of the game. Right here you see him move in to get the loose puck. This kid, I think, can play better than he is right now. He's playing well, but I think he can play much better. You know he had to adjust to many games with the traveling and so on. He hasn't done that in the past. It's only his first year. I think he will be okay in the long run.

Lemaire's hand-picked aides, Larry Robinson and Jacques Caron, remained out of the limelight but each was contributing meaningfully to the club's improvement. Robinson worked with young defensemen Scott Niedermayer and Jason Smith, each of whom was improving monthly. Caron's insightful work had resulted in Brodeur's ability to play competent goal whenever Lemaire gave him the nod.

"Jacques has turned into a terrific coach," said Robinson. "He comes across well and is kind of a player's coach because the decisions he makes and the way he prepares for a game are the way he'd like to be prepared as a player."

Yet the players' view remained a chief focus of the media, most of whom remembered the headlines they obtained writing about Herb Brooks' feuds with his team and the difficulties Jim Schoenfeld and John Cunniff had with their skaters. The reporters waited for the moment when a coach-player feud would erupt during the Lemaire regime, and when it happened they seized the moment.

The dispute developed following a 2-1 loss at Maple Leaf Gardens. This was a solid game in which Toronto took a 2-0 lead until Niedermayer scored at 9:19 of the third period. Throughout the game, Lemaire matched lines with the Tom Chorske-Bob Carpenter-Claude Lemieux checking unit, shutting off the powerful Doug Gilmour-Dave Andreychuk unit. Alexander Semak, Valeri Zelepukin, Stephane Richer, Corey Millen and Bill Guerin spent long stretches on the bench.

In *The Post*, Larry Brooks observed, "There were Devils unhappy with their ice time as Lemaire matched lines. Players making faces on the bench, maybe grumbling."

After the game, Lemaire charged that he had some players "who were looking for excuses when they didn't go on when they thought they should and who stopped working."

By Devils' standards, this was Lemaire's first crisis, if only because the media was making a big deal of it. How the coach handled the unhappiness — and how the players would react to his handling — would go a long way toward determining the Devils' performance in the homestretch.

"I'm not concerned," Lemaire insisted, "because I'm going to solve the problem. If they're not happy, they can watch from the stands."

Before the Devils game with Tampa Bay on February 19, 1994, Lemaire reminded his players that he was the boss. To those who doubted his strategy, he pointed out that in this case he had to play his defensive-oriented players more than his offense-oriented skaters.

"I know as a player, I asked myself what the heck is the coach trying to do?" Lemaire explained. "So, I wanted to tell them. 'When you have played half a season and know certain guys can't play a steady shift against other players, what are you going to do?' Then you hope they bear down, hope they check.

"You can't go into a game hoping. You have to use your best possible players. I want to give a guy a chance to perform, but then they have to give something back."

They did. Captain Scott Stevens became a candidate for the Norris Trophy and was enroute to accumulating the best plus-minus record in the NHL. Scott Niedermayer continued to improve as a sophomore defensive ace and Martin Brodeur began to gain attention as a possible rookie-of-the-year candidate. The Devils maintained their winning pace despite egregious gaps. Lemaire's power play lacked a Brian Leetch-type quarterback; he was bereft of a top face-off winner, and the failure of sophomore Alexander Semak meant that there wasn't a top draw center on the entire team.

"We have a very good team when all the guys are working together," said Lemaire, "and we're getting good goaltending. We've proved so far that we're okay, but there is room for improvement.

"How do you improve? Different ways. The players will get better and play better as a team. They'll understand the game more. And then, on the other hand, you have trades. It's up to the players to decide. If they show they're not good enough to be among the best, they'll make the decision."

On February 24, 1994, the Devils were again defeated by the Rangers. The loss left them ten points behind New York. During the post-game press conference, a reporter asked Lemaire whether he was ready to concede the race for first. "Not yet," he said and left the podium.

Privately, he was concerned. He confided to friends that he was "scared, really scared" because he thought the Devils "could go either way."

Nobody gave the Devils a chance to catch the Rangers, but New Jersey quietly returned to the business of winning and managed to beat the others often. After the loss to the Rangers, the Devils went 12-1-3. Now, the trade deadline was looming and there was the temptation for Lou Lamoriello to make a deal, but he decided to go with what he had and Lemaire accepted the decision without complaint.

In the meantime, the coach continued to evaluate and re-evaluate his players. Every three games he provided a private report to each of his players in which their performance was analyzed numerically, commented upon and graded.

"Players never think they didn't try or play well," Lemaire explained. "Sometimes, maybe, they think they didn't play that well, but they never think they played badly. I know. I was the same way. When I came to New Jersey, I wanted to find a way to let the players know what the coaching staff was thinking. I talked with Lou and my assistants and came up with this."

Lemaire and his staff evaluated each player's effort against his assigned responsibilities. The game was broken down into categories with each player receiving a different report card. Coaches worked from the game and the video.

"I'm very satisfied with it," Lemaire said. "We've gotten good comments from the players. The only problems have come when there's been a typographical error in the office that happens because my handwriting might not be so good."

Bruce Driver: "You always know what's expected of you. There aren't any surprises, 'Oh, I didn't know that's what they wanted.' Every guy has different things they do well. If you don't perform, you're not getting a good report."

Driver's game was broken down into eight categories. "That's what they expect of me. If I do them all, I get 100 percent. If not, then my grade isn't going to be so good. If your report cards aren't good, it's a pretty good indicator there's a problem."

From time to time, there were mildly surprising benchings of certain players. Claude Lemieux, who was suffering through a well-publicized divorce proceeding, was scratched before a 7-2 win over the Red Wings in Detroit. "I'm not satisfied with the way he is playing," the coach asserted. "I told him that I need him to play the way I knew he could play. That's exactly what I need from him. If I don't get that, he won't play."

Lemieux accepted the benching, then returned to the lineup to play his best hockey through the spring. Ditto for Scott Niedermayer who also slumped in the stretch, was scratched and then came back to perform better than he had all season. Lemaire acknowledged that his most significant accomplishment was pulling the Devils together on and off the ice.

"I knew I could get them to play as a group — as a unit," he said, "but I didn't know how long it would take and how good they'd be."

Respect did not come from all quarters. Lemaire took his Devils to Boston and beat the Bruins, 2-1, only to have his club disparaged by GM Harry Sinden. "They looked to me like one of the weakest playoff teams," snapped Sinden. "They have no offense at all. But they're well-coached and they work hard. They make the most of what they've got."

Occasionally, Lemaire himself would tweak his men. After a markedly sloppy 2-1 win over the Lightning, the coach rubbed his abundant brow and chuckled, "It's not often that I get a headache, but tonight I got one. I'm going home with a headache because it looked like the Three Stooges at the end."

Yet, they kept winning and closing the gap with the first-place Rangers. On Sunday, March 27, 1994, they played Quebec in a neutral site game at Minneapolis. A win for New Jersey and a New York loss would bring about a tie for first place, which is precisely what happened.

"They are very happy," said Lemaire. "They are happy with the success they are having. I think they know the importance. They are excited to be winning. They are excited going into the games. It shows."

The Canadiens came to Byrne Arena on March 30, 1994 and the Devils wasted them, 5-2. However, defenseman Ken Daneyko hurt his left shoulder when he was crushed into the boards by Vincent Damphousse early in the third period. Daneyko, who was the NHL's iron man with 388 straight games played, described the check as "definitely dirty [because] he hit me from behind."

Asked whether the Devils would ask the league to review the play, the coach laughed. "No, we'll save our money and the tape!"

Lemaire now had to balance two goals: beating out the Rangers and priming his team for the playoffs. "Finishing first overall would be great," Lemaire said, "but my job is to get our team ready for the playoffs. Certain guys have to get ice time now in case we have injuries. You can't bring a guy in who doesn't play for ten games and expect that he could do the job."

Down the stretch they raced with the Rangers. The climactic meeting of the top two teams would take place at The Meadowlands on Saturday, April 2, 1994. Before that, the Devils would play Washington on Friday night at US Air Arena. "We cannot afford a slip," said Lemaire. "If we slip, maybe the Rangers will get away again."

The slip occurred with 45.8 seconds remaining in the third period at US Air Arena. Tied 1-1 and seemingly enroute to overtime, the Devils permitted Kelly Miller to take advantage of a defensive zone breakdown and drive a 15-foot shot under Chris Terreri's left pad. The defeat ended the Devils four-game winning streak and seven-game unbeaten streak (6-0-1) and was the team's second loss in their last 18 games (13-2-3).

The next night the Rangers beat them, 4-2, to sweep the New York-New Jersey series in six straight games and, suddenly, first place seemed less relevant than the mini-slump. In his post-game press conference, Lemaire was asked if someone could stop the bleeding.

"I don't think we're bleeding right now," he replied, "not if we play in the next game like we played against the Rangers. The guys worked hard and the effort was there. It's so easy to be negative and criticize. To me, it's only one loss. One thing I know is we won't meet the Rangers in the first round of the playoffs, so we'll have time to think about it.

"The guys came away from the weekend knowing what was going on and they were happy. Not because they lost but because they know they are on the right track. These guys are still learning how to win this year. They are still learning." Then, a pause: "AND YOU HAVE GUYS WHO WILL NEVER LEARN AND WHO SLOW THE REST DOWN."

A 3-1 loss to Pittsburgh at The Igloo in the final week of the regular season, inspired a harsh headline in *The New York Post*. "SOME 'SELFISH' DEVILS ON ROCKS WITH JACQUES."

Without naming names, the coach articulated his points, mostly that some of his players were deviating from the team principle. "There are some guys who are more concerned with themselves than with the team," he argued. "I can see it on the bench. Little things. They shake their head if they don't get on the ice on the power play. They make faces if they don't like their ice time. When they do that, they show me they are thinking about one thing — 'me.'

"Do they think they are not on the power play because they are playing well? Don't they understand that? I can understand that players might be concerned about getting their goals and their points because it is how they get their contracts. I know that. But at this time of the year when we can finish first, when it all has to be the team, no, then they are showing they don't know how to win.

"You would think it would be there, but it isn't . . . not from everyone. Not from some guys. A kid, he can learn. But if you think that way when you have played for seven or eight years, it's difficult to change that thinking.

"Let me tell you this about being a team player. It is much easier to be thinking of the team when things are going well. It is easy to be on the wagon for a ride. It is when things get tougher that you see some players thinking of themselves. 'I. Me. I.' That is what I'm looking at. That is what I'm going to learn about the players here —who knows how to win."

Lemaire would inform them without any equivocation that there would be no excuses on the New Jersey Devils.

As it happened, the Rangers beat out New Jersey for first place overall, 112 points to 106.

For the Devils, it was their best season in history, more points, more wins, second-best overall record in the NHL and a new image.

A year earlier they were regarded as underachievers who never would make a mark on the face of big-league hockey.

"If we had predicted this at the beginning of the season," said Devils owner John McMullen, "everyone would have thought we were crazy. Jacques and Larry have inspired the guys. It's a team with a minimum amount of ego. That's all to the credit of the coaches."

Lemaire: "I would love to be able to have a great playoff and to say we had a great year. No doubt if we don't have success in the playoffs I'll be upset. But I just can't forget the season we had, no matter what happens in the playoffs."

LEMAIRE AND THE PLAYOFFS:

"The mental part is most important," the coach explained on the eve of the Stanley Cup round. "The guys have to think about winning. They have to be confident. They have to be calm."

As invigorating as the regular season had been, the Devils as well as New Jersey hockey fans clearly understood that the first 84 games only represented part of the total package. The playoffs were ahead and Buffalo would be the first-round opponent.

Asked whether he was concerned about the playoffs, Lemaire smiled and replied, "Everything worries me because it's my job to worry."

Among his prime sources of anxiety were the Sabres twin scoring threats, Alexander Mogilny and Dale Hawerchuk. To combat them, Lemaire would stack the checking line of Tom Chorske, Bobby Carpenter and Stephane Richer.

"Their role won't just seem more important," said Lemaire, "it *is* more important. They'll have to face the best scorers and the best scorers will play at their top in the playoffs. These guys, the so-called checkers, have to do their job."

But no one was more pivotal than the goaltender. Down through the homestretch, Lemaire appeared more confident in his 21-year-old rookie Martin Brodeur than the veteran Chris Terreri. The coach decided to start Brodeur while reporters wondered whether the rookie could meet the challenge.

"I don't see why not," answered Lemaire, "because he's been put in the lineup against teams he should have been nervous against. Teams like Montreal and Quebec. Even though he didn't do well against the Rangers, he was there and he wasn't nervous because of who they are. I'm more worried about whether the team will play well. Because if the team plays well, he has a chance to play well in goal."

Brodeur played well but his opposite, Dominik Hasek, played even better, shutting out New Jersey, 2-0. It was only the third time in 85 games that a Lemaire team was blanked, yet the coach was remarkably calm about the result at Byrne Arena.

"I can't be disappointed," he exclaimed, "because I thought our guys played well. We had good chances to score and our power play looked better than it did during the regular season, but I give credit to Hasek. He saw nearly every shot and the few rebounds he gave he was in position to stop. He was on top of his game."

When a reporter goaded him by suggesting that the Devils could fall out of the playoffs very easily, Lemaire retorted, "The series isn't over yet. Or, did they change the rules?"

A second loss at home would be devastating to the Devils, and almost as crippling would be a loss of morale. At this critical time, Lemaire was confronted with one of his few personnel crises. Center Corey Millen, who had been benched in Game One to make room for rookie Jim Dowd, sounded off to the media about his desire to play. Teammate Mike Peluso took umbrage with the public pop-off and had serious words with Millen during a scrimmage prior to Game Two.

Lemaire took the embroglio in stride. "Hey," he said, "one player is angry he's not in the lineup. It's no big deal, nothing to be upset about. Players are emotional now. That kind of thing happens. As for my decision, it's no different than in baseball. If a manager puts up a pinch hitter and he strikes out, is it the wrong move? If he doesn't do what you hoped, you still had the right reason."

The Devils struggled again in Game Two — leading 1-0, tied 1-1 in the third — but rallied on a Scott Stevens' power play goal to win 2-1. This enabled them to head for Buffalo, tied at one game apiece. At The Aud, New Jersey won Game Three and then lost Game Four. With the series knotted at two games apiece, the teams returned to The Meadowlands for the critical fifth encounter.

For a time it looked bad as Lemaire's skaters fell behind, 3-1, against the NHL's best goaltender. But they rallied to tie and then, four minutes and 30 seconds into the third period, Claude Lemieux, skating down the right side, took a pass from Scott Stevens, put the puck between the legs of Richard Smehlik, skated around the Sabres defenseman and beat Hasek inside the right post from close range. It was the winning goal in a 5-3 decision and moved the coach to one of his precious few bursts of emotion and even a broad grin.

"Jacques doesn't smile too much," Lemieux said. "But if you get him to smile, it means a lot."

"Claude was so determined," said Lemaire. "He played his best by far. He wanted to win so badly from the first minute to the last."

That Lemieux was the hero proved ever-so-gratifying to Lemaire.

Jacques had singled out Claude as one of his pet projects in September 1993 and stayed with his mercurial forward through some of Lemieux's darkest moments.

"Even when we were down, 3-1, the bench was great," Lemaire recalled. "They were still talking about winning. Sometimes during the year when the other team took control they didn't do that. The bench was at its best of the year and I knew we could skate with them; that's what I asked the players to do. We were so determined. We wanted to win very badly from the first minute to the last."

The series moved back to Buffalo where the Devils were in a position to clinch. Instead, they played a game that was for the ages — a contest that will have historians dissecting it for decades — one that Lemaire called "The best game I ever coached in."

It began normally enough on Wednesday night, April 27, 1994. Neither team scored in the first period, despite many opportunities, nor were there any goals in the second. With 17:14 gone in the third — and the score still tied, 0-0 — New Jersey's Bobby Carpenter was penalized for roughing. The Devils killed the penalty and the game went into overtime — then a second overtime and a third overtime!

Miraculously, goalies Brodeur and Hasek repelled shot after shot as the coaches jockeyed for an advantage. In the first overtime, Lemaire had to adjust to a minor delay-of-game penalty to Stevens as well as a ten-minute misconduct for his captain while Dave Hannan of Buffalo was hit with a tripping penalty at 18:29.

There were no penalties in the second overtime, but Lemaire already had significantly shortened his lineup. Ken Daneyko was benched because, according to the coach, he had lost his composure with a pair of penalties late in the second period and could not be counted upon at this point. Forward Mike Peluso was afflicted with a charley horse and no longer could be used.

In the third overtime period, the Devils were caught with too many men on the ice — a potentially devastating situation, yet somehow they killed the penalty at 12:10 through 14:10. Although the Devils would eventually outshoot Buffalo, 70-50, both teams had scoring opportunities that failed.

For New Jersey, the end came at 1:51 a.m. — at 5:43 of the fourth overtime period — on what started out as an innocent play along the right boards. The Sabres gained control of the puck and moved it to the front of the net where defenseman Tommy Albelin appeared to be in position to clear the rubber. He missed and the puck fell to Dave Hannan, who backhanded the puck over a fallen Brodeur.

The series was tied at three games apiece and would now return to

New Jersey, where it was uncertain how the Devils would rebound from the traumatic defeat. "Everybody was playing as hard as he could," Lemaire concluded, "but guys make mistakes at times."

Asked whether he was able to sleep after the 1-0 loss, Lemaire replied, "I slept because I was just dead. I dreamed about nothing."

He would have pleasant dreams after Game Seven, played at New Jersey. The 1-1 tie was broken at 13:49 of the second period with Buffalo's Doug Bodger just skating out of the penalty box. Stevens slapped the puck from the left point and it was deflected over the net by John MacLean. The puck went into the right corner where Bernie Nicholls centered a pass for Lemieux alone in front.

"Their defensemen were still running around when Bernie got me the puck," Lemieux remembered. "I just shot it on net."

Brodeur stymied the Sabres until there were 13.3 seconds left in the third period. Dale Hawerchuk took a dangerous shot that Brodeur stopped and that cemented the win and the series, sending the Devils up against Boston in Round Two.

If Lemaire's coaching acumen was tested in the opening series, it would be even more severely challenged against the Bruins, especially after Boston captured the first two matches at The Meadowlands, the second of which was lost in overtime after New Jersey had tied the count in the waning seconds of the third period.

Now it was imperative that the Devils win and Game Three saw Lemaire pull off a major coup. He benched goalie Brodeur for the first time and replaced him with Chris Terreri. The veteran who had become a second-stringer responded with a magnificent performance and a 4-2 victory at Boston Garden.

Lemaire looked like a genius again in Game Four, also at Boston Garden. This time he inserted little-used bruiser Ben Hankinson into the lineup and the burly winger delivered a key goal before the 4-4 match drifted into overtime.

But the coaching staff's most memorable move occurred just after the 14-minute mark in the first sudden-death period. Bobby Holik lined up for a face-off with Boston's Adam Oates near the Devils blue line. Lemaire and Larry Robinson signalled from the bench that they had a specific play in mind. Holik caught the signal and told defenseman Bruce Driver he was going to try to push the puck ahead. Driver then told Stephane Richer.

"I cheated a little bit," said Richer, "so I'd be one step ahead of Don Sweeney."

Just as planned, the puck squirted off the face-off to Richer who skated down the middle, cut to his right on his forehand and completely deked goalie Jon Casey, who had been lured far from his crease. Richer easily deposited the puck into the empty net at 14:19 to give New Jersey a 5-4 edge and a 2-2 tie in the series.

"Stephane played a great game," summed up Lemaire. "He was the best player on the ice for me."

Terreri had won the two games he had to win. Logic dictated that Lemaire go with his hot goaltender but the coach had other ideas. He confounded the experts by starting Brodeur in Game Five at Byrne. Not only that but Ben Hankinson, who had delivered a big game in Boston, was replaced by little Corey Millen.

Incredibly, Millen came through with the game's first goal at 1:23 of the second period and Bobby Carpenter, who had become Lemaire's top defensive center, scored with 21.1 seonds left in the second period to make it 2-0. Brodeur was flawless the rest of the way and Game Five ended 2-0.

Now it was back to Boston with the Devils in position for the clincher. Having shut out the Bruins, Brodeur was everyone's favorite to start again but Lemaire again went with his conscience and opted for Terreri.

"He's the best coach I ever played for and it's not even close," Terreri opined. "He's so good that sometimes it gets scary. He's got the ability to dissect things, pick them apart, and then relay it to us in a way that everybody understands."

Yet the media had trouble understanding the man affectionately called Coco. *New York Daily News* columnist Filip Bondy, for one, had this observation: "He could not be a coach in any other pro sport. Jacques Lemaire is too square for basketball, too refined for baseball, too French for American football, but he looks just right for the Stanley Cup playoffs. Hockey fits Lemaire like a padded glove."

The fit was even more snug after his skaters produced a stirring triumph over the Bruins at Boston Garden. Sure enough, Terreri was spectacular when he had to be, protecting a slim lead through the late, tenuous moments of the third period until Tom Chorske provided some breathing room with a late goal.

Thus, the Devils were catapulted into the East Conference finals against the New York Rangers, the President's Trophy-winners and the club which dominated New Jersey — six games to none — through the regular season.

What's more, Lemaire would be matching wits with Mike Keenan, whose iron-fisted style was diametrically opposite to his opponent's. To hockey purists, the coaching contest would be every bit as enthralling as the match-ups between the players.

On paper, the Rangers had the superior team. Mike Richter had been most valuable player in The All-Star Game; Mark Messier was a game-breaker, and Brian Leetch ranked among the premier defensemen. New York, whom John McMullen described as "The finest team money can buy," could afford to keep a dozen reserves in the press box who would be regulars on any other team.

Lemaire understood that he had to neutralize New York's firepower, particularly its power play which was anchored by Leetch and Sergei Zubov. He stressed that his club had to play its patient, checking, defensive, wait-for-the-break game in order to succeed.

"One thing I can assure you," Lemaire asserted. "If we open up we'll be in trouble. Washington opened up against the Rangers and the Islanders opened up against them. You saw the result."

For the most part, Lemaire's plan worked, although the Devils trailed 3-2 late in the third period. With time running out, the coach was able to pull goalie Brodeur and insert an extra shooter. Play moved deep into the Rangers' end as New Jersey pressed for the tying goal. Finally, the irrepressible Lemieux chipped home a shot after a frantic goalmouth scramble to set up overtime.

Once again, an entire first sudden-death expired without a score and more than 15 minutes elapsed in the second extra session before New Jersey caught a break. Bobby Carpenter banked a pass off the left boards to Stephane Richer who outflanked the backtracking Adam Graves. Richer moved in on Richter and sent a shot that richocheted off the goalie's stick and over his shoulder into the net at 15:23. The Devils had won, 4-3.

Game Two was another story. The Rangers pounced quickly on the Devils' defense, scored quickly and maintained a 1-0 lead until early in the third when they overran New Jersey checkers and emerged with a 4-0 win.

When the series moved to The Meadowlands, New York went ahead two games to one on a goal by Stephane Matteau at 6:13 of the second overtime. The Devils were reeling and Lemaire knew that strategy and psychology were imperatives, especially since his crack center Bernie Nicholls had been suspended for Game Four after cross-checking Aleksei Kovalev in the neck during the previous match.

"If you don't take the lead," warned Lemaire, "you'll never win. We have to play our best hockey in the first five minutes."

As Lemaire had hoped, his regiment rallied. They had a good first five minutes and in the 11th minute had their first lead. Richer's power-play goal lifted the 19,040 fans and Bill Guerin's breakaway score sent Richter to the bench in place of Glenn Healy. The final score was 3-1, tying the series at two games.

Nicholls returned to the lineup for Game Five and scored two goals at Madison Square Garden in what was New Jersey's most dominant game so far. They won, 4-1, and played their checking style to perfection. "The key," said Brodeur, "was our checking style. We got the lead, took the crowd out of it. From then on, our defense was superior."

Game Six, which could have been the Devils clincher, was back at Byrne Arena. For the first period and most of the second, Lemaire pulled all the right strings. He had a 2-0 lead which almost was extended to three on a number of scoring opportunities early in the middle frame. The coach had hoped to enter the third period with a two-goal cushion, but a traffic mixup late in the second crushed his hopes.

A pair of Devils became entangled, leaving an opening on the right side for the Rangers Kovalev who seized the opportunity and blasted a shot past Brodeur. Sure, the Devils still had a 2-1 lead at the end of the period but they appeared shaken by the Rangers' thrust.

What had once appeared to be a commanding lead — considering the excellence of Devils checking — now had the strength of a gossamer string. As the Devils reeled, the Rangers regained their firepower and almost in a trice, Mark Messier had tied the score and put the Rangers ahead.

New Jersey got a break with little more than two minutes remaining. A penalty to New York afforded Lemaire an extra skater and that, in turn, provided him with an opportunity for a rare gamble. With the face-off deep in the Rangers zone, he pulled Brodeur and added yet another shooter. Thus, he had two extra skaters and plenty of time to organize — provided that his players performed sensibly.

As planned, the Devils won the face-off and the puck went to usually-reliable John MacLean who was camped near the right circle. MacLean had plenty of time to move the puck to the right point, which would have enabled New Jersey to position at least one — maybe two — players for the precision shot.

Unfortunately, MacLean rushed his move and quickly dispatched a pass to Lemieux, who was well covered in the slot. The puck dribbled to Messier, who aimlessly golfed the rubber down the ice — only this time it had eyes and plunged right into the empty net. The Rangers had tied the series at three!

"We had the game," Lemaire concluded, "and then we threw it away."

So disheartening was the loss that many Devils-watchers wondered whether Lemaire could possibly ressurrect his skaters for the final match. He did, and they played nobly in what now is regarded as one of hockey's classic playoff games for the books.

The Rangers carried a 1-0 lead into the third period, checked feverishly to a point where New Jersey was barely able to penetrate the blue line. So it finally came down to the final minute and, somehow, the Devils managed to fling the puck into New York territory. Once, twice, the Rangers cleared only to have the puck returned for another face-off.

Bernie Nicholls won yet another draw and set a final play in motion. At last, the puck came into the crease area where Valeri Zelepukin — a late insertion by Lemaire — hammered home the tying goal with 7.7 seconds remaining

The arresting comeback was matched only by the profoundly intense first overtime period. In the beginning, the Devils held the upper hand, but could not put a dent in Richter. As the period moved past the ten-minute mark, the Rangers took over and had New Jersey backtracking. Time and again, Brodeur produced key saves.

"Martin was more relaxed than anyone on the team," said Lemaire.

Neither team scored in the first overtime, and when Lemaire returned to his dressing room, he stressed the importance of the subtle plays. "I asked them to pay attention to the little things — like a bad pass — because they could make the difference in the game. That's how you get the two-on-ones. I wanted them to forecheck, go deep in their end."

Surely, New Jersey had its chances to bury the Rangers. On one play, Richter raced to the left boards (his right) to intercept the puck but Bill Guerin pushed it free and would have scored had he maintained sight of the disk which, momentarily, eluded him. Richer had at least one promising opportunity but deked instead of shooting. And then there was the puck that appeared homeward bound before it bounced off Zubov.

Now the puck was in the Devils end. Veteran Slava Fetisov, who had played nobly throughout, tried a clearing pass which bounced off a Ranger. It went to Matteau who sped down the left and moved behind the net. Scott Niedermeyer appeared to have him covered, but the Ranger — still behind Brodeur — tried to move the puck in front. Somehow, it struck the goalie and bounced behind him into the net.

And so the playoffs and season ended for Jacques Lemaire and his Devils.

POST MORTEM: *On the day after his team was eliminated from the playoffs, Jacques Lemaire offered the following commentary on his club, the playoffs and the season in general.*

His Feelings: *"I don't feel badly. My club worked hard and I could see positive results. Time and again, we came back when it seemed we might have lost."*

Surprises: *"I liked their enthusiasm and willingness to win. In the beginning it seemed as if they didn't have any respect for each other. NOW WE HAVE A TEAM. There were not many nights when they didn't show up."*

His Future Needs: *"I'd love to get one or two more offensive players, especially for the power play. Then again, when I look at Los Angeles, Quebec, Detroit and Pittsburgh — all clubs with a lot of offensive talent — I see teams that didn't do much better than us overall. When I say I'd like a goal-scorer, I must emphasize that I don't want one who only plays individually. If that's the case, I'd rather stay with the guys I now have."*

The Rangers' Winning Goal: *"We were tired in the overtime but it was a lucky goal and we were all disappointed."*

His Most Satisfying Game: *"Even though we lost the four overtime game to Buffalo, I was pleased with the way the guys played. That was really something. They went as hard in the overtime as they did at the start. It was just great. Coming from behind the way we did against Boston also was special. And, think about it — when we started the series with New York, we had lost six straight to them. And what did we do; we took them to double-overtime of the seventh game. We worked hard and we came back. Because of that, I have to be proud and satisfied with my hockey club."*

22

DOUBLE-CROSS OR DOUBLE-CROSSED?

"He likes to take responsibility. 'If this is my team, let me run the show here. But if I mess up, you can get rid of me. But don't get rid of me and have my hands tied at the same time. If you're going to blame me for the failure, let me run it.'"

It would be safe to say that the legendary master of deceit, Prince Machiavelli, could not have concocted a more convoluted collection of charges and countercharges, plots and sub-plots involving Mike Keenan between September 1993 and July 1994.

The melodrama began with Keenan taking charge of the Rangers at training camp and, as some believed, he intended to become president and general manager.

Of course, Keenan denied such hanky-panky and said so to us, on tape at the Rye training base. He asserted that he wanted his summers free without any contract-signing hassles and had enough on his plate as coach. Most people believed him.

Keenan's relationship to Smith remained at best polite (when the team was winning) and at worst quasi-nasty when the Rangers suffered a loss. Fortunately for everyone, the Blueshirts emerged as one of the league powers by Christmas and a Stanley Cup favorite in the New Year.

Their partnership weakened considerably as New Jersey's Devils narrowed the gap in late winter. Some of Smith's confederates confided that the GM barely was on speaking terms with his coach and a rupture appeared imminent in the days preceding the March trade deadline.

Keenan had given Smith a check-list of players he wanted. At the 11th hour the GM obtained Keenan choices Stephane Matteau and Brian Noonan from Chicago and Craig MacTavish from Edmonton. Each would play a pivotal role in the club's Stanley Cup crusade.

Although the Devils' first-place charge was repulsed, a startling rumor appeared in *The Hockey News*: If New York won the Stanley Cup, Keenan would have accomplished his objective and move on to yet another job, likely in Philadelphia.

Implausible as it seemed, in light of the Rangers renaissance, the Keenan departure gossip burned like a live ember.

But when the Rangers clinched the President's Trophy, swept the Islanders in four straight playoff games and then butted Washington out in five, the focus returned to the Cup and little else.

Students of New York's hockey politics reasoned that as long as the Rangers won, the delicate Keenan-Smith marriage would remain intact. Keenan had to be content with the winners Smith had obtained and Smith had to accept a coach who had won for him.

However, at this juncture a few new and essential elements had intruded on the scene. To wit:

- Madison Square Garden's parent, Paramount Communications, was taken over by the Viacom Corporation.
- Paramount boss Stanley Jaffee, who many believed had hired Keenan over Smith's veto, was a victim of the takeover, thus depriving Keenan of his closest ally in the high command.
- Garden president Bob Gutkowski, concerned about his future in the new regime, began angling for the best possible position, and carefully eyed the Smith-Keenan relationship in terms of his own power grab.
- Viacom decided to sell the Garden (including the Rangers) leaving Gutkowski, Smith and Keenan as lame ducks for the duration of 1994.

Thus, with the Garden in a state of militant instability the Rangers approached the second half of the playoffs with a scenario that read as follows:

1. If the Rangers are eliminated at any point, Keenan is fired, and possibly Smith.
2. If the Rangers win the Cup, both manager and coach will be retained.
3. If either Smith or Keenan believed they would be victimized by the new general staff, many felt they would jockey for another job.

Already two distinct possibilities quietly surfaced.

Detroit was upset by San Jose, inspiring Red Wings owner Mike Ilitch to move coach Scott Bowman upstairs while Bryan Murray was fired as GM Keenan, close to Bowman, could conceivably enter as GM/coach while Scotty settled for an exalted scouting job.

Meanwhile, St. Louis, a chronic playoff disappointment, was routed in four straight by Dallas. A housecleaning — involving coach Bob Berry and GM Ron Caron — was in order as a prelude to moving into the new

Kiel Center arena. Keenan, of course, would be a natural to replace them.

In the third playoff round the Rangers blitzkrieg was abruptly braked. New Jersey took a three games to two lead and Keenan displayed signs of the pressure. In Game Five he benched superstars Brian Leetch and Mark Messier, claiming they were injured.

At this critical juncture two vital points became evident:
1. Smith distanced himself from the coach, offering no public support.
2. Smith had almost the entire press corps in his corner. Keenan had alienated some members of the New York media.

Game Six at the Meadowlands was a remarkable study in contrasts. New Jersey jumped into a 2-0 lead in the first period leaving the Rangers a thoroughly dispirited bunch. The Devils leaped to the attack in the second period and came perilously close to opening a 3-0 lead.

As the clock ticked down the period, Keenan made a tactical maneuver that suddenly reversed the tide in his favor. Neutralized center Alexei Kovalev was moved from center to right wing on a line with Messier and Adam Graves. Kovalev scored late in the second on a nifty wrist shot. In the third period Messier scored three consecutive goals and the Rangers won 4-2.

However, in the midst of the Blueshirts euphoria, a report on a Prince Edward Island radio station stated that Keenan would be hired by Detroit immediately following the playoffs. Denials and more denials were issued from the Keenan camp. Pressbox denizens reasoned that Keenan had staked the Detroit job in case his Rangers lost to Jersey. New York's double-overtime win in Game Seven merely slowed but hardly stopped the Keenan departure rumors.

New York was expected to rout mediocre Vancouver in the Cup finals. Leading three games to one, the Rangers lost the possible clinching Game Five at the Garden and Game Six in Vancouver.

Throughout the week New York tabloids outdid each other with Keenan-to-Detroit headlines. At first Mike claimed that he was too busy to dignify them with a denial, but on the eve of Game Seven he addressed a record media throng.

Up, down and sideways he denied that he would leave the Rangers. Like General Douglas MacArthur's immortal "I shall return" promise as he left the Philippines in 1942, Keenan vowed that he'd be back on Broadway in 1994-95. Meanwhile, Smith was telling friends Keenan's departure would be the best thing for the Rangers.

Despite an early lead, New York almost blew Game Seven. A bad penalty call against Vancouver and a hit goal post in the third period enabled the Rangers to escape with a one-goal win. Manhattan went berserk as their hockey club ended its 54-year drought.

The triumph was capped by a tumultuous parade on Broadway before an estimated 1,000,000 celebrants. Keenan was King of New York, Smith its Prince.

But no sooner had the champagne dried than the bad blood began flowing. Having returned from a brief European vacation, Keenan called a press conference at *The Sports Network* in Toronto.

Claiming that the Rangers were late with a bonus check, Keenan declared himself a free agent and added that he was exploring other opportunities. A day later he declined a Red Wings offer, ostensibly because Ilitch planned to fire Keenan mentor, Bowman, if Mike was hired.

On Sunday, Keenan met with the St. Louis high command and accepted their offer to be GM-coach for six years at $2 million a year.

Despite weeks of rumors, Keenan's announcement hit Broadway with the impact of a thunderclap. Baseball and football, which normally would have dominated the sports pages, were driven off by "The Adventures of Mike."

Not surprisingly, Keenan was reviled by some members of the Manhattan media. His most persistent adversary, Mark Everson of *The New York Post*, revived the Benedict Arnold charge. Others simply called him "The Rat." Virtually no one supported the coach, except ironically, Rita Keenan, the woman from whom he had been separated.

In an interview with *New York Daily News* reporter Barry Meisel, Mrs. Keenan admitted that their marriage — she is Jewish, he is not — was almost officially over and that the final divorce was impending. Yet, Rita was remarkably supportive of her man.

"Adjectives? Honest. Caring. Sounds funny, because we're getting divorced," she told Meisel. "But I don't have too much bad to say about him. He's also loyal. Which also hurts me to hear people, the New York papers, say he's not loyal."

Rita Keenan even insisted that Mike was not a demanding taskmaster who couldn't get along with people.

"He wasn't like that at home," she asserted. "But he has a strong sense of self, and when he believes something is right, that's important to him. And he doesn't —- how do I say this nicely? — he doesn't pull punches. Mike, as far as I've always known him, I always trusted his word. Whatever he said was the truth. He might not always divulge everything, but he didn't try to lie.

"Mike always says what he thinks. Maybe that isn't always the easiest way to make everybody feel wonderful. But the other thing I know about him is, he likes to take responsibility. 'If this is my team, let me run the show here. But if I mess up, you can get rid of me. But don't get rid of me and have my hands tied at the same time. If you're going to blame me for the failure, let me run it.' That's always been his approach. Maybe that steps on toes."

By this time, Keenan had stepped on more toes than anyone could count, and most of them were at Madison Square Garden where the Rangers lawyers went to court to prevent Mike from breaking his contract and working for the Blues.

Keenan's response was that the Rangers failed to meet a 30-day clause in his contract and that this was a material breach enabling him to become a free agent.

The Rangers countered that the missed payment did not constitute a material breach and that Keenan's contract was valid. Furthermore, the Rangers petitioned NHL Commissioner Gary Bettman to conduct a hearing into the matter.

Soon after the Rangers filed their lawsuit against Keenan in U.S. District Court, the Blues contacted their adversaries and proposed a deal be made to assuage both parties. They finally agreed that St. Louis center Petr Nedved would be dispatched to New York in exchange for Esa Tikkanen and Doug Lidster. With that the Rangers dropped their claim and asked Bettman to cancel the hearing. Instead, the commissioner ordered all parties to his office on a Sunday morning and then levied the following punishment:

- Keenan was fined $100,000 and suspended for 60 days through the summer of 1994 and into training camp.
- The Blues were fined $250,000.
- The Rangers were fined $25,000 for having filed the civil action.
- The Red Wings were fined $25,000 for having negotiated with Keenan on July 16.

"The commissioner looked at the case before him and made that ruling," said Neil Smith. "That should be answer enough."

But that was hardly the end of it.

On Wednesday, July 27, 1994 the staid *New York Times* ran a banner headline: "AS THE RANGERS' BIZARRE WORLD TURNS: CHAPTER 2."

"It is a chapter so peculiar that perhaps only Robert Ludlum could have conceived of it: a devilish conspiracy concocted by two foes, Keenan and Neil Smith," wrote Richard Sandomir.

Radio station WFAN then revealed what it said were the contents of the 12-page brief submitted by Keenan to Bettman prior to the hearing. The brief stated:

- Keenan, his agent Rob Campbell and Gutkowski met June 24 in Gutkowski's room at the Essex House in Manhattan. Keenan presented seven ways of resolving his dispute with Smith. One included replacing Smith with MSG-TV broadcaster John Davidson. Gutkowski rejected all seven options, insisting that Keenan and Smith had better learn to co-exist.

- On June 26, Smith flew to Toronto where he, Keenan and Campbell conceived the late-check scenario to rid Smith of Keenan and let Keenan leave the Rangers. According to Keenan, Smith's private mission was executed without Gutkowski's knowledge. Smith also was alleged to have called three of Gutkowski's superiors from Toronto to request that if Gutkowski wouldn't give Keenan the gate, would they do it for him?

- Keenan charged that Smith signed Keenan's check on July 1, but held it up past July 14 when he was vacationing in Florida. And Gutkowski did not know.

Davidson promptly denied he ever was after Smith's job.

"What happened," said Davidson, "was that during the playoffs, Gut called me and talked about the problem between Mike and Neil. I said I hoped it could be resolved because, despite all the problems, it obviously was producing a Cup contender.

"He said that's what he wanted also, but in case it couldn't be resolved, would I be interested in running the team? I don't even know that I would have been. I have a great job. But at some point during the finals — within the context of a phone conversation with Mike — I did ask him whether he could work with me if I ever got the GM job and he said, 'Sure.'"

The New York fans and the media were perplexed by Keenan's actions. "RANGERGATE" was the *New York Post's* headline. "KEENAN: IT WAS 'TERMINATION BY CONSENT.' SMITH: ALLEGATIONS ARE 'ABSOLUTELY UNTRUE.'"

However, Brown concluded, "But the only guy not following protocol seemed to be Keenan, who seemed to be going over the head of his immediate boss, Neil Smith, by meeting with Smith's boss. It was at this meeting that according to the allegations, the squeeze-out of Smith was discussed — and dismissed by Gutkowski.

While more and more dirt hit the fan in Manhattan, the St. Louis media alternately deified Keenan and drew and quartered the "bad guys" from the New York press for daring to dump on Mike. In the end, the Blues journalistic brigade was ecstatic despite the price of Nedved.

"The Blues handed over the wallets," said Bernie Miklasz of the *Post-Dispatch*, "but won Keenan in the scuffle."

Yet even that wasn't the end of it. Although the corporate group that agreed to pay Keenan a fortune to run the Blues remained ecstatic, the club's captain Brett Hull was less than overjoyed.

At first "The Golden Brett" appeared to endorse Keenan. But during an interview in Los Angeles, Hull declared, "The way I play the game is totally different from the way he would like his players to play the game. Like, I can't play without smiling out there. I can imagine when he sees me smiling out there in Chicago Stadium or Maple Leaf Gardens, he'd absolutely have a conniption fit.

"I find it hard to believe that my personality and his are going to get along too well. Although he's a great man away from the game, from what I understand about his coaching style, I just can't imagine him enjoying the way I play."

To no one's surprise, controversy followed Keenan to his new digs. He somewhat quietly served his summertime suspension, allowing associate coaches Bob Berry and Ted Sator to guide his players into training camp.

It was then that Mike took command at $2 million a year and opened a new chapter in his hockey life.

Unquestionably, a *New York Daily News* headline summed up the saga better than anything — "BOTTOM LINE, ALL ABOUT POWER."

ONE-ON-ONE WITH MIKE KEENAN

SF: Who were the first individuals to mold you into the coach you are today?

MK: I go back to my early days in Toronto. I had a minor hockey coach named Doug Williams, who had played hockey for a very good Canadian amateur team called the Whitby (Ontario) Dunlops. And my uncle Bob Keenan, like Doug, put me in leadership roles when I was still young. Then there was a fellow, Bob Biond, my junior coach at Oshawa, who instilled confidence just by the distribution of ice time. He was a thorough teacher and had a systematic approach. The three of them were very influential.

SF: When did you actually decide that you wanted to make coaching your profession?

MK: It started when I was teaching physical education, geography, and history at the Don Mills School in Toronto and then Forest Hill Collegiate, where I taught at the high-school level for five years. I really started to enjoy coaching although it wasn't hockey, it was box lacrosse. I had been a good box lacrosse player at Don Mills and once went to the finals. At Forest Hill, I coached the hockey and swimming teams and then track and field and basketball. From there I moved to coaching Junior B hockey in Oshawa while I was still teaching.

SF: What did you like about teaching and coaching at the time?

MK: First of all the contact with the children — or adolescents. I enjoyed the aspect of seeing them undertake something and enjoy the improvement. Eventually, I left teaching to become coach and general manager at Peterborough [Ontario]. From there I went to coach Rochester [AHL] for three years and then back to the University of Toronto where I taught and coached.

SF: What's different about you as a coach at Rochester and now?

MK: First of all, I'm a lot more polished than I was then. I had the raw skills when I was younger but didn't have the attributes that I've developed to this point. I've always had a strong intuitive sense for coaching and teaching; in particular the game of hockey; that is, as far as bench strategy is concerned. Over the years I developed my skills to a much greater degree than I had at the start. I'm more understanding and a lot more patient in terms of knowing the learning curve involved. It takes time and it's a hard thing to find because there's so much pressure on you to win every night. Sometimes there's a lot left to learn on those nights that you don't win.

SF: Some coaches believe that they must win every single game —

including exhibitions. Do you feel that way?

MK: No. The way I look at it is like this: It's either you're winning or you are losing; it's not whether you won or lost. And if you're winning, that means you're teaching and there is a learning curve being developed here. It's going to enhance your program and ultimately enhance the performance level of the athletes. They'll be better players. As a result of teaching that takes place.

Sometimes you learn valuable lessons in losses. You have to be able accept the loss in light of the fact that you may have learned a big deal.

SF: Who do you admire most in the NHL coaching fraternity?

MK: Scotty Bowman. When I was in Rochester and he was in Buffalo [Rochester's parent club], I had the opportunity to speak to him almost daily for three years. And just the hockey knowledge and the aspect of preparing the team and his bench work that are so critical at all levels. Scotty knew the league extremely well. He knew each player. He knew the schedule and how much each player was getting in ice time; what the roles were. He knew it for every team. That's incredible knowledge that most coaches don't pay attention to.

SF: What else did he teach you?

MK: The ability to win every night on a consistent basis. Well, maybe not every night but more often then not. Also the ability to get the most out of personalities at the right time. Sometimes you didn't have a superstar and you had to find somebody else that would deliver. In Montreal, Scotty had great teams, no question about that, but he also had to motivate the great players and that can be as difficult — if not more so — as motivating lesser ones. He had the opportunity of coaching more great players then probably any one else. The other thing I learned from Scotty is the ability to change with the times. You don't coach as long he's coached without changing your style. You have to be able to accept change in order to adapt to the different types of players. There are different dynamics to build on different ends. The economics of the game has changed as well, which means there are different requirements and needs of the athletes.

SF: You had other employment options for 1993-94 besides the Rangers. So why did you choose New York?

MK: Philadelphia was one but I chose New York for several reasons. One was the money, but it wasn't the only reason. I believed that the Rangers job provided me an opportunity to coach and have an impact on selling the game in a challenging market place. I feel strongly that the game has to be marketed properly in the U.S. and the greatest thing I could do in that direction would be to win a Stanley Cup for New York. By making the decision, I decided to give it a good shot.

SF: You must be aware that the media and fan attention in New York is different than anything you experienced in Philadelphia or Chicago.

MK: I really don't think too much of it. It bothered Neil [Smith] and Mark [Messier] in terms of their feeling about exposure more than it affects me. They're a lot more sensitive about it. The attention is part of being in New York.

SF: *The Hockey News* picked the Rangers to win the Stanley Cup before the 1993-94 season began. Did you mind?

MK: I like to be the favorite. I enjoy the pressure. I'm at my best when there's pressure. The more pressure, the better. I know the media has been comparing me with Pat Riley of the Knickerbockers. Well, I don't care about the comparisons at all. Pat's Pat and I'm Mike. Pat's coaching basketball and I'm coaching hockey. I've got a great deal of respect for him and his coaching abilities and what he's accomplished. Anytime I can learn from any coach I'm going to be receptive.

SF: What was your biggest concern about New York in terms of the team?

MK: Keeping the players focused with their minds on their responsibilities. And keeping the organization focused. You can't let the media distract you. I had to do what is right for the hockey club.

SF: Did you want to become general manager of the Rangers, instead of Neil Smith?

MK: I turned down jobs as general manager and coach [in Philadelphia] in 1993. I did it for personal reasons. I wanted only to coach for the flexibility in terms of summer free-time.

SF: Did you promise New York Hockey fans a Stanley Cup?

MK: I couldn't do that but I did promise fans that we'd compete and that we'd extract every once of energy to run for the Cup, but you can never promise a Cup. There are too many factors beyond your control: injuries, the competition, etc.

SF: Which player have you enjoyed coaching the most during your NHL career?

MK: Chris Chelios. He loves the game of hockey. You can rely on him every night and he really cares about his teammates. He's a very sensitive individual and he's a winner at all costs. Ronnie Hextall is right up there with Chelios. He'll win at all costs as well.

SF: You made a video in 1993 that depicted the parade-celebration scene when the Rangers finally did win the Stanley Cup. What was the purpose of it?

MK: There are lots of ways of lifting the confidence and expectation level of the players. It's fine to talk about goals but they have to visualize the success they can enjoy if they are willing to see themselves in that setting. If you can't see yourself in certain situations, you're probably not going to achieve them.

SF: Despite your success, a number of players have registered unhappiness with your tough style. Peter Zezel said he learned a lot from you, "but it wasn't worth it." Explain, please.

MK: At the time I was more forceful and demonstrative than I am now. But the lessons were the same: sacrifice and commitment are necessary to win. And it takes a certain amount of courage as well to accept that responsibility. I think Peter would appreciate them more now that's he's 27 than he did when he was 19 and just happy to be in the league.

SF: I t seems to me that you, too, have to have a certain courage to be tough, both as a coach and a parent.

MK: That's called "tough love." You love 'em. You try to do what's right. You explain it to them. Sometimes you have to say "I love you but this time it's no." But that doesn't mean I don't care for them. I care for them a lot more then they can ever imagine. But some times I just have to say "no."

SF: Some of your supporters claim you are misunderstood. Is that a fact?

MK: Quite a bit, there's no question about that. But I'll take some of the responsibility for that because in my younger years I probably didn't take the time to show them that side of me and at the same time it was part of my upbringing. I was taught that you have to be stoic, strong and be there for everyone. As a result, I didn't show them the emotional, sensitive side of Mike Keenan. The players in Chicago saw it but not Philadelphia.

SF: Who influenced you this way?

MK: My mother to a certain extent. I was brought up in an Irish-Catholic home in Toronto and I went to a Catholic School. More often then not, I was put in leadership roles. I was an altar boy for eight years, went to church every Sunday for eight years. I was named captain for every team I've been associated with in athletics, so I've always been in a leadership position. I liked it and I liked the responsibility. I liked the sense of confidence that it gave me but on the other hand, I began to believe you had to be stoic and strong and not show any sensitivity, which was a contradiction in my personality because I am an extremely sensitive and caring. I'm very proud of certain accomplishments I've made since I came from a poor background.

SF: Why did you take that insensitivity with you to the NHL?

MK: Mike Keenan came into the league as an unknown. I had never played in the big league and I had come from out of nowhere. I knew that the tenure for coaches in the NHL at that time was less than two years. It was a matter or survival for me.

SF: What's the best way to handle the press?

MK: Be available to them. They'll respect that and respond. I hope they take an approach that's not totally counterproductive in terms of team performance. I understand that they have papers to sell but not at the expense of the player performances.

SF: You came within three goals of winning the Stanley Cup in 1987, when you took Edmonton to seven games before losing 3-1 in the final. What went wrong?

MK: They were too strong for us and we finally ran out of gas. We took a 1-0 lead on them in the first period of Game 7, but we just couldn't hold them off. We kept it 2-1 until late in the third, but then Glenn Anderson blew a hard one past Ronnie Hextall, and that goal said it all. We were beat up physically and mentally after that. There was nothing left. But we can be proud of our accomplishment.

SF: When you took the Blackhawks to the finals in 1992, it looked like you had Pittsburgh in Game 1. Twice you had a three-goal lead and then Jaromir Jagr tied it by going around three of your four Chicago players.

MK: We were playing them well and I felt that we could have beaten them. I was very disappointed in the league because of that series. It took us four years to get to that position and now that we're there, look what happened: on Jagr's goal, not one, but two penalties could have been called against Pittsburgh on the play. I mentioned that play to John Davidson recently and, without my saying anything, he told me "Two penalties could have been called against them before Jagr scored." Andy van Hellemond was the referee and as far as I'm concerned he's too veteran a referee to allow that to happen in the finals. There were penalties — holding of the stick was one — that could have been called against Mario Lemieux, but none were called. That tells me the league has an influence on who's ultimately going to win. It's a sad situation, but true and it took the heart out of me and my team. We lost in four games, but it didn't have to be that way. It could have been different, and imagine the millions of dollars that were lost by the league because it ended in four games. The league disappointed me.

Part Four:

CHICAGO

STADIUM

23

THE COACHES' ASYLUM

Instead of a substitute practice goalie, Gorman saw a full-sized scarecrow manning the net as if it were a paid goaltender. "The Major's idea," Gorman later related, "was that players would learn to shoot so they could score without hitting the dummy. It was supposed to make them increase their accuracy."

Of all the NHL teams, none had a more bizarre collection of coaches than the Chicago Blackhawks. The franchise started off in a relatively sane manner when Dick Irvin was signed to coach the team at the start of the 1930s.

But when Irvin left the team for the Maple Leafs, a strange collection of leaders followed, mostly because of the bizarre antics of Blackhawks owner Major Frederic McLaughlin.

It was too much to expect Major McLaughlin to follow Irvin with an equally competent coach. Instead, the Major chose a chap named Godfrey Matheson who had absolutely no big-league experience.

The Major was captivated by Matheson's unique game strategy. But the more experienced players immediately sensed that they had acquired a loser. Defenseman Teddy Graham once cited some of Matheson's unique foibles:

"Matheson had coached only kid teams that had just one shift of player — one front line, one set of defenseman, and a goalie. He simply had no experience in changing lines."

When the players reported to their new mentor for game plans, Matheson informed them that only six of them would participate in the regular season action and the rest of them would be able-bodied reserves. That left about 20 players with nothing to do but watch. The nucleus of the team consisted of Chuck Gardiner in goal, Taffy Abel and Helge

Bostrum on defense, and Tommy Cook at center flanked by Paul Thompson and "Mush" March.

The extras were informed that they were to pay close attention to the big team, just in case they had to substitute for any of the regulars. "It was," said Graham, "enough to make a nut house out of any hockey camp."

Matheson added to the improbable situation by referring to each of his hard-bitten pros as "mister." The non-players had to be content with an occasional spin on the ice before and after the special six conducted their practices. The Major had left the pre-season training in Matheson's hands, and the weird arrangement would very likely have remained the same had it not been for Bill Tobin, the business manager of the Hawks. Word had filtered back to Tobin's Chicago office about Matheson's unprecedented plans, and at first Tobin considered the reports as amusing balderdash. It wasn't until he arrived at the training base that he learned the truth.

"We got in touch with Tobin as soon as he arrived," said defenseman Graham, "and let him know what was going on. It was for our good and welfare as much as his."

What followed is something that would have been more appropriate in the screenplay of a W.C. Fields movie of that era. Confronted by Tobin, Matheson promptly turned in his resignation.

The Major now had the opportunity to select any one of several qualified professional coaches to handle the promising team. Instead, he succumbed to one of his quirks — a desire to have Americans rather than Canadians associated with his team. For when he bought the Hawks, McLaughlin had made up his mind that someday he would staff his team with American skaters, although it was well known that the best players were Canadians. The Major wasn't ready to put an all-American team on the ice for the 1931-32 season, but he decided to solve his coaching problem by selecting a United States-born individual.

His choice as Matheson's successor was Emil Iverson, who qualified for the job on the basis of one factor — he was an American. As for his other credentials, they included a stint as a figure skater and experience as a physical culturist. There was no indication that Iverson had ever coached a hockey club.

"The fact is," said Graham, "he was the Blackhawks trainer and never coached a day in his life." With Matheson gone and Iverson at the helm, the Blackhawks headed for Toronto to open the brand-new Maple Leaf Gardens. If they weren't the worst-prepared team ever to open an NHL season, they were very close. Their foes, finely honed to lift the curtain on their handsome new arena, were eagerly awaiting the arrival of the Chicago sextet. The date was November 12, 1931.

The largest crowd to witness an indoor event of any kind in Toronto turned out to see the Chicago massacre. All the trimmings were there, right down to the bands of the 48th Highlanders and the Royal Granadiers playing "Happy Days Are Here Again." The opening ceremonies included the presentation of two floral horseshoes to the Maple Leafs. Eventually, the game started.

When it was over, Iverson's ill-trained, perplexed men were the most surprised people in the building. They had beaten the Maple Leafs, 2-1. But Emil didn't last very long.

In January, 1933, the Major imported Tommy Gorman to manage the team. When Gorman arrived at Chicago Stadium, he immediately realized that all was not quite normal with the Blackhawks. During a workout, Gorman watched Charlie Gardiner guard the pipes at one end of the rink. But when he glanced over at the other end, a strange sight met his eyes. Instead of a substitute practice goalie, Gorman saw a full-sized scarecrow manning the net as if it were a paid goaltender. "The Major's idea," Gorman later related, "was that players would learn to shoot so they could score without hitting the dummy. It was supposed to make them increase their accuracy."

While some observers no doubt could have made a good case for using the dummy, the idea didn't appeal to Gardiner. In fact, he considered it an insult to his profession. But the dummy was there to stay. As Gorman became acclimatized to the new job, he realized that it was but one of an endless list of eccentricities that cloaked the franchise.

But Gardiner, who was bombarded with shots season after season, seethed with resentment during each practice. Finally, in January, 1933, he completely lost his cool. After a workout he skated to the other end of the rink and grabbed the dummy about the waist. Holding the straw man tightly in his grip, Gardiner lifted the pseudo-goaltender over the boards and hauled him right into the Blackhawks dressing room while onlookers watched in amazement. Then he beckoned to trainer Eddie Froelich and called over Bill Tobin.

"Listen you guys," demanded Gardiner, "give that poor fella a good massage. He's worked his feet off. Why, I haven't done a thing today!"

Unquestionably, the Blackhawks' most interesting experiment involved another coach, this one Bill Stewart, an American who was also a Major League baseball umpire. McLaughlin's plan was to stock an All-American-born team, which eventually Stewart would coach.

In the 1935-36 season, the Major began to plant the seeds for his All-American NHL team. He traded Lorne Chabot to the Maroons and decided to go with Mike Karakas, a ruddy-faced goaltender from Eveleth, Minnesota. The Hawks finished third, six points out of first place. Then they lost to the New York Americans in the semi-final round.

Instead of improving, the Hawks deteriorated as the 1936-37 season progressed. As his team plumbed new depths of ineptitude, the Major became more and more determined to fill his lineup with Americans. One of his leading forwards, Johnny Gottselig, expressed the sentiment of the team when he observed, "We thought it [the All-American plan] was pretty ridiculous."

McLaughlin's scouts eventually extracted Albert Suomi, Curly Brink, Bun LaPraire, Butch Schaefer and Ernest "Ike" Klingbeil from the Minnesota-Michigan hockey belt and imported them to Chicago under cover. The Major wasn't quite ready to spring the surprise on the unwitting public, nor did he want to risk a flop. His first project was to condition the athletes, so he sent them to none other than former coach Emil Iverson, who now bore the title of physical director of the Blackhawks.

"His idea of workouts," said Gottseling, "was to have them stand straight with hands on hips. The tips of the toes were to touch. From that position he'd put the guys through bending and stretching exercises."

Borrowing a leaf from the Godfrey Matheson book, the Major ordered his American players to conduct private workouts on the Chicago Stadium ice. It was like having a second platoon completely divorced in strategy and philosophy from the first.

When the Americans finally faced their Canadian teammates, the more experienced veterans treated the newcomers with utter contempt. They refused to sit next to the Americans and ignored them as if they weren't there. When the two teams scrimmaged, the Canadians really laid on the lumber.

"It was awful rough," said Klingbeil in an interview. "They came at us with the works — high sticks and everything." To prevent a bloodbath, the Major agreed to sprinkle the Canadian lineup with the Americans and vice versa. In this way Klingbeil and Schaefer played defense with a Canadian forward line. The integration proved a tonic all around. Suddenly the team's spirits were buoyed, and they began climbing in the standings.

Somehow this integrated lineup didn't appeal to the spectators, though. Despite the Americans, they weren't flocking to Chicago Stadium. The reason, the Major believed, was that all five Americans weren't on the ice at the same time. Yet he was stymied. The Blackhawks were right in the midst of a playoff race, and to put the Americans out all at once would bring almost certain defeat. His only hope, strangely enough, was for the team to be eliminated from contention. Then he could safely experiment with the American line.

It wasn't until the last weekend of the season that the Blackhawks cooperated and finally bowed out of the race. McLaughlin announced that the Yanks would be present in force for the last home game, against the Boston Bruins. As luck would have it, the publicity did a boomerang turn on the Major. Hockey's most beloved star, Howie Morenz, of the Montreal Canadiens, was dying in a hospital at the time and the Blackhawks, though wrongfully so, had been blamed because Morenz had broken his leg tripping over a Chicago player.

When McLaughlin's scheme was made public, the Canadian managers and coaches throughout the league were infuriated. They denounced the Major and demanded his expulsion from the NHL. Nevertheless, McLaughlin persisted with his plan, and when the Blackhawks met the Bruins, they faced a Boston team determined to bludgeon them into the ice. Fortunately Klingbeil and friends retaliated, but even though they held the Bruins to a draw in that department of fisticuffs, they lost the game, 6-2.

In their next challenge the Yanks performed better. They invaded Maple Leaf Gardens in Toronto and emerged with a respectable 3-2 loss. In a way, they had won a victory, because they fought the Leafs on even terms and gave every indication of improving. In their third game Klingbeil's pals finally came out on top by edging Lester Patrick's New York Rangers, 4-3. It was a stirring triumph, because earlier Patrick had derided the Americans, calling them "amateurs."

Although the Hawks were eventually whipped by both the New York Americans and the Bruins, the idea of American-born skaters seemed good enough to be continued as far as the Major was concerned. When the following season began, he hired an American coach, umpire Bill Stewart.

McLaughlin hired Stewart while he was umpiring a ball game in Philadelphia. The major sent a wire to the Massachusetts-born umpire to both manage and coach the Blackhawks. McLaughlin knew Stewart not only for his superb baseball work, but also for his hockey refereeing, which had elevated him to chief arbiter in the NHL. "The Major proposed a one-year contract," said Stewart, "but I was having none of that. When he finally agreed to a two-year contract, I also insisted on an ironclad agreement that I was absolute boss."

Stewart was well aware of the Major's penchant for interfering with the club. And when McLaughlin wasn't around, there always was the threat of Bill Tobin putting his two cents worth. If he could handle this club his way, Stewart believed there would be no problem winning hockey games. "This was the happiest club I ever saw in professional sports," Stewart had said. "And we had some pretty good talent, too.

Players like Gottselig, 'Mush' March, Paul Thompson, Art Wiebe and Doc Romnes. Lionel Conacher once told me he regarded Romnes as one of the finest centers he had ever played with. The biggest reason we won, though, was that we had Earl Seibert on our defense. The big guy played about 55 minutes every game."

Stewart's contract may have been "ironclad," but he found the Major as omnipresent as ever, and the strongwilled pair feuded and feuded. Usually Stewart won.

Most of the time, they argued about the relative merits of certain players. Right off the bat, there was a clash when a choice had to be made between Oscar Hanson and Cully Dahlstrom as his man. The Major won a small concession — Stewart would use Hanson for at least ten games.

Stewart went along with that end of the bargain, but then he simply dropped Hanson. Dahlstrom thoroughly underlined his coach's faith in him by winning the Calder Trophy as the NHL's rookie of the year. Later, when Stewart obtained Carl Voss from the Montreal Maroons, McLaughlin was absolutely convinced that his coach had goofed. After watching Voss in one game, the major insisted that he be cut from the squad as an obvious loser. This time Stewart was adamant. Voss would stay.

And he did. Voss not only stayed, but he played an important part in Chicago's most stirring hockey triumph since the birth of the Blackhawks.

Meanwhile, the Americanized Blackhawks managed to plod along through the schedule at a slightly quicker pace than the Red Wings. The result was that Chicago finished third in the American Division, just two points ahead of its Detroit pursuers, but a good 30 points behind division-leading Boston. Their chances for winning the Stanley Cup were no better than 100 to 1.

To begin with, the Hawks were the only one of six qualifying teams to have less than a .500 record (14-25-9), and their first-round opponents were the Montreal Canadiens, who had a consistently more respectable 18-17-13 mark. Further complicating matters for Chicago was the fact that two of the three games would be played in the Montreal Forum.

Predictably, the Canadiens won the first match, 6-4. But when the series shifted to Chicago, goalie Karakas shut out the Montrealers, 4-0. Suddenly, the Blackhawks were coming on strong. The final game was tied, 2-2, after regulation time. It was decided in Chicago's favor when Lou Trudel's long shot bounced off Paul Thompson and into the Montreal cage, although some observers insisted that the puck was shot by "Mush" March.

Now the Blackhawks were to face an equally aroused New York

Americans sextet that had just routed its archrivals in Manhattan, the Rangers, in three games. Once again the Hawks would have the benefit of only one home game in the best-of-three series. The Americans opened with a 3-1 victory at Madison Square Garden. But when the series shifted to Chicago, Karakas took over again and the teams battled to the end of regulation time without a score.

The game was settled in sudden-death overtime by none other than Cully Dalhstrom, the man McLaughlin had once lobbied against so vigorously. Chicago clinched the series with a third-period goal by Doc Romnes in the third game. The final score was 3-2, and the Blackhawks advanced into the Stanley Cup finals against the Toronto Maple Leafs.

By now the betting odds had dropped considerably in Chicago's favor. But they soared again when it was learned that Karakas had suffered a broken big toe in the final game with the Americans. Karakas didn't realize the extent of the damage until he attempted to lace on his skates for the game with Toronto. He just couldn't make it, and the Hawks suddenly became desperate for a goaltender.

The Leafs were not in the least sympathetic to the Blackhawks' problem and summarily rejected requests for goaltending assistance. So the Chicago brass finally earthed Alfie Moore, a minor league free-agent goalie who reportedly was quaffing liquid refreshment in a Toronto pub when he was drafted to play goal for the Chicagoans. Moore answered the call and went into the Chicago nets on April 5, 1938, defeating Toronto, 3-1, in the opening game of the series at Maple Leaf Gardens.

For the second game, the Hawks decided to try their luck with Paul Goodman, another minor league goaltender. But this time Toronto rebounded with a strong 5-1 decision.

It was obvious that if the Hawks were to win they urgently required the services of Karakas. This was accomplished when he was outfitted with a special shoe to protect his broken toe. Chicago won the game before a record crowd of 18,496 at the Stadium on goals by Romnes and Carl Voss, whom McLaughlin had wanted to discard. The score was 2-1.

By now the Leafs were reeling, and Chicago applied the *coup de grace* with relative ease in the fifth game, routing Toronto, 4-1, on goals by Dalhstrom, Voss, Shill and March. After the game, when the ecstatic Chicago players sought out the Stanley Cup, they finally realized what an upset they had engineered.

"NHL President Calder had earlier caused the trophy to be shipped to Toronto," wrote Edward Burns in the *Chicago Tribune*, "reportedly on the assurance that a hockey team which harbored eight American-born hockey players as did the Hawks couldn't possibly win the Stanley Cup."

The victory was especially gratifying to Stewart, for it vindicated his judgment about several players, especially Voss and Dalhstrom. It appeared that he would be with the Blackhawks for many years, except that with Major McLaughlin around one never knew for sure.

By the 1938-39 season, Stewart was running a fairly solid ship with a record of 19 points in 21 games. Then the Blackhawks played the Canadiens. The coach still recalls the game well, because it catapulted him right out of a job. "We were leading, 1-0, at Chicago with a minute to go," Stewart has said. "They tied it up on a long shot and Toe Blake beat us in overtime. Funny thing about it is that our club was in third place when the Major fired me. I had a two-year contract and they had to pay me every nickel [for the remaining year]. I took off for Florida to spend the Major's money and drown my sorrows in sunshine."